Emerging Military Technologies

International Studies on Military Ethics

THE SERIES IS EDITED UNDER THE AUSPICES OF THE INTERNATIONAL SOCIETY FOR MILITARY ETHICS IN EUROPE (EUROISME)

VOLUME 8

EURO ISME
International Society for Military Ethics in Europe

The titles published in this series are listed at *brill.com/isme*

Emerging Military Technologies

Ethical and Legal Perspectives

Edited by

Bernhard Koch and Richard Schoonhoven

BRILL
NIJHOFF

LEIDEN | BOSTON

Cover illustration: Ample Strike 2021 international exercise in which 700 soldiers participate in Vicenice near Namest nad Oslavou, Czech Republic, September 15, 2021. (Copyright: ANP; CTK Photo/Lubos Pavlicek).

The Library of Congress Cataloging-in-Publication Data is available online at https://catalog.loc.gov

Typeface for the Latin, Greek, and Cyrillic scripts: "Brill". See and download: brill.com/brill-typeface.

ISSN 2214-7926
ISBN 978-90-04-50794-4 (hardback)
ISBN 978-90-04-50795-1 (e-book)

This book is printed on acid-free paper and produced in a sustainable manner.

Contents

PART 3
Drones

PART 4
Enhancement

PART 5
Leadership

Acknowledgements

The editors owe special thanks to the research associate at the Institute for Theology and Peace in Hamburg, Ms. Nicole Pörschmann M.A., for her endless help in publishing this book.

Figures and Tables

Figures

Tables

EuroISME – Introduction

Richard Schoonhoven

On May 13–16, 2018, the 8th EuroISME Annual conference was held in Toledo, Spain, on the grounds of the Spanish Infantry Academy, with over 100 persons in attendance. EuroISME is an offshoot of the original (now, North American-) ISME, itself an offshoot of an earlier series of conferences known as the Joint Services Conferences on Professional Ethics (JSCOPE), which consisted primarily of representatives from the various U.S. service academies and War Colleges. EuroISME held its inaugural conference in 2011 in Paris, and has met every summer since (save in 2020, owing to the Covid-19 pandemic; in 2021 the conference was held as an online event over three days) at various venues around Europe. In that mere ten years, EuroISME has grown to be perhaps the premier international conference devoted to military ethics, bringing together scholars, practitioners, and heads of industry from across Europe and indeed from around the world. The 2018 conference, whose theme was *The Ethical Implications of Emerging Technologies in Warfare*, provides a particularly vibrant example of the range, power, and fecundity of ideas that can be developed when a truly international and interdisciplinary group of thinkers turns its attention to them. The essays in this volume are but a small sample of the papers delivered at that conference. They present a range of perspectives, and often challenge the reader and each other in various ways. But they all show a deep and common concern for grappling with the ethical issues of war, and for making war as humane and moral an endeavor as possible.

The opening address for the conference was delivered by Brigadier General BENOIT ROYAL, then President of EuroISME. In his address, General Royal nicely lays out the four major (partly overlapping) areas in which new military technologies are being developed: human enhancement – physical, cognitive, and psychological; the increasing automation of weapons and weapons systems, including lethal autonomous weapons systems (LAWS); the increased use of and reliance on artificial intelligence (AI) systems on the battlefield for decision-making and control of weapons systems; and the development of cyber weapons and the ever greater activity in the cyber domain. General Royal then succinctly presents the main ethical concerns surrounding these technologies. On the one hand, these technologies all promise greater precision in targeting, and thus a greater ability to discriminate between combatants and non-combatants, as well as reduced collateral damage. Fewer people will be killed who ought not be killed. On the other hand, however, General

 | DOI:10.1163/9789004507951_002

Royal worries that this greater precision may engender more military misadventures and may tend to erode the traditional distinction(s) between war and not-war. Drones, for example, have been widely used in many areas of the world where no legally recognized state of armed conflict exists, and much cyber activity happens "in the shadows," where there is no legal regime and little if any accountability and oversight. Thus, he worries that war might become dehumanized, and that these new technologies may be "starting a new contest between war with rules and war without rules" – worries that animated much of the conference.

The inaugural address was given by H.E. Prof. Dr. MARCELINO OREJA AGUIRRE, honorary President of the Royal Academy of Moral and Political Sciences. In a sensitive and informed piece, Dr. Aguirre stresses the need for ethics, and similarly highlights the major areas of ethical concern: drones, AI, etc. Dr. Aguirre calls attention to the changing and expanding roles of the military: militaries now frequently function as aid workers, assistants, police officers. But he admonishes us not to forget that – whatever changes emerging technologies may bring to the battlefield – combat is still a lethal enterprise that eventuates in the death of human beings. In particular, for example, he warns against the possibility of emotional and psychological detachment among drone pilots. The worry is that with increased distance from the battlefield and with the safety that brings, such pilots will fail adequately to take into account and respect the humanity even of those whom they kill. Thus, they might become indifferent to death, or even develop an excessive readiness to kill, both of which are incompatible with truly ethical behavior on the battlefield.

One of the glories of EuroISME – of ISME generally – is that it seeks out a multiplicity of perspectives – not just those of academics, but of practitioners, politicians, and even leaders of industry. Under this last heading falls EMMANUEL BLOCH, Director of Corporate Responsibility at Thales Group, a major aerospace and defense contractor. Mr. Bloch notes that for a long time, corporate ethics were focused almost exclusively on questions of corruption and harassment in the workplace, but that much has changed over the last couple of decades. Thales has traditionally asked itself three (types of) questions – What do we make? How do we make it? And how and to whom do we sell it? – but they now find themselves answerable not just to governments, but also to NGOs, their shareholders, investors, customers, suppliers – the list goes on. Much of Bloch's paper focuses on tracing out the interrelationships between these various constituencies vis-à-vis ethical issues. He is worried about a shrinking "zone of tolerance" – that area in which a company can operate relatively freely – and argues that the answer lies in clear communication and collaboration between all those involved.

As has already been mentioned, one of the major areas of ethical concern centering on new battlefield technologies is the use of artificial intelligence (AI), and in particular of Lethal Autonomous Weapons Systems (LAWS). There is some debate about precisely what ought to be included under this rubric, but roughly these are weapons systems that would operate without direct human oversight, including the identification of targets. In that sense, machines would be making the decision whether and whom to kill. In an illuminating piece, DEANE-PETER BAKER, who has written extensively on the subject in other venues, identifies what he takes to be the major Western ethical objections to the deployment of such technology, dividing the issues into deontological and consequentialist categories. Baker then carefully dissects several Chinese sources in an attempt to discern the Chinese position on these weapons. He finds echoes of several of the consequentialist objections in the official Chinese communiques, but none of what many – but by no means all – take to be the central deontological objection to their use: that their use would inevitably constitute a massive violation of human dignity. The worry here is that while many of the consequentialist objections may be overcome through improvements in technology, this one stands independent of context. To the extent, then, that the Chinese do not share this concern, they may be more amenable than many – but again not all – in the West to their development and deployment. In any case, Baker also notes the Chinese tendency to use the law to their strategic advantage, and that taken literally the type of ban that the Chinese would apparently support is very narrow, and would allow for a great many weapons systems that would run afoul of many broader, and possibly more reasonable, definitions of LAWS. The issue is of course an important one, given China's increasing dominance on the world stage, and its express interest and investment in AI technologies.

SHANNON FRENCH and LISA LINDSAY share some of the abhorrence of allowing machines to "decide" to kill human beings entirely on their own, and they clearly outline a number of issues that would have to be faced in the development and deployment of AI systems in a military context. They do much to tamp down the unbridled enthusiasm for such systems that results in a rush to develop them as quickly as possible and be the first to field them. But they also recognize the tremendous power and potential of such systems, and are disinclined to throw out the baby with the bathwater. They argue therefore, that the best use for AI on the battlefield is as "option generators" – devices that can present a human commander with a range of options between which he or she can meaningfully decide. But given the "automation bias" – the tendency of humans to default to and trust technology, particularly technology that can seem so powerful and "smart" – to which they themselves call attention, and given that on any technologically advanced battlefield many decisions will have to be made extremely quickly (a fact which they also recognize), it becomes an interesting question whether any meaningful line can be drawn, much less held, between a machine presenting a human with a range of options, and in effect deciding for that human. That is, in order to be maximally useful, the options the machine generates would presumably need to be rank-ordered along some specific set of relevant criteria, and the danger is that the human commander, although nominally making the decision, would tend to default – perhaps even unconsciously – to the top-ranked option. French and Lindsay do point out, however, that the machine could also be programmed to remind the commander at every turn of her legal and ethical obligations, and this might go some way toward alleviating this concern.

Finally, IONNA LEKEA (*et al.*) delves into some of the technical aspects of AI algorithms. At the end of the day, even the most advanced AI system is nothing but a series of algorithms, and so how those algorithms are developed and "trained" becomes vitally important. After briefly rehearsing the basics of *Jus in Bello* – in particular, the notions of discrimination and proportionality – she turns her attention to questions of how well AI can be expected to perform along these dimensions, and to the related questions of responsibility, accountability, and liability for such systems. Lekea and her colleagues developed an artificially intelligent algorithm that was designed to recognize individuals carrying specific weapons in a variety of situations, and then assessed its accuracy and effectiveness. While the accuracy of the algorithm varied according to a number of parameters, the highest success rate they were able to achieve was 82%. As Lekea herself points out, this is certainly not high enough to permit the use of such systems in war. Technological improvement is no doubt possible, and might even get to the point where machines are able to out-perform humans, but they will never be perfect and so we will need to grapple with the question of who should be held responsible, etc., if an AI system goes off the rails, as it were, and violates the rules of war. Finally, she helpfully reminds us that "the fact that AI agents can replace human agents and complete extremely dangerous (and even life-threatening) tasks should not make us accept their currently given technological inability to discern between right and wrong as a secondary problem and use this as a pretense to 'legalize' accidental attacks against civilian targets that should not be under attack." That is, we cannot allow the advantages of AI to lull us into lowering our moral or legal standards.

AI, and LAWS in particular, are fairly new technologies, still under development. Drones, on the other hand, have been widely used for well over a decade.

But the ethical challenges they present are no less important or difficult. Responding in part to an article by Muhammad Idrees Ahmad, PETE BRUNTON clearly canvasses the ethical objections that have been raised against the use of drones in a military context, both *in Bello* and *ad Bellum*. He finds most of the *in Bello* arguments wanting, although he does identify a nice, *in Bello* twist on the Threshold Problem. By allowing almost surgical precision in targeting, drones may encourage commanders to attack targets they otherwise would not, owing to concerns of disproportionate collateral damage. But if the target of such a strike is misidentified, then 100% of the damage done will be collateral. Thus, even if drones offer reduced collateral damage in each individual attack, there is the possibility that overall collateral damage will be increased. Brunton is less sanguine on the *ad Bellum* side of things. Here he worries about the CIA's use of drone strikes in the Federally Administered Tribal Areas of Pakistan. The worry is that these strikes, carried out not by the military but by an intelligence agency, cannot be justified as a form of self-defense, and thus stray from legitimate self-defence or even preemption, into an illegitimate use of preventive force.

In a similar vein, TAMAR MEISELS considers the morality of drone warfare. She carefully separates the use of drones *per se*, from another topic with which it is closely intertwined – *viz.*, targeted killing – wishing to focus solely on the former. Meisels makes the often-overlooked point that drones actually require considerable infrastructure. The day may come when drones are cheap and widely-available enough to be used by terrorists for indiscriminate attacks, but (1) we don't seem to be quite there yet, and (2) that possibility really doesn't tell us much about the morality of drones as they are currently deployed in state-level drone programs. Those programs, as just mentioned, are costly and sophisticated, and this means that drone warfare as currently practiced is highly asymmetrical, favoring states and state-level actors. Meisels sees that as a good thing, for the advantage here is moral as well as strategic. As Meisels notes, "drones are precision weapons, offering the possibility of careful compliance with the laws of war, to those who wish to comply." Thus, while she is sensitive to many of the objections that have been raised, she is largely favorably inclined toward their use, at least as currently practiced by states, like the U.S. and Israel, who generally tend to comply with the laws of war.

DRAGAN STANAR too weighs in on the asymmetry of drone warfare, but whereas Meisels sees it as (often) a good thing, Stanar worries that it undermines the fundamental justification for killing in war. Stanar's concern is that while the history of warfare is the history of developing weapons that allow their operators to strike from greater and greater distances, thereby minimizing risk to themselves, with drones we may finally have entered an era of "risk free" war, where the operators of drones effectively incur no risk whatsoever. A drone operator (though as Meisels notes, not everyone involved in the operation of drones) will often be located thousands of miles from the battlefield, within a secured compound, effectively immune from enemy attack. Arguably, the most dangerous part of his or her job will be the commute to/from work every day. But much of the Just War Tradition is built on the idea of a mutuality and reciprocity of risk: I am justified in killing you, because you pose a threat to me, and you are justified in killing me, because I pose a threat to you. But then when you are no longer a threat to me, what justifies my killing you? Stanar recognizes that Revisionist Just War Theorists will take a rather different view of the situation: they will tend to welcome the asymmetry (assuming that it favors the just side), because they don't think that mutuality of threat is what justifies killing in war in the first place. But then Stanar worries that, to the extent that they allow attacks on people who are not posing a (lethal) threat, they will have no reason to limit their attacks to combatants. Whether this conclusion actually follows, and if so precisely what form it takes, are interesting questions. But Stanar is surely right that drone operators involved in killing, no matter where they are located, would have to be considered legitimate targets under the traditional understanding of war.

Finally, we come to a very interesting and challenging paper by BORIS KASHNIKOV. Kashnikov identifies what he terms humanitarian terrorism, of which the U.S. killer drones campaign is a specific instance (the other two he cites being the French "Reign of Terror" of 1793–1794, and Russian individual terrorism of the late 19th and early 20th centuries). He thus rejects the distinction Meisels makes above between drones *per se* and targeted killing, apparently focusing on the latter. At first glance, humanitarian terrorism would seem to be moral: rather than killing at random, we kill only those individuals deemed deserving of death. This is precisely targeted killing done for moral reasons. Yet it still counts as terrorism, because it relies on spreading terror amongst the enemy: "the terrorists kill the culpable few … and terrorize all the rest into submission." But Kashnikov's worry is that because this killing is personal, because it is based on personal enmity, it is totalizing and leads to "absolute war." That is, to the extent that the enemy is seen as immoral, as evil, reconciliation and compromise become difficult, if not impossible. In the extreme, those under attack may feel themselves to have no choice but to respond with a more "straightforward" terrorism of indiscriminate attacks against the civilians of the opposing side. Thus, things threaten to spiral out of control in a vicious circle of killing.

At something like the opposite end of a spectrum of LAWS operating without human oversight, or even of drones being remotely piloted from thousands of miles away, lies the issue of human enhancement. The desire to build a better soldier, as it were, is probably as old as warfare itself. But only recently has it become possible to directly enhance the human body itself. Enhancement can take many different forms, from the almost wholly non-invasive – exoskeletons, for example – to the extremely invasive – germ-line intervention, in the extreme. How do we ensure respect for notions like autonomy and informed consent in an extremely hierarchical and goal-driven organization like the military? And how would the enhancement of soldiers affect society as a whole? GÉRARD DE BOISBOISSEL builds on and anticipates work done at CREC Saint-Cyr on the subject of the "enhanced soldier," and discusses the ethical implications of enhancement at various stages in the career of a soldier, from recruiting through to his or her reintegration into society after leaving service. The issues are various and complex, but at the end of the day, argues Boisboissel, we must not forget what is truly fundamental: a respect for human dignity.

Thus far, all our authors have focused on newer technologies and/or their use *per se*. But at least until there is a robot uprising, warfare is likely to remain in large part a human endeavor. Thus, the human factor, and in particular human leadership, will remain – and perhaps become increasingly – important. It is this subject that our last several authors address.

ZIPI GUSHPANTZ has extensively studied the sad case of the Kishon River. For decades, Israeli naval special forces conducted diving exercises in the heavily polluted river, despite the "stench ... the profoundly turbid waters ... the sludge ...," and what one would have thought would be the obvious health risks. Over 100 of the troops who had trained there contracted cancer, and at least 27 eventually died. Yet the training continued. Gushpantz traces this tragedy to a number of failures of leadership, and – correctly discerning that many of the newer military technologies will likely first be used by special forces troops – attempts to leverage the lessons learned from the Kishon River case into several cautionary warnings about the deployment and use of such technologies. She notes, for example, that "a high level of cohesion among the commanders of special units might easily create an organizational blindness" to moral and ethical considerations. Loyalty to the unit and to the mission can become paramount, allowing everything else to recede into the background. She closes with several suggestions as to how to implement ethics in the "praxis of command."

The final paper in the volume, also on the importance of leadership, is by CHRISTOPHER LUEDTKE and CHRISTOPHER MILLER. As we have seen, warfare is already very different from what it was a mere generation or so ago, and Luedtke and Miller argue that given the rapidly evolving nature of warfare, the preparation of military leaders is of the utmost importance: indeed, "the development of leaders of character remains the *sine qua non* of military success."

They borrow from Lieutenant General Ervin Rokke the useful idea that the "effective education of a military force requires a continuous, relentless reconciliation of three essential factors: *Immutable values*, the *changing character of successive generations* entering military service, and the *changing character of conflict*." Then, using the United States Air Force Academy as a model, they provide an extended discussion of how each of these factors can be incorporated into the education and development of leaders of character. Different services around the world will no doubt do things somewhat differently, but all will agree on the importance of this goal – as will surely all the contributors to this volume.

PART 1

Introductions/Overviews

CHAPTER 1

The Ethical Implications of Emerging Technologies in Warfare

Opening Speech

BG Benoit Royal

In general, the expression "Emerging technologies" includes:
- The increasing automation of weapons, which we see in everything that we classify as autonomous [and semi-autonomous?] lethal weapons systems (drones, of course, but not exclusively).
- The technologies and biology which lead to increasing military capabilities, which we classify under the umbrella term "the enhanced soldier", including enhanced physical, cognitive, and psychological capabilities.
- The emergence of artificial intelligence and algorithms on the battlefield, especially in the computer systems which help in decision-making – things which help us increase the autonomy and automation of responses in the multitude of electronic decision-making systems.
- The development of cyber technology (to deal with infiltration, hacking, etc.) in cyberspace.

Let us try to identify the main characteristics of the emergence of these new technologies, at a "macro" level. Here are three headings, expanded with a few thoughts:

1. These technologies are potentially less murderous
- They make for increased effectiveness when it comes to targeting, and as far as those focussing on automation of arms are concerned, they no longer require 100 bombs to achieve their aim (as was the case in the 2nd World War), whilst others seek to protect soldiers.
- Reinforced military techniques seek to protect soldiers. [Comment – repeats end of first point]

2. Increasingly covert targeting capabilities, combined with this effectiveness, mean that we can go further, more discreetly, and increase the surprise effect.
- But conversely, these capabilities have the drawback that the ideal tool may look deceiving. US strategists fell into this trap when they were engaged in the drone war in Pakistan and Yemen, which was ultimately extremely lethal in terms of collateral damage, and led John Tierney, President of the House of Representatives' National Security and Foreign Affairs Sub-committee, to

 | DOI:10.1163/9789004507951_003

declare in 2015 that *"the drones' strikes were at best contrary to ethics and at worst counterproductive".*

3. These technologies tend to gradually wipe out defined war frontiers:

A. Beyond the frontiers of the geographical area

This means:

- areas where drones are used, getting in the way of the day-to-day life of populations and countries which did not start the war,
- actions in cyberspace, which of course, has no frontier,
- Drone pilots who are acting from outside of combat zones, staying within their national territory (such as US drone pilots).

So war tends to extend into uncharted territory and other people tend to become involved. We see an inversion of the attempt to reduce combat zones.

B. Beyond the frontiers of the militarised zone

In fact, the dissemination of technologies and their accessibility to government operations encourages this dissemination.

For example:

- the CIA is deeply involved in the drone war
- the cyber war pursued by computer hackers
- dissemination of armed drones in developing countries (e.g., China)

C. Beyond view and control

Here, I would evoke:

- The increasing stealth of aerial vehicles (rather than increasingly invisible bomber aircraft),
- The almost complete invisibility of cyber action,
- The increasing use of special forces and secret operations assisted by increasingly discreet technologies.

What are the consequences of this?

1. The principles of discrimination and proportionality which were the basis for the creation of international law tend to become diluted: after all, what control does the international community have over them?
2. In these increasingly secretive areas, belligerents find room for manoeuvre, where new excesses are allowed, disregarding all rules.
3. Faced with algorithms and automation techniques, man is gradually abrogating some of his intelligence to machines. Nowadays, is he capable of setting their limits?
4. Man's place and his awareness (and so his capacity to regulate the degree of violence) tend to increasingly reduce both in areas where decisions have to be made (top management, decision-making centres) and on the ground. Perhaps man has not yet come out of the loop, but it is certain that he no longer has both feet inside it.

As a result, I consider that the expansion of these new technologies on the battlefield is starting a new contest *between war with rules and war without rules.*

Moreover I believe that there is *a real risk of dehumanisation of war and that our ethical values in future wars will drop* if players on all sides disregard lessons learnt from history and are tempted to return to short-term victories.

Furthermore the values which we are defending are the ones which were identified by humanity's most ancient philosophers as consubstantial with the survival of man. These values, which are felt from within by every one of us and are not imposed from outside by a minority, focus on our love for ourselves rather than our hatred of others. They carry within them the seeds of victory in the face of artificial and deeply exclusive ideologies or hegemonic attempts from another age.[1]

1 In the original: « Elles portent en elles les semences de la victoire face à des idéologies fabriquée de toutes pièces et profondément exclusive d'autrui ou face à des tentatives hégémoniques d'un autre âge. »

CHAPTER 2

EuroISME – Inaugural Address

H.E. Marcelino Oreja Aguirre

1 Introduction

First of all, I would like to express my deep thanks for the invitation to address a few words at the opening session of EuroISME, which meets for the first time in Spain, and brings together scientists, academics and military practitioners, engaged in research as well as in education and training in the field of military ethics.

Our meeting takes place in the Infantry Academy of the Spanish Army, a very distinguished teaching center that provides training, adapted to technological and scientific change, and development, and that maintains high and demanding standards.

As a civilian, I must say that in Spain we have surpassed the distinction between civilian and military long ago and, when we speak of civil society, we also include the Armed Forces. The military have full capacity to freely exercise their rights as citizens. I would like to recall the reflection of a famous Spanish intellectual, Ortega y Gasset, who referring to the Armed Forces expressed the idea that the Military is a spiritual force which has two sides: that of their permanent readiness to combat, and the social side, ready to support the citizens.[1]

Our Armies, as was mentioned recently by my colleague in the Royal Academy of Sciences, General Agustín Muñoz-Grandes, are part of a society that is submitted to frequent change. Therefore, we need a code of conduct that defines, with a spirit of permanence, the fundamental values of the military institution that should always be firmly held, and especially in the uncertain times in which we live.

With all those precedents, you can imagine how honored I feel to address such a prestigious institution as EuroISME.

EuroISME promotes and defends the existence of a specific ethical reflection focused primarily on the exclusive functions of the military profession, and whose last exponent is no other than combat. Military training attempts to create a professional mentality, since the nature of the combat function allows

1 José Ortega y Gasset, *España invertebrada* (Austral 1999).

 | DOI:10.1163/9789004507951_004

one to reflect on the professional exercise of the military. I do think that there is a constant standard of military ethics among military professionals at any time and place, similar to what happens in other social realms.

An important feature, shared by military ethics and the Law of Armed Conflict, which our country has signed and decided to incorporate into our legal system, is communication. Military professionals have the duty of not only expanding the idea of ethics, but also of knowing thoroughly its principles, contents, and application. From the first training center to the last day in the practice of their duties, militaries have the ethical requirement of studying and reaching a comprehensive knowledge of the law of war. This should be carried out through education in academies, instruction in units, advanced courses, training in exercises and individual and collective ongoing preparation. Thanks to EuroISME, this conference will allow us to deepen and incorporate new contents of great ethical and didactic value.

Confronting armed conflict involves the use of military force, which in turn requires the existence of armies. Armies neither seek nor promote war. Because as an institution in societies like Spain, armies are committed to solidarity in the service of peace, freedom, justice and democracy.

Nowadays, these are the values underpinning security in our western civilization, and which must be stressed as a starting point. They constitute the essential ethical principles that must guide the actions of the European military, together with the dignity of the human being.[2]

Today everything is subject to rapid change. Among these changes, technological innovation is one of the most important. This fact has consequences both on the evolution of risks and threats, and on the changes in the nature of the conflicts that armies have to tackle. Therefore, the responses also change in their ethical components. As a result, legality is not only absolutely essential, but also moral legitimacy in the use of force. A force that is lethal, and this is something the military must not forget.

In the end, the changes that are taking place condition the model of the Armed Forces and compel us to consider other instruments besides military means, armies and navies, the defense, in its traditional sense. But, in any case, these Armed Forces and their military must not lose sight of their crucial role as spearheads in the military defense of their democratic societies.

---

2 Article 15 of the Spanish Royal Ordinances for the Armed Forces, approved by Royal Decree 96/2009, 6 February 2009, related to the Primacy of Ethical Principles, states: [The military] *will give primacy to the ethical principles that respond to a requirement which must govern their lives. This will contribute to strengthening the Armed Forces, guarantee of peace and security.*

All this shows that the role of the military has been expanded: that it must assume not only the responsibilities inherent to its essential and prime role of combatant, but also those arising from its new tasks and responsibilities as an aid worker, assistant, or even, occasionally, as a police officer. One could say that the military paradigm does not change, it expands.

And in this expansion, it is worth considering the new role played by technology and new systems incorporated into all military capabilities. Thanks to EuroISME, and during these three days, you will be able to analyze, discuss and consider ethical and legal elements, as well as the nature of the relations between civil society and the military.

1.1 *Technological Development and Ethics*

In our industrialized western societies, the war phenomenon has historically been one of the most important driving forces behind the development of new weapons, fostered by great advances in scientific and technical knowledge.

There has always been 'asymmetric warfare' where irregular combatants participate against conventional forces. However, once the Cold War was over that concept has been broadened to 'hybrid warfare', in which military forces confront conventional and non-conventional contenders (at times including criminal elements). Among other features, these contenders are very difficult to identify and attribute, as they try to use technological capabilities in a surprising way, and they appear and disappear from different scenarios making it impossible to break their will to continue fighting. This means that there is never a classic end to the conflict and that the boundaries between war and peace fade or even disappear.[3] But what is clear is that this menace threatens our shared way of life and the fundamental values that underpin it.

Additionally, at the beginning of the 21st century more than ever, the citizens of Western countries show a profound restlessness towards the victims of armed conflicts, whether they are combatants or civilian victims. They efficiently convey to politicians this consideration, which acts as a moral constraint in the use of military force. A force that by its very nature it cannot be forgotten, produces destruction and death. Yet the contenders to be tackled in the new hybrid conflicts do not have these restrictions.

3 Juan Gamboa, 'Amenaza híbrida, ¿un concepto doctrinal?' (2017) 921 *Revista Ejército* 26. The 'hybrid warfare' concept is introduced in 1998 by Robert Walker in his thesis 'The United States Marine Corps and Special Operations', and it was in 2005 when Mattis and Hofman published *Future Warfare: the Rise of Hybrid Wars*, considered the starting point in the conceptual analysis of hybrid warfare.

When addressing these constraints and challenges, the solutions that science and technological development can provide also have to be considered. Thus, it is common for defense policies to promote advanced technology weapons programs, sometimes relying on civilian research under the umbrella of the concept of dual-use technologies.

The right of our societies to military defense – based on all assumptions of legality and legitimacy – is a public service which contributes to the defense of the values and interests of a political system promoting freedom, human dignity and democratic values. To consign the support that this military defense receives from technology in the search for deterrence, makes it necessary to put this technology at the service of ethical considerations.

It is indispensable to maintain moral standards of warlike conduct in the development of wars and conflicts, not only in the ends, but also in the means and methods, aligned with the values and principles governing the coexistence in their societies. Ethical considerations on the battlefield have always played an important role in military operations. This is why the Geneva and Hague Conventions were developed, and rules of engagement established, taking into account the circumstances in which such operations take place.

That raises the question of whether the doctrine of the use and operation of modern weapon systems, will meet rigorous ethical considerations. The implications of new weapon systems affect, from that ethical perspective, even deeply rooted convictions and moral principles in the professionals of the Armed Forces.

1.2 *The Behavior Changes: Drones*

An essential value to the military pilot is determination. The future combat aircraft will continue to need the pilot's determination, but possibly accompanied by a much more intellectual understanding and psychological preparation. Bravery, understood as a psychological impulse that risk and physical exposure leads to heroic action in combat, requires new considerations. It is therefore important to consider the case of this new type of pilot, who is responsible for the remotely manned aerial systems: the human behind the drones.

Drone pilots who guide drones thousands of miles away, may put at risk a very valuable machine, in technological terms, but not their life. Perhaps they may also expose their prestige and expertise. Their bravery rests on their good judgment, information integration capability, and technical know-how. Something to add to the bravery and boldness of pilots, not afraid to deal with enemy aircraft, missiles and air defense systems.

Faced with these plausible changes in the values and principles of the military ethos, it must be noted that there is one element that must remain, and it is no other than the moral demands imposed by combat. Drone pilots, like aircraft pilots, retain their responsibility with regard to the effects of their actions in employing lethal violence, even though it may well seem that this responsibility disappears because of the huge distance between their position on a computer from which they are conducting their actions, and the results produced on the target.

Consequently, some consider that the fact of following the war through screens and handling it with a remote control would introduce an element of emotional detachment that could translate into indifference to death or even an excessive readiness to kill – both the drone objectives and non-combatant individuals, the so-called collateral victims.[4]

However, if physical distance produces emotional detachment in such a manner that moving away from the objective reduces restraint when making decisions – if also moral restrictions on the use of lethal violence fade away – the ethical justification allowing us to defend ourselves and fight in a just cause, while maintaining certain behaviors in combat, will be lost. Hence, drone pilots cannot allow themselves to be carried away by the feeling that distance and remoteness from the target, as well as the absolute reduction of their own risk, make this target less real and less humane. Particularly, when people are involved. Thus, they cannot allow themselves to be influenced by the thought that this distance also separates them from the demand for adequate involvement and moral attention.

Another ethical problem arises from the example I have just mentioned. Drone attacks are justified by the economic argument of being an inexpensive weapon and by the ethical arguments of 'fewer soldiers die and there are hardly any civilian casualties'.[5] The latter merits reflection.

In conventional wars and conflicts, the principles of necessity and proportionality, the reduction of casualties in the achievement of military objectives and respect for non-combatants, are at the moral bases of war. The use of drones removes the risk of casualties among pilots, but raises concerns about the risk of increasing non-combatant collateral casualties, who according to the international laws of warfare are always innocent victims.

Thus, we have the problem of the time lag between the image obtained from the target and the arrival to the drone operator. In that interim, the target has been able to move and, even worse, be replaced by non-combatants, who

4 Laila Yousef Sandoval, 'La desaparición del combate clásico: un nuevo tipo de guerra. La sustitución del soldado por el dron' in María Gajate y Laura González (eds), *Guerra y Tecnología* (Fundación Ramón Areces 2007) 534.

5 Yousef Sandoval (n 4) 535.

would suffer lethal violence, despite careful screening of targets to avoid affecting non-combatants.

This is a technological problem that perhaps science itself will be able to solve in the future. But, for the time being, warfare has humans lagging behind, even with the most advanced technological systems. And combatants, given their level of responsibility, cannot and must not forget that their actions still lead to the exercise of lethal violence and destruction, so they remain morally and legally responsible for them – in accordance with ethical principles and subject to legal conditions.

1.3 *Artificial Intelligence and Robots*

There is no doubt that scientific developments in artificial intelligence and robotics pose new problems that must also be addressed from the ethical point of view, among other aspects.

In 1942, Isaac Asimov mentioned in his book *I, Robot*, a number of laws as an ethical code for the operation of robots. These laws aimed at ensuring that their operation would guarantee the safety of human beings at all times.

In this sense, as José A. Plaza recalls,[6] we must mention the manifesto that in July 2005 warned about the dangers of artificial intelligence and called for its regulation. This manifesto was supported by prestigious experts such as Stephen Hawking, Steve Wozniak, and Noam Chomsky, among others. In September 2016, the 'Partnership on AI' was created with the participation of Amazon, Apple, Google, IBM, Microsoft and other companies. Other initiatives have expressed concern about the inappropriate, premature or malicious use of new technologies proposing ethical codes of conduct which promote the appropriate use of artificial intelligence.

The new concept of 'Lethal Autonomous Weapons Systems' (LAWS), which some people refer to as 'killer robots', is of particular interest.

As Irene Savio points out,[7] they are at risk of being used in the future as weapons that could make the decision to wound or kill, independently of any kind of human control, and there is currently a gap in international humanitarian law. For this reason, the UN itself held a meeting in Geneva at the end of 2017, within the framework of the Convention on Conventional Weapons, to achieve an international regulatory framework.

---

6 José Ángel Plaza López, 'Lecciones de ética para máquinas que "piensan" y toman decisiones' (*Retina. EL PAIS ECONOMIA*, 19 December 2017) <https://retina.elpais.com/retina/2017/12/19/innovacion/1513661054_305253.html> accessed 26 July 2020.

7 Irene Savio, 'La ONU frente a las 'máquinas asesinas' (*esglobal*, 21 November 2017) <https://www.esglobal.org/la-onu-frente-las-maquinas-asesinas/> accessed 25 July 2020.

The risks of these systems affect ethical as well as legal aspects, such as avoiding innocent victims; the differentiation between civilians and combatants; the responsibility of those who decide on their use and accountability; and their lack of empathy if they have the capacity to 'select targets and attack them on their own in the course of a conflict'.

On the other hand, and in a favorable sense to these developments, it is argued that apart from avoiding military deaths caused by the conflict, 'these machines would not commit rape or war crimes, as they do not fall under the influence of rage, fear or anger'.[8]

In fact, scientists like Ronald Arkin believe that robots with lethal capacity can carry out their work more efficiently and also more ethically than human soldiers. For this scientist: 'The hope is that if these systems can be properly designed and used in situations where they could be correctly employed, they might significantly reduce collateral damage'.[9]

Arkin's main idea is that these systems could be programmed with certain ethical restrictions that would safeguard respect for international humanitarian law on the battlefield without the risk of human error that might lead to illegal and, above all, immoral acts in the conduct of military operations.

Such an ethical model would include the possibility that these systems could leave the mission in the face of unforeseen and unanticipated circumstances, since its execution would be considered immoral and illegal. All this due to the fact that those 'robots' could process more information, faster, and more accurately than humans before considering the use of lethal force.

The critical concept that is being explored and analyzed in international fora is that of 'significant human control'. In other words, that human beings are always ultimately responsible for the performance of a machine, not only in the identification of targets, but also in its selection and final operation.

2 Conclusions

Training and education of the military in our academies and schools must be extended to the ethical and moral field, just as modern technologies and novel missions – other than conventional warfare – demand new capabilities and expertise of our militaries.

---

8 Savio (n 7) 2.

9 Jesús Travieso, 'Las consecuencias de mandar a la guerra a "robots asesinos"' (*eldiario.es*, 17 April 2015) <https://www.eldiario.es/sociedad/debate-torno-robots-asesinos_1_2718731.html> accessed 25 July 2020.

These include training in ethics and military ethics. The justification for the future use of military force will be based on the ultimate argument which is law and moral reason. The Armed Forces will take military action using violence in a rational manner, so as to put an end to irrational violence and not going beyond what is necessary to restore peace.

The transformation of the Armed Forces – the introduction of scientific advances unthinkable a few years ago – requires changes in organization and doctrine, imposes new missions, demands better instruments and calls for open-mindedness. With this, the Armed Forces adapt to the changes of the last decades, so technological, social and even cultural innovations will have to fit into an efficient system, in which tolerance, as well as technology and talent, will definitely become a moral category.

This path of 'positive crisis' has long been followed by the Spanish Armed Forces, which, as an institution, enjoy the highest respect among Spaniards, as revealed by the latest sociological surveys.

All these changes are essential and mentalities need to be adapted for a permanent process of transformation and renewal, since 'constant change and adaptation are in the nature of any military institution'. In short, it is the innovation of the civil and business world to adapt to society and serve more efficiently and rigorously.

These transformations modify the way in which conflicts, military structures, and the psychological disposition of soldiers and sailors to combat are dealt with and managed. Behaviors also change in combat missions, support missions, and of course, in peace missions. Here, the heroic forms that were produced with the means and methods of warfare in earlier times are very different from the current conflicts and operations, and do not prevent the military from demonstrating their heroic value. But this is also expressed in other ways. Heroism only reaches its peak if it leans on the basis of ethically inspired conduct, and does not lose sight of the essential value of human dignity, even in combat.

Another issue that would take us much further is the possibility that one day science will develop machines that escape control and transform into something more intelligent than the human being itself, being able to design and build other devices on its own. The question then would be whether these machines also have the moral judgment to become responsible for their actions on the battlefield. But this issue makes us fear the idea of war between machines and the end of humanity.

References

Gamboa, Juan, 'Amenaza híbrida, ¿un concepto doctrinal?' (2017) 921 *Revista Ejército.*

Mattis, James N. and Frank G. Hoffman. *Future Warfare: The Rise of Hybrid Wars* (2005).

Ortega y Gasset, José, *España invertebrada* (Austral 1999).

Plaza López, José Ángel, 'Lecciones de ética para máquinas que "piensan" y toman decisiones' (*Retina. EL PAIS ECONOMIA*, 19 December 2017) <https://retina.elpais.com/retina/2017/12/19/innovacion/1513661054_305253.html> accessed 26 July 2020.

Savio, Irene, 'La ONU frente a las 'máquinas asesinas' (*esglobal*, 21 November 2017) <https://www.esglobal.org/la-onu-frente-las-maquinas-asesinas/> accessed 25 July 2020.

Travieso, Jesús, 'Las consecuencias de mandar a la guerra a "robots asesinos"' (*eldiario.es*, 17 April 2015) <https://www.eldiario.es/sociedad/debate-torno-robots-asesinos_1_2718731.html> accessed 25 July 2020.

Walker, Robert G. *The United States Marine Corps and Special Operations* (Storming Media 1998).

Yousef Sandoval, Laila, 'La desaparición del combate clásico: un nuevo tipo de guerra. La sustitución del soldado por el dron' in María Gajate y Laura González (eds), *Guerra y Tecnología* (Fundación Ramón Areces 2007).

CHAPTER 3

The Ethical Implications of Emerging Technologies in Warfare

Emmanuel Bloch

The Good, the Bad and the Ugly: lobbying issues over ethics and emerging technologies between States, Businesses, and NGOs

∴

The issue of ethics – or should I say business ethics – gained prominence in the early 2000s at Thales, mainly in relation to two highly specific aspects: ethical business practices (in other words, the fight against corruption), and ethical behaviour (in other words defence against harassment).

We have to remember that, until 1999, when the OECD Convention on Combating Bribery of Foreign Public Officials in International Business Transactions came into force, corruption was not really an issue in most countries, including European countries. Therefore, the entry into force of the Convention in France in 2000 brought something of a shakeup to the business practices of some major groups, including Thomson, Thales's predecessor.

The other major ethical issue of the early 2000s was harassment, whether sexual or psychological. Well before the advent of the #MeToo movement, relationships between individuals in the workplace emerged as a key concern.

The fight against corruption and harassment therefore provided the foundation for Thales's ethics policy in the early 2000s, leading in particular to the introduction of a Code of Ethics, as well as an ethics alert procedure that was revolutionary at the time.

But we have to admit that today this approach is no longer fully suited to our current challenges.

At Thales, we consider that Ethical issues arise at three key moments of the business:
- When creating a product: what do we make?
- When manufacturing a product: how do we make it?
- When selling the product: how and where do we sell it?

 | DOI:10.1163/9789004507951_005

The fight against corruption is most relevant to the third of these aspects: how do we sell it. However, issues relating to the recipient of the product had not been really raised before. Defence contractors like Thales believed that this was not a matter of concern for them, because sales were only possible with authorisation from the State (in the form of a licence from the CIEEMG, the French interministerial commission on defence exports). The decision on whether or not to sell to a given country was therefore taken by the Government, which meant that the company was, *de facto*, freed from its responsibility.

Today, this approach is increasingly being called into question. Firstly, because many products that present a potential threat to individual freedoms do not fall within the scope of defence export licencing. Examples include smart video surveillance systems, or systems used to analyse behaviour for the purpose of detecting banking fraud. And secondly, because today, even if a company has obtained a defence export licence, some NGOs affirm that they may still be held liable for the way its products are used by the end customer. A recent study made by a French law firm tends to support this view, even if it has not been validated by any Court of Justice to date.[1]

Likewise, the consideration of ethical issues in the manufacture of our products focused for a long time on internal questions of harassment, based on the principle that what happened elsewhere, within our suppliers' and partners' factories, was not really within the area of responsibility of Thales. This view is, of course, now completely out of date, notably due to a variety of soft and hard laws which reaffirm that a company's responsibility extends over all its areas of influence. But these areas of influence still need to be defined. The US Dodd-Frank Act on "conflict minerals" and the French law on Due Diligence remind companies that this responsibility extends a long way – right back to the start of the value chain, in fact – and that they are also responsible for the working practices of their subcontractors and suppliers. This is also a game-changer. Defence is maybe less exposed than other sectors such as the textile or the electronic sectors; however, these considerations must be taken into account.

This brings us, finally, to the heart of the matter: the ethics of the product itself. What do we actually make? For a long time, this didn't appear to be an issue either. The only thing that counted was whether the product was legal. In the defence sector, this was, once again, often a matter for the Government to decide. Most defence products were developed with public funding and

---

1 Joseph Breham et Laurence Greig, "Les transferts d'armes de la France dans le cadre du conflit au Yémen, à compter d'avril 2015 jusqu'à la période actuelle" (2018) *Ancile Avocats*, 16th March 2018. <https://www.acatfrance.fr/public/etude-juridique_cabinet-ancile_transfert-d-armes-de-la-france-dans-le-cadre-du-conflit-au-yemen.pdf> accessed 3 September 2020.

State approval. Some major changes have occurred in this area too. Firstly, the increasing use of civil technologies in defence systems brings ethical issues even more to the fore, notably because some civil players object to their innovations being used for military applications. Elon Musk's recent statements on the use of AI in the defence sector, and the mini-rebellion at Google triggered by the possible "militarisation" of some applications developed in-house, are clear illustrations of these changes. Even more disruptive – potentially – is the growing tendency to question the use of technologies strictly dedicated to military uses: treaties banning anti-personnel mines, cluster bombs, and, more recently, nuclear weapons, reflect growing public concern about the ethics of deploying certain types of weapons.

But the question "what do we make?" is not only about weapons. It can also be asked about CCTV systems capable of identifying people on the move or spotting suspicious behaviours, like China is deploying on its territory. It can also be asked about drones capable of identifying participants at a rally by capturing the IMEI numbers of their mobile phones, about AI used to identify suspicious behaviours on the web based on analysis of browsing histories, and so on.

Today, a company like Thales is asked these three questions on an almost daily basis: what do you make? How do you make it? And who do you sell it to? And it's not only NGOs who are asking – it's also our shareholders, investors, bankers, customers, suppliers, employees, lawmakers, and virtually everyone else.

1 Relationships between Companies, States and NGOs

The focus of this paper is to elaborate the relationships between companies, States and NGOs on ethical issues, and in particular regarding new technologies used for defence purposes. Issues regarding Lethal Autonomous Weapon Systems (LAWS) obviously spring to mind, but they are not the only example. Systems to manipulate and incite populations via social media to serve military[2] or political objectives[3] may fall within the same category. So how did we get to where we are today?

2 See "US military studied how to influence Twitter users in Darpa-funded research" The Guardian (London, 8 July 2018) <https://www.theguardian.com/world/2014/jul/08/darpa-social-networks-research-twitter-influence-studies> accessed 3 September 2020.

3 Refer to the New-York Times website dedicated to the Russian involvement in the US Presidential campaign: The New-York Times, "Russian Hacking and Influence in the U.S. Election. Complete coverage of Russia's campaign to disrupt the 2016 presidential election"

Relationships between companies, States and NGOs have evolved significantly over the past twenty years or so, as a result of a number of different political, economic, and technological factors.

When the UN was founded in 1945, it had 51 member states, whose aim was to promote peace and security, economic development, and human rights. In 2015, the UN's mission was extended to encompass 17 Sustainable Development Goals, which include gender equality, an end to world hunger, protection of seas and rivers, etc.

Today, the UN has 193 member states. As a result, its decision-making processes are much more complex. In addition, many people believe that the whole UN "*machin*", as de Gaulle called it, has become much less effective in protecting populations, for example in Syria. And it has lost some of its credibility, given the fact that the UN Human Rights Council encompasses countries close to the bottom of the international rankings in terms of respect for human rights.

This has led to a shift: since States are incapable of ensuring compliance with the treaties they have signed, it's now up to companies to do so. To express it in military terms, power has become more diffuse. Companies now have to ensure that human rights are respected in their countries of operation, and by their subcontractors, throughout the entire value chain, on a global basis. The same applies to the fight against corruption, protection of the environment, gender equality, etc.

This has resulted in a gradual change in the way the non-profit sector works, involving a switch from a highly ideological approach to a more activist approach, with the development of new, particularly effective models of action that combine NGOs, consultancies and certifying bodies, States, and financial institutions.

Let's starts with the NGOs. They have become more structured and more effective, and have cleverly split into two main categories: the "activist" NGOs and the "institutional" NGOs, based on the tasks they aim to accomplish.

The initial aim of activist NGOs is to raise public awareness of a specific issue, such as anti-personnel mines, the use of armed drones, human rights violations, the use of AI in defence, etc. They do this by organising campaigns based on dramatic events such as the "pyramid of shoes" against landmines, trash posters, the occupation of industrial sites, viral videos on YouTube, etc.

(The New-York Times) <https://www.nytimes.com/news-event/russian-election-hacking> accessed 3 September 2020.

Their objective is clearly to get coverage of their issues in the mainstream media. And of course, they also rely heavily on the use of new technologies and particularly social media, such as Facebook, Twitter, etc. to spread their message. In fact, widespread dissemination of messages via the Internet and social media has played a crucial role in the rapid growth in visibility and effectiveness of these NGOs.

Institutional NGOs operate at a different level – their role is not to mobilise opinion, but to raise awareness of a given issue among institutions at UN, national, or political levels. They naturally rely on the work done by activist NGOs, enabling them to contact politicians directly: "Dear Member of Parliament, as you can see from the widespread press coverage, artificial intelligence is currently a major issue ..." They have to identify the right "client" (a State, a prominent individual, a political party or politician) who is ready to champion the cause for ideological or personal reasons. Among the States who supported the Treaty on the Prohibition of Nuclear Weapons, some of them clearly did so for political reasons –as a negotiating tool, or as a means of striking back at Western countries who are perceived as arrogant and moralistic – rather than for ideological reasons.

For example, if we look at the full-time staff of ICAN, the International Campaign to Abolish Nuclear Weapons, which was awarded the Nobel Peace Prize in 2017, we can see that they are far from being the bearded tree-huggers of popular legend. Many of ICAN's personnel have university degrees, mainly in Law or Political Science, and some of them have worked or completed internships at major international institutions, in particular the UN. In short, they are talented professionals with real international experience.

Once the subject appears on the political scene, the next step is to draft a treaty or standard to define the scope of the cause. It is at this stage that the major consulting and law firms become involved. Their expertise is essential in formalising the initial ideological concept, particularly since they often make their best experts available *pro bono* to participate in the working groups that draw up the future hard or soft laws. They do this, of course, because they support the initiative, but also perhaps because they are in the exceptional situation of being involved in the definition of the standard "from the inside". This situation may be particularly profitable when it comes to supporting actors who will subsequently have to comply with it: the businesses. A cynic might even say that they are, to a certain extent, creating their own market.

Finally, there is the question of implementation. Not all of these initiatives result in binding laws or treaties. The journey from the launch of a campaign by an NGO to the production of a universally recognized binding treaty can take years. But that isn't necessarily a problem for the NGO. It is sufficient for the issue to be taken on board by financial institutions.

Take for example the case of the United Nations Global Compact, an initiative that brings together businesses, UN agencies, labour groups, and civil society around ten principles in the areas of human rights, the environment, and anti-corruption. The organisation recently reviewed its integrity policy to exclude sectors such as tobacco and "controversial" weapons, a category which includes anti-personnel mines, cluster bombs, and nuclear weapons. As a result, companies associated with the manufacture of such weapons are unable to sign up to the Global Compact, and can be excluded from it.

The initial consequence of exclusion is, of course, reputational. But that's not all: many banks and investors use the Global Compact as a basis for defining their investment policies. This means that if you are excluded from the Global Compact, you risk losing shareholders, and you may have increasing difficulty obtaining the funds you need for your business. This threat is real and it is highly effective, and that is why NGOs are increasingly targeting financial institutions.

Finally, States pass legislation … or they do not. But legislation is often just the final part of a process that is already well advanced.

In the sector that interests us, I would like to come back to the concept of "controversial weapons". This vague notion now underpins the policy initiatives of NGOs. The fact is that many financial institutions, rather than providing precise details of their exclusion policy, simply refer to the concept of "controversial weapons". All the NGOs have to do is to apply the broadest possible interpretation to the concept, which was initially linked mainly to chemical and bacteriological weapons, and then to anti-personnel mines and cluster bombs, with the aim of imposing *de facto* constraints on certain companies.

This is how white phosphorus, armed drones, nuclear weapons, and now assault weapons (where they are on sale to the general public) have become "controversial weapons". And Lethal Autonomous Weapon Systems will probably soon be included too.

It's also interesting to note that the concept of "controversial weapons" is a highly political one: white phosphorus and armed drones (as well as cluster bombs) are linked to the Israel-Palestine conflict, nuclear weapons to the Treaty on the Prohibition of Nuclear Weapons, and assault weapons to the recent shootings in Parkland, Florida.

2 How Should Companies and States Respond?

Should companies – and, to a certain extent, States – simply stand back and take the hit every time? Because that's what seems to be happening at the moment.

The easiest way to visualise the situation is to consider the notion of a "zone of tolerance". Companies operate within a regulatory, political, economic, and societal environment which is, in principle, positive. This environment can be viewed as a "zone of tolerance", the playing field on which a company is able to function. However, this zone of tolerance can change significantly over time. It can expand, giving companies greater scope for action, or it can shrink, if increasing constraints are imposed. Take the example of the pharmaceutical industry: twenty years ago, it was considered the industry of the future, and was attracting all the young talent. Over the past five or six years, however, its reputation has been tainted, and regulation in the sector has increased considerably. In short, the zone of tolerance has shrunk. A more recent example is the technology sector, and in particular social media. The "zone of tolerance" of Facebook or Google has really shrunk, particularly in Europe.

Today, some NGOs are aiming to restrict the zone of tolerance for defence activities; our role is to ensure that this doesn't happen, or at least to minimise it. This means that we have to take action, bearing in mind the current context. Because the world has changed.

For a long time, companies and States showed a degree of disdain toward NGOs and "minor States", who were perceived at best as day-dreamers, and at worst as being manipulated by "hostile" forces.

In my view, the adoption by the UN of the Treaty on the Prohibition of Nuclear Weapons, and its subsequent signing by a significant number of countries (59 to date),[4] owes a great deal to this kind of behaviour. For a long time, some of the "nuclear" states displayed certain contempt for the discussions around that issue, and the companies involved did not appear to care at all. This recently changed when legal experts began taking a serious look at the consequences associated with the treaty's potential entry into force. That quickly led to a degree of concern, not to say agitation.

Today, the same question arises with regard to the use of artificial intelligence. And this time we must not simply stand on the sidelines of a debate that concerns us. I say "us" because this naturally affects industry, as well as governments and, obviously, the armed forces. To borrow an expression that

4 As of August 31st, 2018.

I find particularly relevant to this kind of discussion: if you're not at the table, you're on the menu.

What we need, therefore, is a "doctrine". This is why, at Thales, we decided to set up an internal "Artificial Intelligence and Digital Transformation" working group, which quickly identified two main obstacles:

1. Any discussion of the use of AI in defence and security applications, and in particular of the issue of Lethal Autonomous Weapon Systems, immediately comes up against personal moral principles. There is a great temptation to react instinctively, and express strong individual opinions on the issue – on either side of the argument – without first having reflected on its nuanced nature.
2. Artificial intelligence is an extremely complex subject that combines ethical, technological, political, and economic aspects, and requires in-depth analysis. It is not possible to make a genuinely constructive contribution to the debate on AI without first having examined all of these different aspects.

The working group includes people from many of Thales's areas of expertise – and not just engineers. It will also call upon external experts specialising in operational matters, philosophy, sociology, geopolitics, etc.

Our aim is not to arrive at a clear-cut position, whereby we say a firm "yes" or "no" to Lethal Autonomous Weapon Systems, but to define the limits of what we consider to be acceptable in relation to this topic.

Obviously, this work only has value if it is shared with all of our stakeholders, including the NGOs who are also focusing on these issues. Ideally, it could perhaps provide a benchmark for our sector.

What we are trying to show with this example is that ethics ultimately lies at the heart of these new challenges. We have an array of emerging new technologies which will probably revolutionise the way wars are fought – in addition to Lethal Autonomous Weapon Systems, of course, there's also the use of Big Data in control systems, the Internet of Things, cyber weapons, etc. – and we have to identify what is actually possible, with the help of all the stakeholders. Opportunities for discussion, like conferences, are essential in this respect.

Because that's what, according to us, ethics is about. It's not about ensuring compliance with standards, or saying what's right and wrong. It's an instrument of arbitration between all our stakeholders' opinions to ensure that we can continue to work efficiently in the event of a conflict of values. In any case, that's how we perceive it.

3 Conclusion

In conclusion, we want to be clear about our approach. It's not about confrontation, but collaboration. The world has changed. Public opinion and civil society want to take part in these debates, and are developing the capabilities that allow them to do so.

It would be not only unethical but also highly dangerous to ignore this. The time when quoting the "national interest" was sufficient to silence dissenting voices has passed. And that's no bad thing.

We have stepped squarely into the era of responsibility, once and for all.

Companies are responsible to their stakeholders. We have to be capable of assessing, as objectively as possible, the positive and negative externalities, in other words the benefits and the consequences, which arise from our products and solutions.

States are responsible to their populations; they also have responsibilities in respect of the treaties they have signed. It's high time that the international community had the courage to ask States finally to comply with the many treaties and conventions they have committed to. It is an easy task when these States are designated as "rogue States" by the most powerful countries in the world. It is obviously less simple when you have to tell an "ally" that it has been going too far.

The armed forces also have responsibilities. Most of the armed forces are acutely aware of that fact; unfortunately, however, this is not the case everywhere.

Last but not least, NGOs have their own responsibilities. They can't shirk them just because they are non-governmental organisations. On the contrary, it seems to me: great causes go hand-in-hand with great responsibilities. They have to be professional and attach a permanent attention to the truth. The defence of a cause, whatever it is, should never rely on lies or public opinion manipulations.

At Thales, we firmly believe that this collaborative approach will enable us to define an ethical environment that is acceptable to everyone. Excluding stakeholders is not appropriate or effective. Neither is it ethical.

References

Breham, Joseph et Laurence Greig, "Les transferts d'armes de la France dans le cadre du conflit au Yémen, à compter d'avril 2015 jusqu'à la période actuelle" (2018) *Ancile Avocats*, 16th March 2018. <https://www.acatfrance.fr/public/etude-juridique_cabinet-ancile_transfert-d-armes-de-la-france-dans-le-cadre-du-conflit-au-yemen.pdf> accessed 3 September 2020.

"Russian Hacking and Influence in the U.S. Election. Complete coverage of Russia's campaign to disrupt the 2016 presidential election" (*The New York Times*) <https://www.nytimes.com/news-event/russian-election-hacking> accessed 3 September 2020.

"US military studied how to influence Twitter users in Darpa-funded research" *The Guardian* (London, 8 July 2018) <https://www.theguardian.com/world/2014/jul/08/darpa-social-networks-research-twitter-influence-studies> accessed 3 September 2020.

PART 2

AI/LAWS

CHAPTER 4

Exploring Western and Chinese Responses to the Ethical Challenge of Lethal Autonomous Weapons

Deane-Peter Baker

1 Introduction

In recent times a vigorous debate has developed over the appropriateness of lethal autonomous weapons systems (LAWS). These discussions have emerged as a result of advances in weapons technology and, more specifically, the decision in the United Nations to launch a process under the Convention on Certain Conventional Weapons (CCW) to engage a Group of Governmental Experts (GGE) to evaluate whether autonomous weapons should be regulated or banned within the scope of the CCW. From that debate, several ethical challenges to the use of these weapons have emerged, primarily from Western think tanks and academics. As a High Contracting Party to the CCW, China has been a participant in the meetings of the GGE, and has made a number of statements to the GGE. Given that analysts of China's defence posture have reported considerable enthusiasm for the potential military employment of Artificial Intelligence, including seemingly in autonomous weapons, it came as some surprise when it was reported that during the April 2018 meeting of the GGE in Geneva, the Chinese delegation expressed a "desire to negotiate and conclude" a ban on "the use of fully autonomous lethal weapons systems", a position that was reiterated in the March 2019 meeting. In this paper I set out the predominant ethics-based arguments for and against lethal autonomous weapons which have emerged from Western sources, and attempt to plot China's articulated position against it. I also suggest ways scholars of Chinese ethics might construct an authentic Chinese ethic on this topic which is consistent with the Chinese just war tradition.

The definition of what constitutes an autonomous weapon remains disputed, as is the distinction (which some parties deem significant) between 'automated' and 'autonomous' systems. Nonetheless, there is increasing acceptance that they are "robot weapons that once launched will select and engage

 | DOI:10.1163/9789004507951_006

targets without further human intervention"[1] or, as the ICRC puts it in their version:

> Any weapon system with autonomy in its critical functions. That is, a weapon system which can select (i.e. search for or detect, identify, track, select) and attack (i.e. use force against, neutralize, damage or destroy) targets without human intervention.[2]

Despite being widely accepted, this definition is not without its shortcomings. In particular, some of the terminology is, arguably, loaded. 'Select' carries an implication of deliberate cognitive activity which may not be an appropriate description of how many autonomous weapons do or will function – 'discern' or 'identify' would be a more neutral alternative. Likewise, 'attack' is a loaded term in this context, given the importance of the question of at which point human agency is relevant – 'engage' would again be a more neutral alternative. Nonetheless, for the purposes of this paper, I will take it that the ICRC definition is a sufficiently accurate description of the phenomenon under consideration.

2 Western Responses to Lethal Autonomous Weapons

Taking actions designed to kill fellow human beings is, to state the blindingly obvious, extremely morally risky. It is for this reason that we have a range of instruments in international law which restrict the use of military force by states and non-state actors, as well as a demanding framework for ethics (the Just War Tradition) which applies to such actions in the context of armed conflict. The moral seriousness of killing underpins the international community's ongoing efforts to evaluate the appropriateness of new methods and means of warfare, as we are seeing now in the case of autonomous weapons. The arguments for and against the employment of LAWS have, by and large, emerged from among the ranks of Western scholars, policy-makers and advocacy groups. In their paper 'Meaningful Human Control over Autonomous Systems: A Philosophical Account', Filippo Santoni de Sio and Jeroen van den

1 Jürgen Altmann, Peter Asaro, Noel Sharkey and Robert Sparrow; 'Armed military robots: editorial' (2013) 15(2) *Ethics and Information Technology*, 73–76.

2 International Committee of the Red Cross, 'Autonomous Weapon Systems: Implications of Increasing Autonomy in the Critical Functions of Weapons' (Report) Expert meeting, Versoix, Switzerland, 15–16 March 2016, 8.

Hoven helpfully sum up the three main ethical objections which have been raised in the debate over AWS:

> (a) As a matter of fact, robots of the near future will not be capable of making the sophisticated practical and moral distinctions required by the laws of armed conflict …: distinction between combatants and non-combatants, proportionality in the use of force, and military necessity of violent action. The delegation of military tasks to robots may therefore raise the number of wrongs and crimes in military operations. …
> (b) As a matter of principle, it is morally wrong to let a machine be in control of the life and death of a human being, no matter how technologically advanced the machine is … According to this position, which has been stated among others by The Holy See …, these applications are *mala in se* …
> (c) In the case of war crimes or fatal accidents, the presence of an autonomous weapon system in the operation may make it more difficult or impossible altogether, to hold military personnel morally and legally responsible …[3]

Where the summary provided by Santoni de Sio and van den Hoven leans towards (though is not exclusively drawn from) the philosophical literature on the topic, the ICRC's focus leans more towards the legal and policy literature in this regard. Nonetheless, though they only use a two-part distinction, the ICRC's summary of the ethical objections to AWS that have come to the fore is very similar:

> Ethical arguments against autonomous weapon systems can generally be divided into two forms: objections based on the limits of technology to function within legal constraints and ethical norms; and ethical objections that are independent of technological capability.[4]

The latter set of objections include the question of whether the use of autonomous weapons might lead to "a responsibility gap where humans cannot uphold their moral responsibility"; whether their use would undermine "the human dignity of those combatants who are targeted, and of civilians who

3 Filippo Santoni de Sio and Jeroen van den Hoven, 'Meaningful Human Control over Autonomous Systems: A Philosophical Account' (2018) Front. Robotics and AI 2.

4 ICRC, 'Ethics and autonomous weapon systems: An ethical basis for human control?' (April 2018) 9.

are put at risk of death and injury as a consequence of attacks on legitimate military targets"; and the possibility that "further increasing human distancing – physically and psychologically – from the battlefield" could increase "existing asymmetries"[5] and make "the use of violence easier or less controlled".

The ICRC also provides a succinct summary of the ethical arguments in favour of AWS:

> The primary argument for these weapons has been an assertion that they might enable better respect for both international law and human ethical values by enabling greater precision and reliability than weapon systems controlled directly by humans, and therefore would result in less adverse humanitarian consequences for civilians. ... Another ethical argument that has been made for autonomous weapon systems is that they help fulfil the duty of militaries to protect their soldiers by removing them from harm's way.[6]

A guiding principle which has gained increasing support in the debate over AWS in and around the meetings of the GGE is the concept of 'meaningful human control.' First introduced into the international debate over the regulation of AWS in 2014 by the British advocacy group Article 36 (Article 36 2014), 'meaningful human control' is seen by many as the fundamental test for the appropriateness of these weapon systems. However, despite the popularity of 'meaningful human control' as a non-negotiable requirement for weapons systems incorporating autonomy, there remains a lack of clarity over what, precisely, meaningful human control entails.

An issue not directly mentioned either in Santoni de Sio's and van den Hoven's paper or in the ICRC's account of the ethical challenges raised by LAWS, but one which has been raised by a number of Western commentators and which, broadly speaking, has an ethical dimension, is the potential that these systems will threaten strategic stability or lower the threshold for the use of force, thus potentially leading to greater violence. For example, Jürgen Altmann and Frank Sauer have argued in the journal *Survival* "that AWS are

5 It is not obvious to me why this is an ethical issue. I am reminded of Conrad Crane's memorable opening to a paper "There are two ways of waging war, asymmetric and stupid" (Conrad Crane, 'The Lure of Strike' (2013) 43 (2) *Parameters* 5) – it doesn't seem to me to a requirement of ethics that combatants 'fight stupid'.

6 ICRC, 'Ethics and autonomous weapon systems' (n 4) 8.

prone to proliferation and bound to foment an arms race resulting in increased crisis instability and escalation risks."[7]

In sum, then, the ethical objections to LAWS raised by Western analysts fall broadly into the following categories:

Consequentialist/Prudential

1. LAWS cannot be relied upon to act consistently with the laws of war
2. LAWS will lower the threshold for war and cause strategic instability

Deontological

1. Allowing LAWS to make the decision to kill a human being is a violation of human dignity
2. The use of LAWS undermines moral and legal responsibility for battlefield killings

3 China and the Development of AWS

Arguably, the most prominent open-source analyst of China's approach to, and development of, military-use artificial intelligence is Elsa B. Kania, a fellow at the Center for a New American Security. In her November 2017 report, 'Battlefield Singularity: Artificial Intelligence, Military Revolution, and China's Future Military Power', Kania contends that China's military, the People's Liberation Army (PLA), is seeking to capitalise on what they view as a new military revolution, one emerging from advances in Artificial Intelligence (AI) by investing in an "expansive research and development agenda while leveraging private sector progress through a national strategy of military-civil fusion."[8] This revolution is seen as coming about as warfare becomes "intelligentized" (智能化), and will be as, or more, significant in shaping the balance of military power as has been the advent of today's "informatized" (信息化) warfare. The significance of this perception of the future of warfare for China is evident in the fact that the PLA "is already funding a range of military applications of AI under the 13th Five-Year Plan, including through the CMC Equipment Development Department and service-level equipment departments and research projects."[9]

7 Jürgen Altmann and Frank Sauer, 'Autonomous Weapon Systems and Strategic Stability', (2017) 59 (5) *Survival* 117, 118.

8 Elsa B. Kania 'Battlefield Singularity: Artificial Intelligence, Military Revolution, and China's Future Military Power' (November 2017) Washington D.C. Center for New American Security, 12.

9 Kania, 'Battlefield Singularity' (n 8) 12.

The planned uses of next-generation AI by the PLA includes command decision making support, assisted military analysis, and as an enabler for military equipment. This includes what the PLA calls 'artificial intelligence weapons', which the *People's Liberation Army Military Terminology* manual defines as "a weapon that utilizes AI to automatically [...] pursue, distinguish, and destroy enemy targets; often composed of information collection and management systems, knowledge base systems, assistance to decision systems, mission implementation systems, etc."[10]

Kania quotes Lieutenant General Liu Guozhi, Director of the Central Military Commission's Science and Technology Commission, as anticipating that advances in AI

> ... will accelerate the process of military transformation, causing fundamental changes to military units' programming, operational styles, equipment systems, and models of combat power generation, ultimately leading to a profound military revolution. As he warns, "facing disruptive technology, [we] must ... seize the opportunity to change paradigms (弯道超车). Whoever doesn't disrupt will be disrupted!"[11]

While Kania reports that the PLA's perspective on the military use of AI has been influenced by its study of the U.S. military's approach, particularly the 'Third Offset Strategy' of the US DoD,[12] there are nonetheless significant differences. Where the U.S. military has thus far shown a significant degree of caution in embracing AI, and particularly autonomous weapons systems, writing by PLA academics and officers displays a far greater enthusiasm for these systems. Kania reports that

> In the spring of 2016, AlphaGo's initial defeat of Lee Sedol in the ancient Chinese game of Go (weiqi) seemingly captured the PLA's imagination at the highest levels, sparking high-level seminars and symposiums on the topic. The continued success of AlphaGo, including its recent victories over China's top Go players, is considered a turning point that demonstrated the potential of AI to engage in complex analyses and strategizing comparable to that required to wage war – not only equaling human

10 Elsa B. Kania, 'China's Strategic Ambiguity and Shifting Approach to Lethal Autonomous Weapons Systems' (*Lawfare Blog*, 17 April 2018) <https://www.lawfareblog.com/chinas-strategic-ambiguity-and-shifting-approach-lethal-autonomous-weapons-systems>.

11 Kania, 'Battlefield Singularity' (n 8) 13.

12 Kania, 'Battlefield Singularity' (n 8) 14.

cognitive capabilities but even contributing a distinctive advantage that may surpass the human mind."[13]

U.S. military writing on the topic has tended to focus a great deal on potential legal and ethical concerns arising from the employment of AI enabled systems including AWS, while Kania reports that "there has been relatively limited discussion of these issues to date by the PLA."[14] PLA thinkers posit that a point will be reached that they refer to as battlefield singularity (奇点), when human thought will be unable to keep up with the pace of warfare. "Under such conditions, human commanders would no longer have capacity to remain directly 'in the loop' (人在回路中) but rather possess ultimate decision-making authority (e.g., a model of a "human on the loop," 人在回路上), without actual involvement in each decision in combat."[15] To adapt to this environment, PLA thinkers foresee military forces shifting to a structure in which wars are fought by intelligent machines (AWS) under the command of, and directed by, human commanders, planners and administrators.[16]

Kania does, however, see cultural factors working somewhat against this possible future. She suggests that the culture in the PLA is such that there is a "reluctance to delegate authority downward", which could extend to a reluctance to trusting weapons systems to operate autonomously, or a reluctance to rely on the guidance of AI systems in general.[17] Despite this possibility, the PLA seems to be moving ahead rapidly in the development of AI enabled systems. For example, in February 2018 an article published in the *South China Morning Post*[18] reported that "China is working to update the rugged old computer systems on nuclear submarines with artificial intelligence to enhance the potential thinking skills of commanding officers ..." Described as a system capable of "thinking its own thoughts" this planned upgrade is intended as a means to compensate for the danger that "if the 100 to 300 people in the sub's crew were forced to remain together in their canister in deep, dark water for months, the rising stress level could affect the commanding officers' decision-making powers, even leading to bad judgment." While the unidentified senior

13 Kania, 'Battlefield Singularity' (n 8) 15.
14 Kania, 'Battlefield Singularity' (n 8) 14.
15 Kania, 'Battlefield Singularity' (n 8) 16.
16 Kania, 'Battlefield Singularity' (n 8) 16.
17 Kania, 'Battlefield Singularity' (n 8) 21.
18 Stephen Chen, 'China's plan to use artificial intelligence to boost the thinking skills of nuclear submarine commanders' *South China Morning Post*, (Hong Kong, 4 February 2018, updated 6 February 2018).

scientist interviewed for the article insists that for reasons of 'safety redundancy' there is no intention of reducing the crew on China's nuclear submarines, and that "There must be a human hand on every critical post", that rings somewhat hollow against the backdrop of the PLA's notion of 'battlefield singularity.' Kania reports that some PLA thinkers believe that AI may "eventually supplant human cognition and decision-making on the battlefield", and postulates that the shift to greater autonomy for AI enabled systems may be driven by bureaucratic competition as well as the PLA's ongoing struggle to recruit a high-quality workforce.[19] Indeed, Kania reports that "Within the foreseeable future, PLA strategists expect that autonomous combat by unmanned systems and the joint operations of unmanned and manned systems will disrupt traditional operational models."[20]

As mentioned at the beginning of this paper, this apparent embrace of AI and autonomous weapons by the PLA meant that there was considerable surprise by analysts when China's delegation to the GGE seemed to express support for a ban on the use of these systems. In the next section I unpack the delegation's submissions and analyse the ethics-relevant content thereof.

4 China's GGE Position Papers on AWS

China's first formal statement to the GGE was at the Fifth Review Conference, which took place from 12 to 16 December 2016 in Geneva.[21] The statement recognizes that the weaponization of technologies related to "the autonomous warfare platform" has "caused humanitarian concerns." A central concern expressed in the statement was China's view that a significant obstacle to making progress on the topic of AWS is that "there is currently still a lack of a clear and agreed definition of [Lethal Autonomous Weapons Systems]". China's statement goes on to call for definitional clarity over "levels of autonomy and criteria for their determination", "relations and distinctions between automation, autonomy and remote control" and "the mode of human involvement and the human role". Of particular interest regarding the latter requirement is the insistence in the statement that a "strict definition" is required rather than "such vague concepts as 'human judgement' or 'meaningful human control'."

19 Kania, 'Battlefield Singularity' (n 8) 16–19; 36.

20 Kania, 'Battlefield Singularity' (n 8) 22.

21 The position paper submitted by the Chinese delegation to CCW 5th Review Conference <https://www.unog.ch/80256EDD006B8954/(httpAssets)/DD1551E60648CEBBC125808A005954FA/$file/China's+Position+Paper.pdf> accessed 11 December 2010.

The Chinese delegation goes on to reiterate that the use of AWS must be governed by existing International Humanitarian Law and the core principles of distinction, proportionality and what they refer to as 'restriction', which is likely the principle of necessity. They acknowledge, in this regard, uncertainties regarding the ability of AWS to fulfil the requirements of these constraints on the use of force. First, they state that the ability of AWS to distinguish between legitimate and illegitimate targets (distinction) "remains doubtful". Later in the submission this is reiterated in even stronger terms: "Such systems cannot effectively distinguish between soldiers and civilians and can easily cause indiscriminate killing or wounding of the innocent." Second, they state unambiguously that "such a weapons system is incapable of proportionate decisions". And third, they contend that ensuring accountability for the use of force if LAWS are employed "presents difficulties." The statement recognizes some positive role for "the new weapons review process of states" in ensuring that AWS are kept accountable to IHL, but notes that these reviews "vary from state to state and the relevant evaluations have no binding legal force". It seems that what is in view here is the requirement in Article 36 of Additional Protocol I to the Geneva Conventions that states must conduct reviews of new weapons, means, and methods of warfare to ensure their compliance with IHL before opting to use them. As a consequence of this perceived lack of binding force inherent in Article 36 reviews, in the 2016 statement China records its support for "the development of a legally binding protocol on issues related to the use of LAWS, similar to the Protocol on Blinding Laser Weapons", though it does not specify any details of what the content of such a protocol might be.

The 2016 statement also states that "the development and use of LAWS will lower the threshold and cost of war, thus making the outbreak of wars easier and more frequent." While not stated explicitly, this seems clearly to be raised as a point of ethical concern. Not everything in the statement is, however, negative about AWS. In the middle of the statement is a sentence that is seemingly disconnected from everything else: "LAWS with its high adaptability to the environment is especially suited to highly dangerous missions in environments where threats exist from nuclear, biological or chemical weapons."

China's 2018 position paper[22] is, in some respects, an expanded version of the 2016 position paper. It reiterates the previously expressed concern about

22 Group of Governmental Experts of the High Contracting Parties to the Convention on Prohibitions or Restrictions on the Use of Certain Conventional Weapons Which May Be Deemed to Be Excessively Injurious or to Have Indiscriminate Effects. Geneva, 9–13 April 2018 (first week) Item 6 of the provisional agenda (Position Paper) <https://www.unog.ch/80256EDD006B8954/(httpAssets)/E42AE83BDB3525D0C125826C0040B262/$file/CCW_GGE.1_2018_WP.7.pdf> accessed 11 December 2019.

the lack of "a clear and agreed definition" and adds that "many countries believe such weapon systems do not exist." A new feature of the position paper is that some parameters are given for China's view of what a definition of LAWS should include. It is proposed that LAWS "should be understood as fully autonomous lethal weapons systems" and that a definition should include five key characteristics, namely

1. lethality ("sufficient pay load (charge) and for means to be lethal");
2. autonomy ("absence of human intervention and control during the entire process of executing a task");
3. 'impossibility for termination' ("once started there is no way to terminate the device");
4. Indiscriminate effect ("the device will execute the task of killing and maiming regardless of conditions, scenarios and targets"); and
5. evolution "through interaction with the environment the device can learn autonomously, expand its functions and capabilities in a way exceeding human expectations".

The statement does not specify whether or not all of these characteristics must be in place for a system to be considered a Lethal Autonomous Weapons System, though that might perhaps be inferred from the statement that a definition "should include but not be limited to" these characteristics.

The 2018 statement also reiterates the previously expressed concern to ensure the "prevention of indiscriminate killing and maiming by LAWS" and reiterates the firm view that "LAWS are not capable of effectively distinguishing between soldiers and civilians" and "lack the capability of making decisions regarding proportionality"; and furthermore that "it is difficult to establish accountability when this type of weapon systems are used". The earlier criticism of the notions of meaningful human control and human judgment is repeated, though in a toned-down form – these concepts are described as "rather general" and in need of being "further elaborated and clarified". The slightly odd emphasis on the suitability of LAWS for "dangerous operations in an environment where threats of nuclear, biological and chemical weapons are involved" is also reiterated, as is the concern about their potential for "lowering the threshold of war, and the cost of warfare on the part of the user countries." Scepticism over relying on "national reviews on the research, development and use of new technologies" is raised again, as is the importance of LAWS being subject to existing IHL.

What is new in the 2018 statement is a comment about the potential positive societal benefits of progress in AI and the related concern that "there should not be any pre-set premises or prejudged outcome which may impede the development of AI technology." What's more interesting, however, is what is missing from the 2018 statement that was in the 2016 statement. Gone is any direct statement of support for a legally binding protocol on LAWS. Instead, there is something much weaker: "pending an appropriate solution, we call on all countries to exercise precaution, and to refrain, in particular, from any indiscriminate use against civilians."

Despite this lack of a statement of support for a legally binding protocol on LAWS, it was announced with some fanfare by opponents of LAWS that China had become the first permanent member of the UN Security Council to support new international law to regulate LAWS. This arose primarily from the Campaign to Ban Killer Robots, which quoted (in a now deleted tweet) from their transcript of the official UN recording of the April 2018 meeting, which has the China delegation giving the following somewhat garbled statement:

> We are in favor of efforts on the basis on a wide participation by all parties to reach a common understanding on the definition of LAWS and, on this basis, to negotiate and conclude a succinct protocol on the prohibition to ban the use of fully autonomous lethal weapons …

5 Analysis

So what should we make of China's submissions to the GGE of the CCW so far? The first thing to note is that there are no unique concerns of an ethical nature which have not also been expressed in the Western contributions to the debate. But there is also a noteworthy omission in China's list of concerns, an issue that is very prominent in the Western discourse. The table below plots the ethical concerns raised in China's submissions against the framework of reference provided and discussed in the first part of this paper.

The glaring gap, of course, lies in the lack of any statement to the effect that allowing LAWS to kill combatants would constitute a violation of human dignity, that it would be (as Santoni de Sio and van den Hoven put it) *mala in se*. This is particularly noteworthy given the stated view by the ICRC that "While there are concerns regarding the technical capacity of autonomous weapons systems to function within legal and ethical constraints, *the enduring ethical arguments against these weapons are those that transcend context* – whether during armed conflict or in peacetime – and transcend technology – whether simple or sophisticated."[23] The implicit view being expressed here is that, barring the issue of human dignity, the questions raised by LAWS, while difficult,

23 ICRC, 'Ethics and autonomous weapon systems' (n 4), 1 emphasis in original.

TABLE 4.1 Comparison of China's GGE statements to Western objections to autonomous weapons

Western ethical objections	*China's 2016 GGE Statement*	*China's 2018 GGE Statement*
CONSEQUENTIALIST/ PRUDENTIAL		
LAWS cannot be relied upon to act consistently with the laws of war	"Such systems cannot effectively distinguish between soldiers and civilians and can easily cause indiscriminate killing or wounding of the innocent."	"LAWS are not capable of effectively distinguishing between soldiers and civilians"
	"such a weapons system is incapable of proportionate decisions"	"lack the capability of making decisions regarding proportionality"
LAWS will lower the threshold for war and cause strategic instability	"the development and use of LAWS will lower the threshold and cost of war, thus making the outbreak of wars easier and more frequent."	[potential for] "lowering the threshold of war, and the cost of warfare on the part of the user countries"
DEONTOLOGICAL		
Having LAWS make the decision to kill a human being is a violation of human dignity	N/A	N/A
The use of LAWS undermines moral and legal responsibility for battlefield killings	[Legal accountability] "presents difficulties"	"it is difficult to establish accountability when this type of weapon systems are used"
	"the new weapons review process of states [Article 36 reviews] ... vary from state to state and the relevant evaluations have no binding legal force"	[Scepticism regarding the binding force of] "national reviews on the research, development and use of new technologies"

are not impossible to answer. Is it possible that autonomous weapons, employing current or foreseeable technology, will be able to be used in a manner that comports with the legal and ethical constraints on the use of force (discrimination/distinction, proportionality, and necessity)? It is certainly easy enough to imagine scenarios where this would not be possible or likely given current or near future technology (e.g. identifying and engaging individual human irregular combatants in a crowded urban environment), but at the same time it does seem that we can imagine other scenarios where meeting these constraints would be possible (e.g. in situations of 'boxed autonomy', such as the use of autonomous air-superiority combat aircraft to provide 'top cover' for a naval task force on the high seas in the context of a high intensity conventional interstate war). Can autonomous weapons be used in a way that maintains human responsibility? That may be challenging, but is not, it seems to me insurmountable. Does the use of autonomous weapons result in human distancing from the battlefield, making the use of violence easier or less controlled? The question of whether using violence is 'easy' is irrelevant (weapons development has for centuries been making the use of violence easier); what matters is whether or not force is used appropriately, which collapses into the earlier question about using force within the bounds of law and ethics.

Of course that is far too quick, and many will disagree with my assessment of the correct answer to these questions. But my point here is that it is not infeasible that contextual factors could mitigate or obviate the ethical concerns that have been raised about LAWS – all of them, that is, barring the concern over human dignity. This issue transcends context – if it is the case that having LAWS making the 'decision to kill' is a violation of human dignity (and if it is indeed the case that LAWS make the 'decision to kill'), then that's that, no contextual adjustments can make it otherwise.

The other issue of note emerging from the comparison of the two statements submitted by China is the apparent backpedalling on the issue of support for a legally binding protocol on LAWS, which is absent in the more recent statement. Given this shift, which is hardly likely to be an oversight given the close attention that is given to the wording of documents of this type by diplomats, it is at least questionable that claims by anti-LAWS activists that China has joined a "growing list of countries calling for a ban on fully autonomous weapons",[24] based on the rather garbled and unclear statement quoted from

24 Campaign to Stop Killer Robots, 'Convergence on retaining human control of weapons systems' (13 April 2018) <https://www.stopkillerrobots.org/2018/04/convergence/> accessed 11 December 2019.

the meeting transcript by the Campaign to Ban Killer Robots, holds all that much water. Adding to the confusion is the further claim by the Campaign that "In response to the campaign's queries, the delegation of China confirmed its ban call, but stressed that it is *limited to use only*."[25]

Kania suggests that China may be being 'strategically ambiguous'. She notes that

> The Chinese military does not have a legal culture analogous or directly comparable to that of the U.S. military. It's also important to recognize that Beijing's military has traditionally approached issues of international law in terms of legal warfare, seeking to exploit rather than be constrained by legal frameworks. The military's notion of legal warfare focuses on what it calls seizing "legal principle superiority" or delegitimizing an adversary with "restriction through law."[26]

Kania also rightly points out that China's position must be considered in the context of the key definitional features of 'fully autonomous lethal weapons' that they provide in the 2018 submission. While on the surface reasonable, if we take it that all of these features must be present (as discussed above, this is unclear from the submission) these elements combine to create a very narrow definition of what might, or might not, be subject to a ban. For example, if the criteria are applied strictly, then any robotic weapon system that could be recalled once deployed would not be covered because 'impossibility of termination' is a definitional feature of 'fully autonomous lethal weapons'. Likewise, if it were the case (as I have suggested above is feasible, whether through design or restrictions on operational environment) that a system could be employed without 'indiscriminate effect', that would not be covered either. The definition also includes the ability to 'learn autonomously', which excludes a wide range of systems which would meet the ICRC definition of a lethal autonomous weapon.

Arguably, by leaving the door open to the *development* of 'fully autonomous' LAWS, and defining these systems in such a narrow way, China effectively is allowing itself the scope to ultimately employ systems that would be LAWS by any broader definition. It is very telling that, as Kania also points out, the definition of "an artificially intelligent weapon" that appears in the Chinese military's internal dictionary, and which was quoted at the beginning of this paper, is itself considerably broader.

---

25 Campaign to Stop Killer Robots 2018 (n 25).

26 Kania, 'China's Strategic Ambiguity' (n 10).

6 Towards a Distinctively Chinese Ethical Position on LAWS

If, as seems to be the case, China's contribution to the discussion over LAWS in the GGE is driven more by strategic positioning than ethics, are there any other sources that might be drawn on to develop an understanding of a distinctive and authentic Chinese ethical position on the ethics of LAWS? In this final section of the paper, I suggest two possible sources within the Chinese ethical tradition from which such a position might be drawn.

First, as I argue elsewhere,[27] the current debate in the West over the ethics of LAWS closely parallels the debate over the ethics of employing mercenaries. In an earlier work[28] I identified the primary ethical objections that have been raised against (to use the less value-laden term I prefer) contracted combatants. Broadly speaking these objections fall into the following categories:

a. Objections over motivation (inappropriate motivation or lack of appropriate motivation);
b. Objections over accountability;
c. Objections over trust/reliability.

It is an interesting question whether historical Chinese sources raise similar objections to the use of mercenaries, or whether a significantly different view is evident. Given the parallels between the use of mercenaries and LAWS, this body of literature (if it exists) would be a valuable source for drawing out an authentic Chinese position on the ethics of LAWS.

Second, an even closer parallel to the use of LAWS in warfare is the employment of weaponised animals. In the Western context two of the more notable cases of this were, first, the 1930's and 1940's Soviet program to turn trained and explosive-laden dogs into guided anti-tank munitions, and second, the ultimately abandoned project in the latter part of WWII to release large numbers of Mexican free tailed bats, carrying incendiary devices, over Japanese cities in an attempt to start fires in the mostly wood and paper buildings characteristic of Japan at that time. There is at least one unsubstantiated claim of the use of weaponised animals in ancient Chinese military history. According to an unsubstantiated Wikipedia source, monkeys were used as a military weapon during the early part of the Southern Song Dynasty. At that time, the Chinese Imperial Army, led by Zhao Yu, was engaged in battle with rebels from the Yanzhou province. During this battle the army allegedly employed monkeys

27 Baker 2021.

28 Deane-Peter Baker, *Just Warriors, Inc.: The Ethics of Privatized Force* (Bloomsbury Academic, Sydney 2011).

as incendiary weapons. It is claimed that bundles of oil-soaked straw were attached to the monkeys and set alight as the monkeys were released into the rebel camp. The enemy's tents were thus set alight, throwing their force into chaos. The similarity of this tale to the Biblical account of Samson's use of weaponised foxes against the Philistines does, however, raise questions over the likely authenticity of this story:

> So he went out and caught three hundred foxes and tied them tail to tail in pairs. He then fastened a torch to every pair of tails, lit the torches and let the foxes loose in the standing grain of the Philistines. He burned up the shocks and standing grain, together with the vineyards and olive groves.[29]

If, however, this claimed Chinese use of weaponised animals is legitimate, or if there are other such accounts in the historical literature, then any discussion by Chinese scholars of the ethics thereof could provide a valuable source in drawing out an authentic Chinese position on the ethics of Lethal Autonomous Weapons.

7 Conclusion

The question of whether the employment of Lethal Autonomous Weapons (LAWS) can be ethical is one of the burning issues of military ethics today. In this paper I have outlined the general trends in Western ethical objections to LAWS, and compared that to the position articulated in the formal statements presented by China to the United Nations Group of Governmental Experts addressing LAWS under the terms of the Convention on Certain Conventional Weapons. I noted that a significant difference is the lack of any emphasis on human dignity in China's statements. I noted further that there are good reasons to view China's position as being more motivated by strategic positioning than ethics, and that reading between the lines of the definition of LAWS provided in China's statements suggests that China may not in fact be seeking to support a meaningful ban on these weapons systems. I went on to suggest two sources scholars of Chinese military ethics might draw on to develop an authentic Chinese position on the ethics of LAWS, namely any discussion in the relevant literature on the ethics of mercenaries and the ethics of weaponised animals respectively.

29 Judges 15 v 4–5, New International Version.

References

Altmann, Jürgen and Frank Sauer, 'Autonomous Weapon Systems and Strategic Stability', (2017) 59 (5) *Survival*.

Altmann, Jürgen, Peter Asaro, Noel Sharkey and Robert Sparrow, 'Armed military robots: editorial' in *Ethics and Information Technology* (2013) 15 (2) 73.

Baker, Deane-Peter (2021), 'The Robot Dogs of War' in Jai Galliott (ed.), *Lethal Autonomous Weapons: Re-Examining the Law & Ethics of Robotic Warfare* (Oxford University Press).

Baker, Deane-Peter, *Just Warriors, Inc.: The Ethics of Privatized Force* (Bloomsbury Academic, Sydney 2011).

Campaign to Stop Killer Robots, 'Convergence on retaining human control of weapons systems' (13 April 2018) <https://www.stopkillerrobots.org/2018/04/convergence/> accessed 11 December 2019.

Chen, Stephen, 'China's plan to use artificial intelligence to boost the thinking skills of nuclear submarine commanders' *South China Morning Post*, (Hong Kong, 4 February 2018, updated 6 February 2018).

Crane, Conrad, 'The Lure of Strike' (2013) 43 (2) *Parameters*.

Group of Governmental Experts of the High Contracting Parties to the Convention on Prohibitions or Restrictions on the Use of Certain Conventional Weapons Which May Be Deemed to Be Excessively Injurious or to Have Indiscriminate Effects. Geneva, 9–13 April 2018 (first week) Item 6 of the provisional agenda (Position Paper) <https://www.unog.ch/80256EDD006B8954/(httpAssets)/E42AE83BDB3525D0C125826C0040B262/$file/CCW_GGE.1_2018_WP.7.pdf> accessed 11 December 2019.

International Committee of the Red Cross, 'Autonomous Weapon Systems: Implications of Increasing Autonomy in the Critical Functions of Weapons' (Report) Expert meeting, Versoix, Switzerland, 15–16 March 2016 <https://www.icrc.org/en/publication/4283-autonomous-weapons-systems> accessed 11 December 2019.

International Committee of the Red Cross, 'Ethics and autonomous weapon systems: An ethical basis for human control?' (April 2018) <https://www.icrc.org/en/document/ethics-and-autonomous-weapon-systems-ethical-basis-human-control> accessed 11 December 2019.

Kania, Elsa B. 'Battlefield Singularity: Artificial Intelligence, Military Revolution, and China's Future Military Power' (November 2017) Washington D.C. Center for New American Security.

Kania, Elsa B., 'China's Strategic Ambiguity and Shifting Approach to Lethal Autonomous Weapons Systems' (*Lawfare Blog*, 17 April 2018) <https://www.lawfareblog.com/chinas-strategic-ambiguity-and-shifting-approach-lethal-autonomous-weapons-systems> accessed 11 December 2019.

Santoni de Sio, Filippo and Jeroen van den Hoven, 'Meaningful Human Control over Autonomous Systems: A Philosophical Account' (2018) *Front. Robotics and AI* <https://doi.org/10.3389/frobt.2018.00015> accessed 11 December 2019.
The Holy Bible. New International Version.
The position paper submitted by the Chinese delegation to CCW 5th Review Conference <https://www.unog.ch/80256EDD006B8954/(httpAssets)/DD1551E60648CEBBC125808A005954FA/$file/China's+Position+Paper.pdf> accessed 11 December 2019.

CHAPTER 5

Artificial Intelligence in Military Decision-Making

Avoiding Ethical and Strategic Perils with an Option-Generator Model

Shannon E. French and Lisa N. Lindsay

There is little doubt that artificial intelligence (AI) will become widely deployed in military decision-making. There is still time, however, to determine how to do it right, in both the ethical and practical sense. There are clear perils to avoid when integrating AI into military decision-making, but also some potentially promising opportunities. Above all, human decision-making should not be ceded to machines, for a number of reasons that we will present. However, there are ways in which AI could help humans make better decisions in military contexts. We will argue that the most ethical and valuable role for AI in military decision-making is as an option generator.

1 Automation Bias

The growing push toward integrating AI into military decision-making is fueled in part by the widely held position that AI technology will decrease errors in military decision-making and lead to fewer overall deaths during warfare. The errors in question include both practical and moral failures. Practical failures can result from inaccurate or incomplete information, faulty analysis, inadequate training, and a host of other factors, while moral failures tend to be produced by a toxic combination of psychological stressors, character flaws, poor leadership, and a lack of discipline. Defending the use of robots and other automated systems in the military, Ron Arkin has essentially argued that humans are too emotionally vulnerable to be trusted to do the right thing in combat conditions. Citing surveys in which military personnel admit to unethical views about the importance (or lack thereof) of obeying the laws of war, Arkin asserts that humans are too often overcome by intense feelings such as rage and fear (or terror) that effectively hijack their brains and can lead even to the perpetration of war crimes. In his book *Governing Lethal Behavior in Autonomous Robots*, Arkin avers that, '... it seems unrealistic to expect normal human beings by their very nature to adhere to the Laws of Warfare when

 | DOI:10.1163/9789004507951_007

confronted with the horror of the battlefield, even when trained.'[1] He believes robots can do better.

Others lean less on the claim that automated systems would be more ethical than human troops and focus instead on the idea that technology can simply make faster decisions than humans, and that that speed in itself creates a strategic advantage for the side that deploys it. This of course depends on whether it is empirically true that speed of decision-making actually does produce an advantage. Boyd's well-known OODA loop concept of military decision-making encourages the belief that rapid decisiveness wins engagements. However, Boyd's critics have pointed out that the OODA loop model is only applicable in certain specific tactical settings (such as air-to-air combat), and does not translate well to, for example, the urban combat domain where decision-making happens simultaneously across many levels of command and a bad decision made quickly is *not* always better than a delayed decision.[2] A more nuanced version of the argument that technology-derived decision-making in combat may be superior to human decision-making suggests not that mere speed is the decisive factor, but that programmed systems are capable of making complex calculations that take into consideration more data or aspects of a problem than most human minds could manage to weigh at any one time. This is an idea to which we will return later.

Intentionally replacing human decision-making with AI decision-making is ill advised from both an ethical and a strategic perspective, and we will say more about that shortly. However, there is a serious and often unappreciated risk of *unintentionally* overriding human decision-making with AI decision-making that needs to be confronted first. Widespread use of AI – as well as other automated technology – in military settings can proliferate a phenomenon called automation bias. Automation bias occurs when humans are in an automated environment that orients them to be mostly observers rather than agents.[3] In this environment, humans exhibit an increased trust in automated systems, and often seek neither to confirm nor deny the validity of an evaluation or decision made by a computer or other automated system. They simply accept the automated system's judgment as final (and superior).

The presence of AI systems creates an environment where military members are likely to trust judgments of AI over their own and those of their human

1 Ron Arkin, *Governing Lethal Behavior in Autonomous Robots* (Taylor & Francis Group 2009) 36.

2 See Jim Storr, 'A Critique of Effects-Based Thinking,' (2005) *The RUSI journal*, Volume 150, Number 6, (December 2005), 32.

3 Linda J. Skitka, Kathleen L. Mosier, Mark Burdick, 'Does automation bias decision-making?' (1999) 51 *International Journal of Human-Computer Studies* 991.

peers. In the late 1990s, Linda Skitka did a study on automation bias using a flight simulator. Her study showed that in a test environment with an automated computer aid specifically stated *not* to be 100% accurate, participants would often still trust the computer over the other instruments in the cockpit that *were* stated to be 100% accurate.[4] This is worrisome because the participants seemed blinded by their own assumptions or notions about the accuracy and reliability of the automated aid, despite being specifically told that it was fallible (and less reliable than the other systems).

Alongside this, the study reached the conclusion that people in an automated environment were less vigilant about checking the accuracy of their systems and indicators than those in a non-automated environment. Participants in an environment with an automated flight aid only noticed 59% of problems unannounced by the automated aid, whereas participants without any automated aid noticed 97% of the same problems.[5] The type of error committed by those in the aided environment is one of omission, where a human not alerted to a problem by an automated system will not notice the problem, nor check to make sure that no problems in fact exist. The high level of success in noticing unannounced problems by those participants without an automated aid can be attributed to their vigilance in checking dials and indicators, and processing that information to determine the existence, type, and severity of a problem.

The other type of automation bias error is that of commission, in which a human acts according to the prescriptions of an automated system, even when other non-automated systems are indicating something different or contradictory to the automated system. An example of this type of error can be seen in a small 1992 study done in the NASA Ames Advanced Concepts Flight Simulator.[6] This study, which Skitka references in her own work on automation bias, included one scenario in which an 'auto-sensed checklist' suggested that the flight crew shut down the #1 engine due to fire damage. However, 'traditional engine parameters indicated that the #2 engine was actually more severely damaged.'[7] Three-quarters of the crews in the auto-sensed checklist scenario shut down the #1 engine, while only one quarter of participants using a paper checklist did the same.

This shows how an automated aid can quickly diminish the vigilance and diligence of people in verifying information given to them. Any crew in the

4 Skitka, Mosier and Burdick (n 3) 991.

5 Skitka, Mosier and Burdick (n 3) 991.

6 Kathleen Mosier, Everett Palmer & Asaf Degani, 'Electronic checklists: Implications for decision making' (1992) *Proceedings of the Human Factors Society 36th Annual Meeting* 7.

7 Skitka, Mosier and Burdick (n 3) 991.

auto-sensing scenario could have chosen to look at the analog dials and indicators in the cabin to determine if in fact the #1 engine was severely damaged. However, rather than carefully reading the analog dials and other indicators in the cockpit to form a judgment based on information and experience, the crews often opted instead to follow directions from a computer they had placed a high level of trust in. The analog devices could communicate the same information to an experienced pilot as a computer, but it takes more mental work on the behalf of the pilot to conclude that information from the indicators given to them.

When discussing this study, Skitka says, '[a]nalysis of the crews' audiotapes also indicated that crews in the automated condition tended to discuss much less information before coming to a decision to shut down the engine, suggesting that automated cues short circuited a full information search.'[8] This short-circuiting is one of the most dangerous aspects of automation bias. The presence of automated systems makes it less likely that those working with them will be vigilant in routinely checking nonautomated systems, nor will they put much effort into using other available tools to verify a decision reached by an automated system. These lapses are symptoms of the increased trust humans have in computerized or automated systems. This trust itself can also have perilous repercussions, both for the human *in situ*, and those who are affected by his or her actions – or inactions.

In July 1988, the crew of the USS *Vincennes* fell prey to the effects of automation bias with grave consequences. The ships' Aegis radar system (which was at the time set to a semi-automatic mode wherein humans worked with the system to decide what to fire upon and when) misidentified an Iranian passenger jet as an F-14 Iranian fighter jet. Despite other data indicating that the plane was not a fighter jet – including the plane broadcasting civilian radar and radio signals – no one in the command crew of eighteen disagreed with the computer's classification. They authorized the system to shoot, and only afterwards realized their horrific mistake. All 290 passengers and crew onboard the civilian plane were killed.

Peter Singer recounts this event in *Wired for War*, as well as a similar incident during the 2003 invasion of Iraq in which U.S. Patriot missiles shot down a pair of allied planes that the system misidentified as Iraqi rockets. The soldiers in this event had 'veto power,' over the system, but unfortunately they were 'unwilling to use [it] against the quicker (and what they viewed as better) judgment of a computer.'[9] Elke Schwarz describes this kind of environment,

8 Skitka, Mosier and Burdick (n 3) 991.

9 Peter Singer, *Wired for War* (The Penguin Press 2009) 125.

saying, '[s]et against a background where the instrument is characterized as inherently wise, the technology gives an air of dispassionate professionalism and a sense of moral certainty to the messy business of war.'[10]

Now, over twenty years after the Skitka study highlighted the dangerous existence of automation bias, humans have increased the use of automated systems in all areas of life, both civilian and military alike and, if anything, are more trusting than ever before of automated guidance. Artificial intelligence, as a technology that is little understood by the general public and often sold as 'better' than human ability, puts us at even higher risk for automation bias. Despite documented failures, people focus on reports that seem to suggest that artificial minds are superior to organic ones, including news of computers beating humans at strategy games like chess and Go. While television advertisements find humor in people following incorrect Google maps directions straight into a lake, the reality of overreliance on automation is much less amusing. In a military context, automation bias can have life or death consequences. Just as infantry check the proper functioning of their weapons, those using AI systems in their military roles are obligated to make sure their tools – both automated and not – are working correctly, too.

It is also vital to remember that no matter how advanced or capable of 'machine learning' they are, AI and other automated systems were originally programmed by humans, and we are fallible, biased creatures. Rather than freeing us from our natural weaknesses, such systems unfortunately have the potential to establish them more firmly – to 'bake them in,' as it were. There are already many recorded cases of algorithms that were designed with the goal of providing superhuman objectivity, but instead merely amplified human prejudices and replicated character flaws. One example that shows this effect clearly was the attempt in 2016 by the company Beauty.AI to program a computer to judge an international beauty contest. The results turned out to be dramatically biased in favor of lighter-skinned contestants. Analysis revealed that the programmers who had provided the original images to the system for it to 'learn' what beauty was had relied almost exclusively on photos of young white women:

> Beauty.AI – which was created by a 'deep learning' group called Youth Laboratories and supported by Microsoft – relied on large datasets of photos to build an algorithm that assessed beauty. While there are a

10 Elke Schwarz, 'Technology and moral vacuums in just war theorising' (2018) *Journal of International Political Theory* 1.

> number of reasons why the algorithm favored white people, the main problem was that the data the project used to establish standards of attractiveness did not include enough minorities, said Alex Zhavoronkov, Beauty.AI's chief science officer.[11]

In another famous case, Microsoft created an AI 'chatbot' which it named Tay and allowed it to 'learn' how to communicate from interactions with real humans on Twitter. The results were deeply disturbing, as Tay soon started sending out hate-filled racist, anti-Semitic, misogynist, and otherwise extremely offensive tweets.[12] And as journalist Sam Levin notes, '[A]fter Facebook eliminated human editors who had curated "trending" news stories ..., the algorithm immediately promoted fake and vulgar stories on news feeds.'[13] It, too, copied the worst aspects of the content it encountered.

This is a problem commonly referred to as 'garbage in, garbage out,' but it cannot be solved just by keeping AI systems away from the more pernicious elements on social media. Bias can be more difficult to keep out of AI programming than one might at first imagine. As legal scholar Jerry Kang has exhaustively documented, human bias is extremely difficult to avoid and is quite often unrecognized or unconscious. As one illustration, Kang cites the following study:

> Shooter Bias. Social cognitionist Joshua Correll created a video game that placed photographs of a White or Black individual holding either a gun or other object (wallet, soda can, or cell phone) into diverse photographic backgrounds. Participants were instructed to decide as quickly as possible whether to shoot the target. Severe time pressure designed into the game forced errors. Consistent with earlier findings, participants were more likely to mistake a Black target as armed when he in fact was unarmed (false alarms); conversely, they were more likely to mistake a White target as unarmed when he in fact was armed (misses). Even more striking is that Black participants showed similar amounts of 'shooter bias' as Whites.[14]

---

11 Sam Levin, 'A beauty contest was judged by AI and the robots didn't like dark skin,' *The Guardian*, (8 September 2016).

12 James Vincent, 'Twitter taught Microsoft's AI chatbot to be a racist asshole in less than a day,' *The Verge* (24 March 2016).

13 Levin (n 11).

14 Jerry Kang, 'Trojan Horses of Race,' *UCLA Journal of Scholarly Perspectives* (1 January 2007) 3, 43.

Thus, as long as humans program AI, bias and other human vices will come along for the ride, and sometimes be amplified. While this does not make it certain that AI will make any worse decisions than people would, it is a warning that AI systems should never be assumed to be more accurate or objective than a person would be. They should certainly not be trusted to be anything like infallible. In another recent example of a high-profile AI failure, IBM marketed its Watson supercomputer to doctors as a source of medical guidance for treating cancer patients (as 'Watson for Oncology'). However, the results were strongly criticized by real doctors as worse than useless:

> One example in the documents is the case of a 65-year-old man diagnosed with lung cancer, who also seemed to have severe bleeding. Watson reportedly suggested the man be administered both chemotherapy and the drug 'Bevacizumab.' But the drug can lead to 'severe or fatal hemorrhage,' according to a warning on the medication, and therefore shouldn't be given to people with severe bleeding. ...[15]

Interestingly, when the negative study results came back to IBM, they blamed Watson's failures on the way that he was 'trained' by doctors at Memorial Sloan Kettering (MSK) Cancer Center, using synthetic data:

> According to the report, the documents blame the training provided by IBM engineers and on doctors at MSK, which partnered with IBM in 2012 to train Watson to 'think' more like a doctor. The documents state that – instead of feeding real patient data into the software – the doctors were reportedly feeding Watson hypothetical patients data, or 'synthetic' case data. This would mean it's possible that when other hospitals used the MSK-trained Watson for Oncology, doctors were receiving treatment recommendations guided by MSK doctors' treatment preferences, instead of an AI interpretation of actual patient data.[16]

Whatever the source of Watson's errors, this case highlights the danger of organizations that manage risk on the level of life and death giving in to the temptation to rush to adopt AI systems that offer guidance that sounds authoritative but may in fact be at least as likely to be mistaken as human judgment

15 Jennings Brown, 'IBM Watson reportedly recommended cancer treatments that were "unsafe" and "incorrect,"' *Gizmodo* (25 July 2018).
16 Brown (n 15).

(if not more so). All that does is introduce another possible point of failure into the system.

2 Ethical Deskilling of the Military

Another potential way in which the integration of artificial intelligence into a military decision-making role could prove to be harmful if not handled correctly is if it leads to the 'moral deskilling' of the military.[17] Deskilling occurs when the opportunity for a skill to be practiced is diminished or eliminated, leading to the decreased ability of a human to perform that skill well. Both practical and ethical skills are put at risk with the introduction of artificial intelligence or other automated aids in military decision-making. For our purposes here, we will focus on ethical deskilling, though many of the same arguments and conclusions will apply to practical deskilling, as well.

In many militaries around the world, the expected professional military ethic is communicated and taught through virtue ethics. There is a code promoting particular virtues that is inculcated into all new recruits and (ideally, if not always successfully) reinforced until it becomes core to the identity of every person who serves. This particular brand of thinking is popular in the United States, where virtue ethics are the backbone of the professional military ethic in all military branches. Virtue ethics differs from other styles of ethical thinking, such as duty-bound deontology or greatest-good-for-the-greatest-number utilitarianism, in that it calls upon each agent to act ethically in everything they do as a matter of habit, as a way of embodying certain key virtues (e.g. courage, commitment, integrity, honor, loyalty, discipline, etc.). By this approach, troops (and especially those in leadership roles) are encouraged not simply to reference a rule or perform a calculation to make ethically charged decisions, but instead to act according to the military virtues instilled within themselves. Virtues are expected to be an intrinsic part of each action and decision in which a member of the military engages. More than guiding principles, virtues are meaty and deep character traits that shape a person and the way they move through the world. Acting ethically should be not second- but first-nature to a truly virtuous person.

17 This phrasing of the concept was first brought to our attention by Shannon Vallor, 'The Future of Military Virtue: Autonomous Systems and the Moral Deskilling of the Military,' (2013) *2013 5th International Conference on Cyber Conflict* (*CYCON 2013*) Tallinn, 1. For more in-depth analysis, see Vallor's excellent *Technology and the Virtues*, 2016.

In his *Nicomachean Ethics*, Aristotle says, '... moral virtue comes about as a result of habit.'[18] Habituation of ethical behavior is essential to both properly forming and maintaining good character. As Shannon Vallor notes, Aristotle '... also reminds us that virtue is *more* than just skill or know-how; it is a state in which that know-how is reliably put into action when called for, and is done with the appropriate moral concern for what is good.'[19] This state cannot be attained, or maintained, in an environment where humans are denied the opportunity to practice their virtues. The passive observer role that artificial intelligence systems can easily push humans into is one such environment.

Use of autonomous systems in any facet of military work performed by a person takes away the opportunity for military personnel to practice their virtues in that role. Just like muscles in the body, virtues must be exercised in order to maintain their strength and effectiveness. In the specific context of military decision-making, handing this role – in whole or in part – to autonomous systems will reduce the ability of military personnel to practice all of their virtues and skills honed for that purpose. This could very well lead to a decreased ability of troops to respond to any ethically fraught issues that arise when the AI is not available.

Ethical deskilling of the military is something to be avoided for several reasons. First, the longer that autonomous systems are used in decision-making capacities and humans are excluded from that role, the more likely it becomes that the humans will feel less sure of themselves when it comes to questioning the autonomous system and challenging its authority. As discussed previously, automation bias makes people much less likely to question automated systems or to try to verify their conclusions. The people who work around autonomous decision-making systems will grow used to not having to make any decisions themselves, and thus will be much less prepared to do so than people who are consistently and actively practicing their virtuous habits and decision-making skills.

There is an additional concern. Due to what some scholars refer to as the 'black box' nature of how AI makes decisions, currently it is almost if not totally impossible to determine what reasons or justifications an AI has for making a particular decision.[20] This makes it impossible for most humans (who are not

18 Aristotle, *Nicomachean Ethics* Book II, 1 (trans. W. D. Ross) <http://classics.mit.edu/Aristotle/nicomachaen.2.ii.html> accessed 12 May 2020.

19 Vallor (n 17) 1, emphasis original.

20 However, there are some efforts underway to find out what's going on inside the 'black box,' see https://futurism.com/third-wave-ai-darpa/ 'DARPA is funding research into AI that can explain what it's "thinking."' <https://futurism.com/third-wave-ai-darpa/> accessed 12 Mai 2020.

programmers and the designers of algorithms) to understand an AI system's decision-making process and possibly learn something from it. We do not want a result where soldiers are neither practicing their own ethical decision-making skills, nor are they able to learn from the new entities that are making the decisions. This essentially leaves soldiers in a mere observer-caretaker role in which they watch AI systems make decisions and perhaps are also responsible for ensuring their proper functioning.

This can be problematic when a soldier who has not had to make a decision in a long time is working with an artificial intelligence that may be malfunctioning and making unethical decisions. How able will the soldier be to see if an AI is creeping towards the edges of legally and ethically permissible action? A lack of practice in having to carefully weigh objectives, costs, and benefits of an action within legal and ethical restraints makes it less likely that a soldier will see when an AI is currently or is about to act unethically. For an analogy, consider how the United States Naval Academy struggled with the decision to keep or remove courses in celestial navigation in the era of GPS navigation systems. In the end, after taking the course out their requirements for midshipmen, they ended up restoring it, because they received feedback from the Fleet that celestial navigation was both a good back-up skill in case of a failure of electronic navigation (or tampering with it by an enemy) and a way for sailors to recognize when their GPS systems might be malfunctioning:

> The Navy and other branches of the U.S. military are becoming increasingly concerned, in part, that they may be overly reliant on GPS. … In a big war, the GPS satellites could be shot down. Or, more likely, their signal could be jammed or hacked. … [Rear Admiral Michael] White, who heads the Navy's training, says there is also a desire to get back to basics. Over the past decade, electronic navigation systems on ships have become easier to use, so less training is required. He says the Navy is bringing back celestial navigation to make sure its officers understand the fundamentals. 'You know, I would equate it to blindly following the navigation system in your car: If you don't have an understanding of north/south/east/west, or perhaps where you're going, it takes you to places you didn't intend to go,' he says. In fact, there has been at least one incident in the past decade when a Navy ship ran aground partly because of problems with the electronic navigation system, investigators say.[21]

21 Geoff Brumfiel, 'U.S. Navy Brings Back Navigation By The Stars For Officers' NPR, Science, Morning Edition (22 February 2016) <https://text.npr.org/s.php?sId=467210492> accessed 12 May 2020.

Ethical decision-making – including when and how to show moral courage – will also become an area of vulnerability if it is not taught and practiced.

The most detrimental peril of ethical deskilling of the military is that it takes something valuable away from military personnel. Virtues and the habituation of good character stay with a military member long after they have left the service. It seems safe to say that most people do not join the military to become a worse person – they join to become a better person and a better member of society for having served their country. Denying them the opportunity to cultivate virtues and character properly and fully is depriving them of one of the aspects of military culture that is intrinsically beneficial to military members. While the military teaches many valuable skills – such as survival, navigation, and marksmanship – habituated ethical virtues and the ability to make ethical decisions under pressure can provide someone with benefits in all areas of their life, military and civilian. In order to maintain an ethical military, all its members must be able to properly habituate and inculcate virtues as a benefit to themselves, as well as the institution of the military, and society as a whole. While in reality this goal remains aspirational (and the many challenges of professional military education (PME) are beyond the scope of this discussion), it certainly should not be rendered nearly impossible by the overuse of AI systems.

3 Ceding Strategic Advantage

There is a reliable pattern in human history, in which the development of a new military technology by any group or nation sparks an 'arms race' among competitors to at least catch up with or ideally leap ahead of all others to deploy the latest tool in combat. It is therefore unsurprising that there are some panicked voices in NATO or among its allies insisting that the determination of governments in, for example, China and Russia, to focus resources on the speedy advancement and utilization of AI in military applications represents a serious threat that can only be answered by wholeheartedly diving into an AI arms race. So we see statements like these in a memo from Deputy Secretary of Defense Patrick Shanahan, released in June 2018:

> This effort is a Department priority. Speed and security are of the essence. I expect all offices and personnel to provide all reasonable support necessary to make rapid enterprise-wide AI adoption a reality.[22]

22 Official memorandum from Deputy Secretary of Defense Patrick Shanahan (27 June 2018).

These are the closing words of the memo, emphasizing speedy and extensive AI adoption for the Department of Defense. However, it should be noted that earlier in the same memo, Shanahan cautions that, 'we must pursue AI applications with boldness and alacrity while ensuring strong commitment to military ethics and AI safety.'[23]

The lessons of history do not definitively support the idea that a 'be first, or be last' approach is strategically sound. There are four key points to remember: (1) being one of the first to adopt a new military technology does not guarantee immediate advantage or ultimate supremacy in the wielding of that technology, (2) even if technological superiority is achieved by the earliest adopters, being the technologically superior side in an asymmetric conflict is absolutely no assurance of victory, (3) introducing any new technology introduces new potential points of failure, and (4) taking time to develop a new technology more carefully and deliberately can allow you anticipate potential weakness and both harden your own systems against them and identify how to exploit the flaws in your opponents' systems.

Being the first out of the gate to field a new weapon has produced a mixed bag of outcomes. Gunpowder was invented by China in the 9th century AD, but was not really used effectively until the 13th century when Islamic troops in Egypt were armed with small cannon and other gunpowder-based projectile weapons.[24] Certainly, the English army benefited tremendously from the edge that the use of the longbow gave them against the French at Agincourt. However, the first submarine, used by the Colonials against the British in the American Revolution, was a dismal failure. On the other hand, it could be argued that the development of the tank helped break the stalemate in World War I. The Germans flew the first jet fighters in World War II and were generally innovative and early adopters, but, due to many factors, they ultimately lost the war. Meanwhile, both radar and the atomic bomb were new technologies vital to the victory of the Allies. The Soviet Union had many technological firsts, and yet they lost the Cold War, in part because they were outspent and driven to extremes (such as the Caspian Sea Monster) in their attempts to outpace the West.

Similarly, while it seems counter-intuitive to doubt that superior technology will yield victories, this has simply not been consistently the case in asymmetric conflicts. In ancient times, the technologically inferior Gauls defeated the Romans (and the Celts gave them a run for their money). The ill-equipped

23 Shanahan (n 22).

24 Michael Marshall, 'Timeline: Weapons Technology,' *New Scientist* (7 July 2009).

Colonials beat back the British army (although arguably they might not have been able to do so without the support of the French fleet). And more recently, the United States found itself unable to dominate the conflict in Vietnam, despite having objectively superior weapons and technology across the board. It is simply not the case that low-tech always loses against high-tech. Small modern drones can be knocked out of the sky by a simple hand-thrown spear or a trained falcon. Asymmetric advantage is a red herring. The seemingly technologically inferior side in an asymmetric conflict quite frequently wins, against the odds.

This is not to say that developing new technology is a waste of time. It can be an essential component to victory, particularly in more evenly matched conflicts. The caution here is only against the dangerous assumption that it will always provide a decisive edge. To put this in more positive terms, there is no need for a country like the United States to be made nervous or intimidated by news of the aggressive pursuit of AI by its rivals. The correct response is to focus on research, not to rush anything into the field. Researching new military technology is necessary, if only to be prepared with countermeasures against whatever opponents might design. The approach should not be to mirror the enemy's moves, but to carefully identify all the potential advantages and flaws of this new technology: not to do it first, but to do it better. Such research should simultaneously focus on effective countermeasures to exploit the vulnerabilities in the new technology. If some forms of AI are a bad idea, the smart move is not to waste resources copying those forms, but to design tools to defeat them. In this way, the hastiness of others becomes more an opportunity than a threat.

All programmed and automated systems introduce two potential points of failure: predictability and hackability. Human troops cannot easily be reprogrammed to turn against their own side. It is possible to do so, but it will never be as straightforward as changing a few lines of code. At the same time, humans can be astonishingly adaptable and creative. Artificial systems may have success against people within the strict confinement of a rule-based game like chess or Go. In the real world, rigid rules are replaced by ever-changing circumstances and seemingly irrational or unpredictable but often surprisingly effective human responses to extreme peril. Perhaps advances in quantum computing will ultimately yield artificial intelligence that is as flexible as the human mind and capable of leaps of intuition and imagination. Until that time, however, talented human strategists, with that elusive quality Clausewitz referred to as the *coup d'oeil*, will prevail. It is incumbent on military leaders not to allow themselves to be carried away by the siren song of the latest breakthroughs in emerging technology and hand over actual military decision-making to AI. This would be foolishly ceding a strategic advantage for the fashion of the season.

4 Moral and Legal Responsibility

While new technologies are being integrated into both civilian and military society, often ethical and legal standards regarding their use lag behind. Artificial intelligence is a tool that many fields, from banking to defense, have wanted to get their hands on and use as quickly, and as much, as possible. There have been some early successes that have added to the excitement, such as the use of AI to stitch together and extrapolate from archeological data to give more detailed images of the past than were ever possible and to decipher ancient manuscripts.[25] New technology that is appraised as better than current tools is often rapidly implemented with little thought to the human, social, or political repercussions of its longer-term or more extensive use. This has been particularly true with AI, which seems to have endless capabilities and possible applications. It is unfortunately both common and dangerous that questions of legality and morality surrounding the use of new technology are typically left to be debated only after something problematic has occurred. This overall trend needs to be fought against, and many are already doing so, with vigor, as seen in the robust scholarship around the legal or ethical permissibility of using autonomous weapons systems and so-called 'killer robots.'[26] For all emerging tech, but especially any with potentially lethal consequences, conversations about the possible consequences of the use of emerging technology need to happen early in the R&D phase, so that appropriate safeguards can be built into the design (rather than having to be retrofitted in response to documented harms). As Damon Horowitz says, '[w]e want the people building the technology thinking about what we should be doing with the technology.'[27]

The 'should' is important here, and points to the inherently normative nature of creating and introducing, let alone widely implementing, any new technology. Deeply considering how a new technology could be used or

---

25 *News Network Archaeology*, 'Using AI to Uncover Mysteries of the Voynich Manuscript' (26 January 2018).

26 See: Bradley Jay Strawser (ed), 'Killing by remote control: The ethics of an unmanned military' (2013); Patrick Lin, Ryan Jenkins, and Keith Abney (eds), 'Robot Ethics 2.0, From Autonomous Cars to Artificial Intelligence' (2017); Noel Sharkey, 'Saying 'No!' to Lethal Autonomous Targeting,' (2010) *Journal of Military Ethics*, Volume 9 Issue 4, 369.

27 Damon Horowitz, 'We need a "moral operating system," ' TEDxSiliconValley talk (2011).

abused, particularly outside its original scope or purpose, helps to anticipate problems and, where possible, design them out of existence. Even when it is impossible to block a potentially harmful use (or misuse) of a product, having forewarning of the issue at least allows for clear communication (advance warning is far preferable to surprise) and the development of countermeasures in advance. This is important not only when the concern is about new technology getting into the 'wrong hands,' but also even when it will be in the right hands. The U.S. military has a troubling history of implementing systems without ample time for them to be carefully studied and tested from a safety perspective, let alone from a legal or ethical standpoint. The Bradley fighting vehicle and the osprey are just two well-known examples of flawed systems rushed into use. There are also the tragedies of service personnel who were sent into irradiated areas before the effects of nuclear weapons were understood or the combat troops who were given unreliable, jam-prone M-16s in Vietnam: 'from Gettysburg to Hamburger Hill to the streets of Baghdad, the American penchant for arming troops with lousy rifles has been responsible for a staggering number of unnecessary deaths.'[28]

It is not enough, however, to take steps to anticipate what might go wrong with a new system. It is also important to consider in advance how accountability can be determined when something does go wrong. Is it possible to determine what should be attributable to the new tool and what is the fault of the operator? If AI is given too great a role in military decision-making, such determinations of legal and moral responsibility may become quite murky. In the case of the *USS Vincennes* described earlier, did the crew members decided to shoot down the aircraft the Aegis system identified as an enemy fighter? Or did they allow the system to act from its own findings? In that event, the Aegis system required a human to approve its findings and authorize it to fire, so attribution of responsibility for the catastrophe can reasonably be tied to the crewmembers who gave the go-ahead to the system. Still, the influence of the system on the crew's decision was significant. It is not difficult to imagine even more nuanced circumstances in which an AI system assumed to operate exclusively within algorithmically determined targeting parameters in line with the relevant laws of war and rules of engagement offers only one targeting option to troops, and innocents die as a result. Those seeking to assign blame could choose to take aim at the manufacturer, the code writers, the system technician on the ground, or a myriad of other possibilities. In the end, no one might truly be held accountable. The less human oversight and the greater

28 Robert H. Scales, 'Gun Trouble,' *The Atlantic* (January/February 2015).

decision-making influence AI systems have, the greater the problem of legal and ethical responsibility grows.

Patrick Lin has argued that, 'as robots become more autonomous, a case could be made to treat robots as culpable legal agents.'[29] He goes on to examine how autonomous robots may fit into a category he calls 'quasi-agents,' which typically includes children and the mentally disabled in today's legal understanding. Legal quasi-agents are not expected to have the same faculties of judgment as a full agent, and thus have 'diminished responsibility' for their actions.[30] Any consideration of how to treat artificial intelligence in the legal realm will likely follow from determinations about the legal status of robots generally. However, it is not necessarily a good idea for robots, or AI, to be given any legal status. What societal benefits would be reaped from being able to legally prosecute a robot or automated system? Surely humans would not feel safer after a robot has been punished (whatever that may entail), but only when the cause for a robot's harmful, unethical, and/or illegal actions is discovered and corrected. Keeping automated systems, and AI in particular, out of any decision-making role eliminates the need to consider them in any legally culpable sense. If these systems cannot be said to be legally responsible for errors, then it is the humans in charge who will be culpable. This puts the onus on the humans to closely observe automated systems as they work, and emphasizes the need for humans not to take the determinations of an automated system as the last word on any matter.

Not permitting AI to make decisions in a military context will help guard against automation bias, the dangers of which we explored earlier, and will keep humans in an ethically-charged role wherein they can be held to appropriate legal and moral responsibility for their actions. Elke Schwarz saliently describes what happens when humans are not the decision-makers:

> [there is a] moral vacuum that technologies of ethical decision-making create in their quest to 'secure' moral risk. A moral vacuum opens when certain parameters of harm are no one's responsibility; when the decision that harm is permissible has been determined through technological means.[31]

---

29 Patrick Lin, George Bekey, and Keith Abney, 'Autonomous Military Robotics: Risk, Ethics, and Design,' Report for the Department of the Navy, Office of Naval Research (2008).

30 Lin, Bekey and Abney (n 29).

31 Schwarz (n 10).

5 The Promise of AI as an Option-Generating Advisor

Artificial intelligence is not an inherently unethical creation. While it can cause myriad different problems if permitted to make its own decisions or to overly influence the decisions of human operators, this does not mean it cannot be used well in more appropriate manners and contexts. AI can be a positive supplement to military operations if it is employed as a tool to help humans, rather than as a replacement for or authority over them. There is a specific role in which military decision-making that AI could be immensely beneficial – that of an option generator. In this role, an automated system could even be, to borrow language from the responsibilities of military chaplains, 'an ethical advisor to command.'[32]

One of the well-documented strengths of AI is that it can process large amounts of information faster than humans.[33] This capability of AI makes it well suited to assist with time-sensitive and data-heavy tasks, both of which are easily found in military contexts. We have explained the perils of having AI systems control military decision-making, but AI could enhance human decision-making. By flagging logical fallacies, challenging assumptions, exposing blind spots in reasoning, and by processing information quickly it may provide a number of potential courses of action. This could help guard against common impediments to good decision-making by humans under stressful conditions.

There are many factors that can derail effective and ethical decision-making in high-pressure situations. For example, Kevin Mullaney and Mitt Regan have done in depth analysis of one single minute of the 19 November 2005 incident in Haditha, Iraq, in which U.S. Marines ultimately killed 24 unarmed civilians.[34] Among many other valuable insights, they have determined that the marines in question, due to their emotional state following the death of one of their own from an IED, failed to detect various visual cues that should have indicated essential information such as that the civilian car involved in the incident was

32 OPNAVINST 1730. (See (5) 'The chaplain shall serve as the principal advisor to the commander on all matters related to religious ministry and shall advise on ethical and moral matters and issues pertaining to the command.') And as Rev. Dr. Nikki Coleman has noted, there are generally not enough chaplains to go around to perform this role for all commands.

33 Lin, Bekey and Abney (n 29).

34 Prof. Mitt Regan (Georgetown Law and the US Naval Academy) and CDR Kevin Mullaney, Ph.D. (US Naval Academy), 'One Minute in Haditha: Morality and Non-Conscious Decision-Making,' presented at the North American ISME (International Society for Military Ethics) conference, Case Western Reserve University, Cleveland, Ohio (25 January 2018).

riding too high to have been filled with weapons and explosive equipment. An AI system could conceivably be designed to make a rapid scan of the surroundings and pass that kind of information on to human decision-makers in a neutral way that would not predetermine what action should follow from that information (thus avoiding the risk of undermining human authority through automation bias). In other words, the AI system might simply register something like, 'Apparent civilian car detected. Not carrying a heavy load.'

Of even greater value might be a well-timed, calm reminder by the automated system of the rules of engagement: 'Likely civilians detected; current rules of engagement prohibit firing unless fired upon; no incoming rounds detected.' Rather than being a spur to lethal action, as in the *USS Vincennes* case, the automated system could serve as a backstop against impulsive behavior. In conducting variations of his famous experiments about obedience and human responses to authority, Stanley Milgram discovered that the negative influence of a corrupt authority could be overcome by the introduction the competing influence of a rebellious peer or secondary authority.[35] By just asking questions (e.g. 'Are you sure we should be doing this?'), they were able to 'break the spell' of the original authority and awaken the conscience of the experiment subjects. Without giving direct contradictory orders, an AI advisor could provide a valuable second opinion or voice of reason to remind troops of their true mission and core values.

In cases where time permits those in command to weigh different options, AI systems could present the pros and cons of different options – again, aiding decisions, not making them. This could be used in operational settings and to help military leaders think through non-combat-related ethical issues and perhaps avoid the reckless violations and waves of corruption that have at times seemed to sweep through and decimate the service (e.g. the 'Fat Leonard' scandal in the U.S. Navy). It is clear that some commanders could use an AI voice of reason: their own automated 'Jiminy Cricket.'

Such systems must be programmed never to provide only one potential course of action. The moment AI offers just one option, it becomes the voice of authority, and all of the previously detailed perils to human autonomy and accountability return. While AI could be programmed to know and remind members of the military about such guidance as the Uniform Code of Military Justice (UCMJ), the Law of Armed Conflict (LOAC) or International Humanitarian Law (IHL), and particular Rules of Engagement (ROEs), the

35 Stanley Milgram, *Obedience to Authority: An Experimental View* (New York: Harper Perennial Modern Thought 2009) 107 and 118.

interpretation of these laws and principles must be left up to the humans themselves. Beyond the concerns already raised, the door must always be left open for human agents to decide that something is unethical, even if it is technically legal and permitted. Human moral agents have the capacity to recognize gray areas and nuance, to feel empathy, and sometimes to know instinctively when something 'just isn't right.' No AI system should undermine that ability. What we commonly think of as instinct or conscience is more than likely the result of the lived experience of navigating a complex world and the well-engrained, habituated virtues acquired through that experience.

Without interfering with instinct or blocking the nudge of conscience (and in some cases even by being the source of the latter), artificial intelligence can present multiple viable options in moments of decision that could help reduce the negative impact of the psychological and physiological effects of combat stress, such as tunnel vision, becoming trapped in a false dilemma, and experiencing paralyzing sensory overload. For example, tunnel vision can impede troops' ability to think 'big picture' and consider effects beyond their current engagement, possibly leading to actions that may solve an immediate problem, but create other, greater problems within the mission. Using AI as an option-generator could be programmed to work within and support strategic, operational, and tactical objectives. While programming would have to account for how to balance among these objectives, they all would be considered in the option-generation process to create viable choices for troops or leaders to consider.

Similarly, artificial intelligence as an option-generator could help prevent soldiers from falling into the trap of false dilemmas: believing themselves to be in binary, 'either/or' scenarios, when in fact other options for action exist. Implementing AI as an option-generator in the military decision-making context will guard against this phenomenon by consistently presenting a range of appropriate options. AI as an option-generator could alleviate some of the pressure from the amount of data that troops must gather and process when attempting to develop solutions to a pressing problem. This would address the issue of sensory overload.

The combination of time-sensitivity and data-leadenness in military decision-making make artificial intelligence attractive as a means to produce appropriate options. This is not to say that troops and military leaders are not adept at or capable of formulating solutions to pressing mission problems, only that they might benefit from using AI to generate options quickly that balance legal, ethical, and practical restraints, especially in chaotic conditions or within layered domains. Situating artificial intelligence as an option-generator and not as a decision-maker keeps it in the realm of tools to be used by human service members, not as a replacement for them.

6 Conclusion

Much of the language around AI references the position of a human in or out of a decision-making 'loop.' Yet even in situations where a human is 'somewhere in the loop,' supposedly checking and observing the system to make sure it is working properly, artificial intelligence should never be allowed to make decisions or to offer only one option to the people it advises. Humans are far too trusting of computers and other advanced systems. While technology is often implemented to reduce human error, AI systems can manifest new kinds of errors for humans to make that are just as deadly as the old ones. Artificial intelligence can make mistakes on its own, as well, and the people who work around it may not be vigilant enough to catch them in time.

This does not mean that there is no opportunity for the military to benefit from the use of AI, but rather that it should be designed and deployed as an option-generator for decision-making humans, not an artificial authority figure. AI should not tell service members what to do (let alone do it for them), but should instead provide them more information and perspective than they might be able to access themselves. As an option-generator, taking myriad factors into consideration, AI could act as a bulwark against the natural psychological pressures that can drive humans to make poor or unethical decisions in the stress of combat or other high-stakes situations. Automated systems could even serve as a sort of artificial conscience, reminding military leaders of the ramifications and possible consequences of their decisions.

War is an enterprise with profound human costs. As such, it should be conducted primarily by humans. As autonomous agents, humans can bear the moral responsibility for their actions and be held accountable for them. Technology cannot be used as a shortcut to perform roles using less effort or expenditures than the moral weight of those roles demands. There is too much at stake, including resisting the moral and practical deskilling of the military, avoiding the hidden bias that can be deeply embedded in automated and machine-learning systems, and maintaining strategic advantage.

Any new technology that is implemented in military decision-making can have serious and far-reaching consequences, and ought to be used only as an aid or tool for human operators – never as a replacement for them. There are ways that AI could assist humans in making ethical decisions in the complex context of modern warfare, by presenting information quickly in a digestible manner and offering a range of options to the human decision-maker. Yet AI systems remain fallible and their advice should never be privileged over human judgment, instinct, and experience. War is not chess or a game of Go, and any military that sublimates human decision-makers to AI systems will lose more than its soul.

References

Aristotle, Nicomachean Ethics Book II, 1 (trans. W. D. Ross) <http://classics.mit.edu/Aristotle/nicomachaen.2.ii.html> accessed 12 May 2020.

Arkin, Ron, Governing Lethal Behavior in Autonomous Robots (Taylor & Francis Group 2009).

Brown, Jennings, 'IBM Watson reportedly recommended cancer treatments that were "unsafe" and "incorrect,"' *Gizmodo* (25 July 2018).

Brumfiel, Geoff, 'U.S. Navy Brings Back Navigation By The Stars For Officers' NPR, Science, Morning Edition (22 February 2016) <https://text.npr.org/s.php?sId=467210492> accessed 12 May 2020.

Horowitz, Damon, 'We need a "moral operating system,"' TEDxSiliconValley talk (2011).

Kang, Jerry, 'Trojan Horses of Race,' *UCLA Journal of Scholarly Perspectives* (1 January 2007).

Levin, Sam, 'A beauty contest was judged by AI and the robots didn't like dark skin,' *The Guardian*, (8 September 2016).

Lin, Patrick, George Bekey, and Keith Abney, 'Autonomous Military Robotics: Risk, Ethics, and Design,' Report for the Department of the Navy, Office of Naval Research (2008).

Lin, Patrick, Ryan Jenkins, and Keith Abney (eds), *Robot Ethics 2.0, From Autonomous Cars to Artificial Intelligence* (Oxford University Press 2017).

Marshall, Michael, 'Timeline: Weapons Technology,' *New Scientist* (7 July 2009).

Milgram, Stanley, *Obedience to Authority: An Experimental View* (New York: Harper Perennial Modern Thought 2009).

Mosier, Kathleen, Everett Palmer & Asaf Degani, 'Electronic checklists: Implications for decision making' (1992) Proceedings of the Human Factors Society 36th Annual Meeting.

News Network Archaeology, 'Using AI to Uncover Mysteries of the Voynich Manuscript' (26 January 2018).

Official memorandum from Deputy Secretary of Defense Patrick Shanahan (27 June 2018).

Regan, Mitt and Kevin Mullaney, 'One Minute in Haditha: Morality and Non-Conscious Decision-Making,' presented at the North American ISME (International Society for

Military Ethics) conference, Case Western Reserve University, Cleveland, Ohio (25 January 2018).

Scales, Robert H., 'Gun Trouble,' *The Atlantic* (January/February 2015).

Schwarz, Elke, 'Technology and moral vacuums in just war theorising' (2018) *Journal of International Political Theory*.

Sharkey, Noel, 'Saying 'No!' to Lethal Autonomous Targeting,' (2010) *Journal of Military Ethics*, Volume 9 Issue 4.

Singer, Peter, *Wired for War* (The Penguin Press 2009).

Skitka, Linda J., Kathleen L. Mosier, Mark Burdick, 'Does automation bias decision-making?' (1999) 51 *International Journal of Human-Computer Studies*.

Storr, Jim, 'A Critique of Effects-Based Thinking,' (2005) *The RUSI journal*, Volume 150, Number 6, (December 2005).

Strawser, Bradley Jay (ed), *Killing by remote control: The ethics of an unmanned military* (Oxford University Press 2013).

Vallor, Shannon, 'The Future of Military Virtue: Autonomous Systems and the Moral Deskilling of the Military,' (2013) 2013 5th International Conference on Cyber Conflict (CYCON 2013) Tallinn.

Vallor, Shannon, *Technology and the Virtues* (Oxford University Press 2016)

Vincent, James, 'Twitter taught Microsoft's AI chatbot to be a racist asshole in less than a day,' *The Verge* (24 March 2016).

CHAPTER 6

Discussing Issues of Responsibility, Accountability and Liability When AI Agents Decide and Act During War

The Case of Training Algorithms for Attacking Possible Targets

Ioanna K. Lekea, Panagiotis Karampelas, George Anthimou, and Konstantinos Michail

1 Introduction: Artificial Intelligence and the New Battlefields

Nowadays, the possibility of a partial replacement of humans by AI systems/agents is under investigation from different scientific disciplines. When we refer to an AI agent we talk about a powered machine that senses, thinks (in a deliberative, non-mechanical sense), and, acts; AI agents can be operated semi or fully autonomously, but cannot depend entirely on human control.[1] On the other hand, when we talk about *autonomy*, we refer to the capability of an AI agent to operate in the real world environment without any form of external control, once it is activated and, at least, in some areas of operation, for extended periods of time.

In this context, the use of autonomous robotics systems[2] in a war is expected to have significant operational and tactical advantages. For instance, robots are capable of rapid data processing, and quick reaction to a situation without the restrictions, that a human being would naturally have, like lack of sleep, stress, high adrenaline, and low morale. Also, the use of AI systems/agents is expected to reduce human losses (in terms of the lives of soldiers engaged in war operations). To this end, AI systems/agents are expected to make serious and even lethal decisions, such as when to fire upon a target, without any human

---

1 For instance, unmanned aerial vehicles used by the Air Force, the Navy or the Army, could possibly qualify as AI agents as far as they make some decisions on their own, such as distinguishing and surveilling suspicious targets, but a toy car remotely controlled definitely doesn't fall under this category since its control depends entirely on the operator.

2 George Bekey, *Autonomous Robots: From Biological Inspiration to Implementation and Control* (MIT Press, Cambridge MA 2005); Jai Galliott, *Military Robots: mapping the moral landscape* (Ashgate 2015).

 | DOI:10.1163/9789004507951_008

intervention; and, if technology guarantees that AI agents are capable of completing those lethal tasks without mistakes or with a very low percentage of mistakes and collateral damage, AI agents could even replace human soldiers in a range of dangerous missions, such as: securing urban streets, clearing roads from IEDs (improvised explosive devices), investigating the existence of biochemical weapons in hostile areas, guarding borders and buildings, or controlling hostile crowds.

However, as we know, technology always implies a number of perceived risks, whether functional, physical, financial, or social. In our case, we have to deal with a serious risk, and that is the potential damage (lethal or non-lethal) caused by AI agents to third parties; AI agents producing deliberate or collateral damage, for example due to manufacturing error, malfunction, or mistaken analysis of the situation by the algorithms used, may not be intended by the manufacturers, but still is a breach of the applicable moral and legal framework that has secondary side-effects to specific persons (those who manufactured the system) and to society as well.[3] Therefore, issues related to ethics and law[4] (especially as far as responsibility, accountability, and liability are concerned for unwanted, intentional or unintentional damage produced by AI systems/agents) should be resolved for all parties involved in the development, construction and use of AI technology, before robots are given lethal power[5] and used on a real battlefield.[6]

3 Peter M. Asaro, 'How just could a robot war be?' (2008) *Current issues in computing and philosophy*, 50–64; Peter M. Asaro, 'What should we want from a robot ethic?' (2006) 6 *International Review of Information Ethics*, 9.

4 Eleanor Bird, Jasmin Fox-Skelly, Nicola Jenner, Ruth Larbey, Emma Weitkamp and Alan Winfield, 'The ethics of artificial intelligence: Issues and initiatives' (2020) European Parliamentary Research Service, March 2020 <https://www.europarl.europa.eu/RegData/etudes/STUD/2020/634452/EPRS_STU(2020)634452_EN.pdf> accessed 11 November 2020.

5 In this chapter we discuss the possibility of mistakes made by AI agents with lethal power, but there is much more to it. AI agents are used for a variety of non-lethal missions (surveillance, verification of targets etc), which have undisputable operational and tactical benefits, but also entail ethical and legal considerations. Those cases are not included in this work, therefore, the relevant considerations are not addressed in this paper.

6 Nicholas Michael Sambaluk, *Conflict in the 21st Century: The Impact of Cyber Warfare, Social Media, and Technology* (ABC-CLIO 2019).

2 Discussing Ethics and Law of War. A Short Version of a Long Story

2.1 *The Principle of Discrimination*

According to the just war theory, two principles govern just war conduct: the principle of discrimination and the principle of proportionality. The principle of discrimination defines who and what one can justly attack in a war.[7] It is considered immoral to deliberately kill non-combatants who are 'morally and technically innocent, that is, harmless'[8] and pose no threat whatsoever; this idea also forms the moral baseline of international legislation relating to war issues: therefore, civilians' lives should be protected in the best possible way, while, on the other hand, it is justifiable to attack the enemy's armed forces and military targets, such as military installations, military airfields and naval bases, military factories and munitions. Furthermore, some civilian targets such as railways, roads and bridges, could be destroyed, if they have verified combatant functions, as long as the non-combatants are excluded from direct, intentional attack and their property is not intentionally harmed.[9] Intentionally attacking non-combatants,[10] for example medical personnel and equipment, either military or civilian is strictly forbidden.[11]

The principle of distinction prohibits any direct attacks on non-combatants or their property; those who are not directly participating in the fighting are not to be targeted. In the context of current military operations and/or interventions, given the fact that they happen in populated areas, non-combatant immunity is a very important factor to be taken into consideration when planning and executing military action; let us not forget that amongst the usual and fundamental reasons for justifying military action of any kind is the protection

7 Nicholas Fotion, 'Who, What, When and How to Attack' [Paper presented at the *Joint Services Conference on Professional Ethics* (JSCOPE): 1996] <http://isme.tamu.edu/JSCOPE96/fotion96.html> accessed 11 November 2020.

8 David R. Mapel, 'Realism and the Ethics of War and Peace' in Terry Nardin (ed), *The Ethics of War and Peace. Secular and Religious Perspectives* (Princeton University Press 1996) 54–77; Robert L. Holmes, *On War and Morality* (Princeton University Press 1989) 104.

9 Geneva Convention (IV) relative to the Protection of Civilian Persons in Time of War of 12 August 1949, Articles 4, 27–34; Protocol Additional to the Geneva Conventions I of 8 June 1977, Article 52.

10 Common Article 3 of the 1949 Geneva Conventions of 12 August 1949; Protocol Additional to the Geneva Conventions I of 8 June 1977, Article 48.

11 Geneva Convention (I) for the Amelioration of the Condition of the Wounded and Sick in Armed Forces in the Field of 12 August 1949, Articles 19–21, 24–25; Geneva Convention (II) for the Amelioration of the Condition of the Wounded, Sick and Shipwrecked Members of Armed Forces at Sea of 12 August 1949, Articles 22–35; Protocol Additional to the Geneva Conventions I of 8 June 1977, Articles 12 and 23.

of fundamental human rights and the prevention of widespread human suffering. This means that, if the military forces harm civilians on purpose, then the humanitarian perspective of any military operation is overlooked.

In other words, military action, in order to be justified, should concentrate on constantly adhering to the principle of distinction and in no case should civilians be the direct target of military action on purpose. The protection of civilians is also dictated by International Humanitarian Law.[12] Combatants should be well trained and willing to accept an increase in risk to their own safety in order to protect non-combatants;[13] they should also take every possible step to protect them. This is a very difficult task indeed, especially given the fact that terrorists or insurgents dress the same way civilians do and hide among them. Soldiers need a lot of training to effectively discriminate in urban terrain and, during the military operations, they can also get assistance by receiving and using fresh data to clear up situations, when things are not apparent or unambiguous.

People throughout the ages have managed to successfully accomplish – at least to an acceptable point – all the above mentioned stages (effective training, critical thinking, asking for guidelines in grey areas cases, use of updated data). But what about AI agents?[14] What kind of training or use and processing of data could possibly guarantee that a machine can actually follow the rules of engagement? How can a programmer or a military commander be certain that an AI agent is capable of distinguishing and targeting only confirmed targets without any interference or human control?[15]

2.2 *The Principle of Proportionality*

Even if we accept that it is almost inevitable to harm civilians during the course of a military operation, we still need to take positive steps in order to ensure

12 Nathalie Durhin, 'Protecting Civilians in Urban Areas: A Military Perspective on the Application of International Humanitarian Law' (2016) 98 *International Review of the Red Cross*, 177.

13 Sebastian Kaempf, *Saving Soldiers or Civilians?: Casualty-Aversion versus Civilian Protection in Asymmetric Conflicts* (Cambridge University Press 2018); Thomas W. Smith, 'Protecting Civilians … or Soldiers? Humanitarian Law and the Economy of Risk in Iraq' (2008) 9 *International Studies Perspectives*, 144; Noam Zohar, 'Risking and Protecting Lives. Soldiers and Opposing Civilians' in Helen Frowe and Gerald Lang (eds), *How we Fight: Ethics in War* (OUP 2014).

14 William H. Boothby, *New technologies and the law in war and peace* (Cambridge University Press 2019).

15 A. van Wynsberghe & S. Robbins, 'Critiquing the Reasons for Making Artificial Moral Agents' (2019) 25 *Science and Engineering Ethics*, 719.

the best possible way that civilians will not get hurt on purpose (or by mistake) and their properties will not be damaged. Within this context, the principle of proportionality is a central assessment of the conduct of war. The reason is that it looks into ways one should use for attacking the enemy. It is used to resolve issues such as how one should attack and what kinds of weapons one might use in order to achieve the military objectives set without causing disproportional collateral damage,[16] i.e., civilian casualties or damage to civilian objects.

In non-clear-cut cases, where the enemy is surrounded by civilians or uses them as disguise, and there is a possibility of harming or killing non-combatants as a result of the military operation, the principle of double effect is invoked.[17] A high-level approach to this principle-granted that on the battlefield things can get really complicated- is that if we are planning to perform an act that is likely to harm non-combatants, we proceed only if the following four conditions stand:[18]

- The act must be good in itself; it must be a legitimate act of war.
- The direct effect must be morally acceptable (so, the target must be legitimate).
- Any bad effect must not be intended.
- The intended outcome must be proportional to the foreseen bad effect. This means that the good effect coming from the military achievement should outweigh any negative consequences of the attack.

Even when the aforementioned conditions are met, still the foreseeable bad consequences must be eliminated as far as possible.[19]

It follows that both principles of discrimination and proportionality create the obligation for military commanders and other people involved in planning a specific military operation to think carefully about the results of any military

16 Michael N. Schmitt, 'State-sponsored Assassination in International and Domestic Law' (1992) 17 *Yale Journal of International Law,* 609–685.

17 Stefano Predelli, 'Some Comments on Double Effect and Harmful Involvement' (2004) 3 *Journal of Military Ethics,* 16; Gary D. Brown 'Proportionality and Just War' (2003) 2 *Journal of Military Ethics,* 171; Joanne Lekea, 'Missile Strike Carried Out With Yemeni Cooperation' – The War Against Terrorism: A Different Kind of War? (2003) 2 *Journal of Military Ethics,* 230.

18 Emanuel Gross, 'Self-defense against Terrorism-What Does It Mean? The Israeli Perspective' (2002) 1 *Journal of Military Ethics* 96; James Turner Johnson, *Morality and Contemporary Warfare* (Yale University Press 1999) 132–133; Richard J. Regan, *Just War, Principles and Cases* (The Catholic University of America Press 1996); Michael Walzer, *Just and Unjust Wars, A Moral Argument with Historical Illustration* (*4th edn,* Penguin Books 1984) 153.

19 Walzer (n 18) 155.

operation; civilians and their property should be protected in the best possible way. It is not permissible to harm civilians and destroy non-military targets, except for when harm and destruction is accidental or not intended and is proportional to the overall goal of the operation. The logic of this would be that every effort has been taken to not harm non-combatants.

Does technological change and its recent advancements in AI allow us to include non-human agents in the chain of decision-making, defining right and wrong or even choosing between possible actions and means of attack?[20] Who should be deemed responsible for the choices and actions of AI agents? What if mistakes are made or unsuccessful choices lead to terrible results? Let us discuss the scheme of responsibility-accountability-liability in the chain of command and see if including AI agents in military operations is possible and where AI agents could fit.[21]

3 Responsibility – Accountability – Liability: Who Will Take the Blame for Any Mistakes?

Responsibility is an ethical and legal term related to accountability.[22] However, these two words are not synonymous, they mean different things; responsibility means that one is responsible for his/her actions, while accountability simply means that he/she will be called to account for them. The person who is responsible for a task should, first, decide whether or not he/she should actively be involved, and, if taking action is his/her initial choice, identify the best possible action to accomplish their goal and then execute it. If anything goes wrong, then, he/she will be asked to give an account for his/her actions or inaction, because he/she didn't manage to fulfill the responsibility he/she had.

Accountability is a higher-level concept than responsibility, as it does not just demarcate who is responsible for an action, but it also requires that the person who commits to a task can be called to account for his/her action (or inaction, if that is the case); he/she must provide a reason or give an explanation

20 Patrick Hew, 'Autonomous Situation Awareness: Implications for Future Warfighting' (2007) *Australian Defence Force Journal,* 71; Bill Hibbard, 'Avoiding unintended AI behaviors' (2012) *Artificial General Intelligence,* 107.

21 Colin Allen & Wendel Wallach, 'Moral machines: Contradiction in terms of abdication of human responsibility?' in P. Lin, K. Abney, & G. A. Bekey (eds), *Robot ethics: The ethical and social implications of robotics* (MIT Press 2011).

22 Marc Cornock, 'Legal definitions of responsibility, accountability and liability' (2011) 23 *Nursing Children and Young People,* 25.

for his/her action/inaction. Giving an account for a decision and/or an action doesn't always mean that something went wrong; in certain cases, monitoring the decision-making process or training new employees or just sharing information for the benefit of others may be the reason behind holding someone accountable for his decisions and actions. No matter the case, however, giving an account is an obligation which is usually related to a formal procedure.

Liability is more of a legal concept and implies that there is a disadvantage to the person who is liable: that the person has to account for his/her actions to a legal body within a legal framework.[23] Liability is, therefore, a form of legal or legislative accountability, and the person who is liable for something has a legal obligation to answer to the law through the courts or to a regulatory body; and, of course, following the legal procedure, the possibility of a sanction or punishment is always present.

When the person, who is held accountable for an action/inaction, can reasonably give a valid explanation for his/her decision and behavior, he/she may be considered as responsible, but not liable for the negative result. Let us think of the following incident: a soldier is under lethal attack and decides that he should respond to the attack by targeting the enemy with lethal force. This is considered an acceptable choice and form of action under International Law and the Rules of Engagement (RoE);[24] therefore, it is expected that the soldier will not get punished, because he wounded or killed an enemy in self-defense (that is the right for people to use reasonable force or defensive force for the purpose of defending their own lives or the lives of their comrades). On the other hand, consider a situation where a soldier decides to immediately use lethal force against a suspected person, who has not attacked him/her yet nor has implied by any means that he/she will attack the soldier. In that case, the soldier is expected to be held accountable, because his decision to attack someone, who is not a confirmed target nor poses an imminent threat to the soldier or his comrades, is a breach of the RoE.[25] In the absence of an immediate attack or threat of an imminent attack, other actions should be considered as more appropriate and suitable; in this case, before a lethal attack another

23 R. A. Duff, *Answering for Crime. Responsibility and Liability in the Criminal Law* (Hart Publishing 2007) 19.

24 Michael N. Schmitt, 'Deconstructing Direct Participation in Hostilities: The Constitutive Elements' (2010) 42 *New York University International Law and Politics*, 697.

25 Camilla Guldahl Cooper, *'Introduction' in NATO Rules of Engagement* (Brill/Nijhoff 2019); Christopher M. Ford, 'Personal Self-Defence and the Standing Rules of Engagement' in Winston S. Williams and Christopher M. Ford (eds) *Complex Battlespaces: The Law of Armed Conflict and the Dynamics of Modern Warfare* (OUP 2018).

more suitable action, such as an inspection, arrest, or even use of non-lethal force. Therefore, it is very likely that the soldier will get punished for his misjudgment and for the negative results on the individual he/she attacked without sufficient justification. If, during the legal procedure, it is proved that the soldier did not receive the appropriate training, his/her superiors could get punished as well. And of course, if the case is that the soldier followed an illegal order to shoot someone who posed no threat at that moment, the person who issued the illegal order will get punished as well.

This is a very short and simplified version of how responsibility/accountability/liability works within a structured military organization: anyone within a certain hierarchical order is responsible for himself and his subordinates:[26] even when the commanding officer is not present, if a war crime is committed, most probably he/she will be held accountable too for his/her subordinates' actions.[27] Commanders have the responsibility to train their personnel, to provide them with guidance and to decide what the proper action is in ambiguous situations; they can also be held accountable and be considered liable for both their actions and their subordinates' actions, when they don't fulfill their obligations or when they misguide their subordinates or issue illegal and immoral orders.

These situations[28] can prove to be very complex, especially when they cease to be just hypothetical scenarios for use in class, but happen in real life. With AI[29] in the scheme of things, the practical, ethical, and legal issues can get even more complex. AI agents are trained to decide and act upon a situation without any external human interference. A lot of people contribute to the development of AI agents and it is quite an issue to prove who is to be held responsible, accountable, or liable for misconduct, when something goes wrong.[30]

For example, a major challenge for programming an AI agent is to decide whether a top-down ethical theory or a bottom-up process of learning is the

26 Darryl Robinson, 'A Justification of Command Responsibility' (2017) 28 *Criminal Law Forum*, 633.

27 Darryl Robinson, 'How command responsibility got so complicated: A culpability contradiction, its obfuscation, and a simple solution' (2012) 13 *Melbourne Journal of International Law*, 1.

28 Patrick Lin, Georg Bekey & Keith Abney, *Autonomous military robotics: Risk, ethics, and design* (California Polytechnic State University 2008).

29 Heather M. Roff, 'Responsibility, liability, and lethal autonomous robots' in Allhoff, Fritz, Evans, Nicholas G. and Henschke, Adam (eds), *Routledge Handbook of Ethics and War: Just War Theory in the 21st Century* (Routledge 2013).

30 Roff (n 29) 352; David C. Vladeck, 'Machines without Principals: Liability Rules and Artificial Intelligence' (2014) 89 *Washington Law Review*, 117.

most effective approach for building artificial moral agents.[31] A top-down approach would program rules into the AI agent and expect the AI agent to simply obey those rules without change or flexibility. The downside, is that such inflexibility can easily lead to bad consequences, when situations unforeseen by the programmers occur, causing the AI agent to perform badly and act in an unacceptable way.[32] A bottom-up approach, on the other hand, depends on robust machine learning: an AI agent is placed into various situations and is expected to learn through trial-error (and feedback) what constitutes an acceptable action and what is unacceptable. But this approach can also become problematic, particularly if the AI agent is introduced to brand new situations, as it cannot fall back on any rules to guide it beyond the ones it knows from its own experience.[33] If the situations used by the programmer for training the AI agent are insufficient, then the AI agent will likely perform poorly as well. Perhaps a hybrid architecture should be the preferred model for constructing ethical autonomous agents.[34] Some top-down rules are combined with machine learning to best approximate the ways in which humans actually gain knowledge and expertise.[35]

For all the above-mentioned advantages and disadvantages, human developers and programmers are responsible to choose the best option,[36] but if an AI agent fails to perform its task correctly, and, within a given ethical and legal background, who is to blame for the failure along with any damage it may entail as well?[37] AI agents constantly receive data during a military operation, but what will happen, if they choose to disobey an order, because of conflicting information? This may stop or damage the whole operation; it could kill innocent people and destroy property. AI agent is considered the perpetrator in this case, but how can we punish a machine? On the other hand, a number

---

31 Wendell Wallach, *Moral Machines: Teaching Robots Right from Wrong* (OUP 2008).

32 Colin Allen, Gary Varner, and Jason Zinser, 'Prolegomena to Any Future Artificial Moral Agent' (2000) 12 *Journal of Experimental & Theoretical Artificial Intelligence*, 251.

33 Daniele Amoroso and Guglielmo Tamburrini 'The Ethical and Legal Case Against Autonomy in Weapons Systems' *Global Jurist* 18.1 (2017).

34 Martin Ebers, Susana Navas, *Algorithms and Law* (Cambridge University Press 2020).

35 Wendell Wallach, Colin Allen, & Iva Smit 'Machine Morality: Bottom-up and Top-down Approaches for Modeling Human Moral Faculties' (2008) 22 *AI & Society*, 565; Ugo Pagallo, Pompeu Casanovas & Robert Madelin, 'The middle-out approach: assessing models of legal governance in data protection, artificial intelligence, and the Web of Data' (2019) 7 *The Theory and Practice of Legislation*, 1.

36 Matthias Scheutz, 'The need for moral competency in autonomous agent architectures' in Vincent C. Müller (ed) *Fundamental Issues of Artificial Intelligence* (Springer 2016).

37 Jacob Turner and Robot Rules, *Regulating Artificial Intelligence* (Springer 2019); Spyros G. Tzafestas, *Roboethics: A Navigating Overview* (Springer 2016).

of persons can be considered as instigators or accessories, because they developed and programmed the machine or they allowed it to take part in the operation. So, who will take the blame? And on what grounds? The manufacturer and the programmer for a faulty or defective machine, the military organization for relying on a machine (even an intelligent one) to do the job, or the legal advisors who advised and accepted the participation of AI agents in military operations, giving them the power to use lethal force against people? Should more be added to this who-can-be-blamed-for-what-list too? As there is no point to punishing a machine, that is why it is very important to think and try to solve any foreseeable problems,[38] before introducing AI agents in real operations.[39]

4 Technological Maturity for an AI Autonomous Robotic System

4.1 *Technological Challenges*

Autonomous military robots as previously mentioned and analytically described[40] are considered machines, which are able to sense the environment through a variety of sensors, assess the input of the sensors and make decisions using complex algorithms and, finally, act based on their decisions.

Since robots are primarily advanced machines, there are several technological risks and challenges pertaining to the manufacturing, the testing, the deployment, the operational use and the maintenance of those machines. Figure. 6.1 summarizes potential risks per robot life-cycle.

Starting from the manufacturing stage,[41] as in all military systems, there is a series of risks that involves the specific life-cycle stage. Since each part and sensor of the robot may ship from different manufacturers, it is very important to ensure that all parts and sensors are fulfilling all the security standards during their manufacturing in order to ensure the minimum malfunction of the circuits or that all the parts will react as they are designed and expected during the operational use of the robot. Since most of the parts and sensors contain circuits, it is essential to ensure that no hardware virus will be injected during the manufacturing stage and the parts and sensors are behaving as they expected to do by their design.

38 Vincent C. Müller, 'Autonomous Killer Robots Are Probably Good News' in Ezio Di Nucci and Filippo Santoni de Sio (eds) *Drones and Responsibility: Legal, Philosophical and Socio-Technical Perspectives on the Use of Remotely Controlled Weapons* (Ashgate 2016).

39 Heather M. Roff, 'The Strategic Robot Problem: Lethal Autonomous Weapons in War' (2014) 13 *Journal of Military Ethics*, 211.

40 Lin, Bekey & Abney (n 28).

41 Lin, Bekey & Abney (n 28).

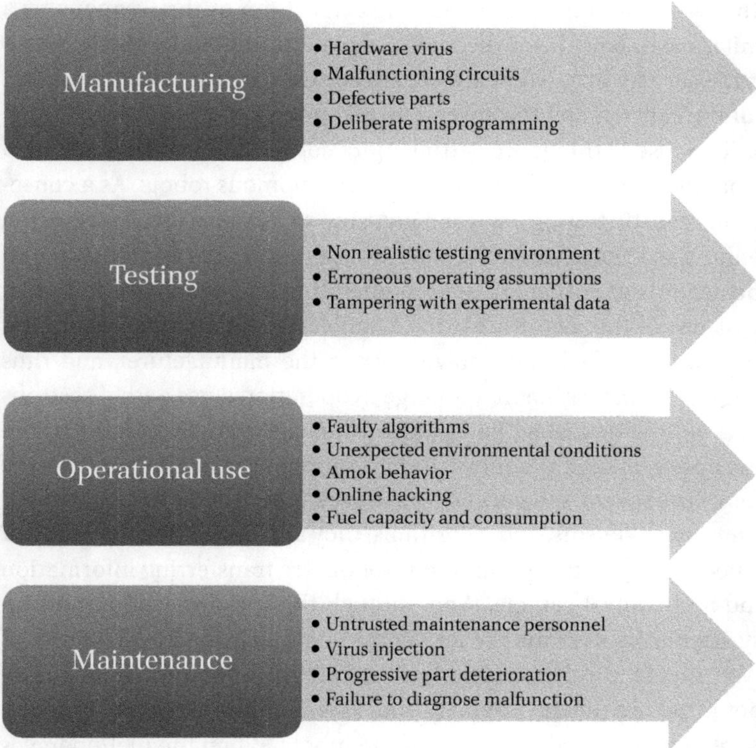

FIGURE 6.1 Autonomous Military Robots potential risk in their life-cycle

Moving to the testing stage,[42] there are a lot of risks regarding the conditions of operation. Depending on the mission of the robot, the corresponding testing environment should be set and the appropriate testing conditions should be developed in a way such that the experiments will simulate the real operational conditions of the robot. Failing to do so, may cause collateral damage or losses on the battlefield, as for example if the robots are meant to protect a target in a desert and the temperature is higher than the one in which they have been tested, this may lead to faulty behavior and as a result endanger the security of the target. Another phenomenon that has been observed in military systems is that sometimes the manufacturer has tampered with the experimental results in an effort to demonstrate better or improved performance

42 Lin, Bekey & Abney (n 28); George R. Lucas Jr, 'Industrial challenges of military robotics' (2011) 10 *Journal of Military Ethics*, 274.

vis-a-vis other rivals, and thus influence the acquisition of the weapons by a nation. Similar cases have been recently observed in other situations, as for example in the car industry, where intelligent software manipulated the diesel emissions of the cars to meet the appropriate standards.

In operational use,[43] things are getting more complicated since there are a lot factors that may affect the behavior of the autonomous robots. As a consequence of non-realistic testing environments, the robots may face unexpected environmental conditions when they are in operation and demonstrate an expected behavior; e.g., run amok or stop operating and endanger their mission. In most cases, the algorithms that enable the autonomous operation of the robots are classified and known only to the manufacturer, and thus potential bugs in the algorithm may emerge in operational use with disastrous outcomes. As will be described below, algorithms are very important in the autonomous operation of a robot and if they fail then the actual operation of the robot may raise several ethical and legal issues. Since robots are extensively based on computers, sensors, and algorithms, they are susceptible to viruses or hacking. Especially when the autonomous robots are transferring information to command-and-control centers, then, through the communication link, an enemy may attempt to override the legitimate commands and take control of the robot. Another factor that may seriously affect the operation of an autonomous robot is the fuel/energy capacity and consumption, since fuel is necessary to ensure uninterrupted operation of the robots. When the fuel/energy is depleted, the robot cannot continue its mission.

Finally, at the maintenance stage,[44] it is important to allow only authorized personnel to work with the robot and update the critical systems. There is always the risk of infecting a subsystem of the robot with a virus when the robot is under maintenance, as in the case of the stuxnet worm, which contaminated the supervisory control and data acquisition (SCADA) system during the maintenance stage, ruining a certain number of Iran's nuclear centrifuges. Other risks pertaining to the specific stage may come from the continuous use of the robots in extreme situations, which may lead to the deterioration of critical parts of the robot. If the maintenance personnel fail to diagnose the problem during maintenance stage, this will have as a result the robot operating at a lower level of performance than expected.

---

43 Roberta Arnold, 'The Legal Implications of the Use of Systems With Autonomous Capabilities in Military Operations' (2015) *Issues for Defence Policymakers*, 83.

44 Shozo Takata et al, 'Maintenance: changing role in life cycle management' (2004) 53 *CIRP Annals*, 643.

4.2 *Experimental Assessment of Technological Maturity*

Having in mind all the potential risks that the use of autonomous robots may have, now we will focus on those factors that affect the ethical and legal aspects of their operation.

Our experiment took place at the War Games Lab at the Hellenic Air Force Academy, and two academic divisions participated: the Division of Leadership-Command, Humanities and Physiology, and the Division of Informatics & Computers. The experiment took place between April 2016 and May 2017 and it was part of a dissertation.

Our main objective was to test algorithms that are trained to decide on the risk against potential targets and how our systems should attack. The basic question we wanted to address was if and in which ways ethics could be programmed so as to become part of an AI autonomous system.

The experiment was conducted by applying well-established supervised learning computer vision algorithms in detecting potential threats. We attempted to:

- recognize targets carrying specific guns in diverse situations and, then,
- assess the accuracy and effectiveness of the algorithms used, and, finally,
- investigate whether they can function autonomously, taking into consideration the ethical and legal limitations.

In this effort, we have tried to understand if and in which ways ethics could be programmed so as to become part of an Artificial Intelligent robotic system that could decide to react to potential targets, and to measure its performance and decide whether the technology is mature enough to start using such an autonomous robotic system. In order to reach a concrete conclusion, we set up an experiment using an automated artificially intelligent algorithm that was able to recognize targets carrying specific guns in diverse situations. Then, we attempted to assess the accuracy and effectiveness of the algorithm based on the recognition rates, and finally we investigated whether the algorithm could be used in a robot to function autonomously, taking into consideration the ethical and legal limitations.

As previously mentioned, a real autonomous targeting algorithm is usually classified and thus it is very difficult to get access to such technology. In order to overcome this obstacle, we resorted to open-source algorithms that are used for object recognition in diverse situations such as in the case of license plate recognition on toll roads.[45] The specific algorithms belong to the broader category of pattern recognition which is a branch of machine learning.

---

45 Ankush Roy & D. P. Ghoshal, 'Number Plate Recognition for use in different countries using an improved segmentation' (2011) in *2nd National Conference on Emerging Trends*

The algorithm adopted and customized to recognize targets carrying guns is implemented taking advantage of the functionality offered by the openCV library.[46] The algorithm is based on the Viola-Jones object detection framework[47] which implements the Adaboost learning algorithm[48] and utilizes Haar-like features[49] to speed up the recognition process. The Viola-Jones algorithm was initially created to recognize faces and thus the Haar-like features originally referred to facial properties. Taking advantage of the aforementioned techniques, we customized the algorithm which was then tested using a dataset of images that were collected from open-source databases. All the images contain weapons that share similar features – e.g., a gun barrel – and thus the first step in weapon detection was the selection of these features (Haar-like feature) which referred to the properties of the selected guns. Then the algorithm produced an integral image which consists of all the rectangular areas collected by the Haar features. Then Adaboost was used to select the best features to train the classifiers, and in the last phase, the produced sub-images were checked to determine whether a weapon exists or not in an unknown image. Since the algorithm is a supervised machine-learning algorithm, it requires training with a test set of images and then the system is able to classify a new image either as positive when the object in question has been detected or negative when the object has not been detected. To improve the accuracy level of the algorithm, it is very important to train the system with the appropriate image set.

In general, object detection can be seriously affected by four parameters that can upgrade or degrade the detection accuracy of the algorithm.[50] These parameters are:

---

and Applications in Computer Science (*NCETACS*), 1; M. Rhead, R. Gurney, S. Ramalingam & N. Cohen, 'Accuracy of automatic number plate recognition (ANPR) and real world UK number plate problems' (2012) in *2012 IEEE International Carnahan Conference on Security Technology* (*ICCST*), 286.

46 Gary Bradski, 'The OpenCV Library' (2000) 25 *Dr. Dobb's Journal: Software Tools for the Professional Programmer*, 120.

47 Paul Viola & Michael Jones, 'Rapid object detection using a boosted cascade of simple features. In Computer Vision and Pattern Recognition' (2001) in *Proceedings of the 2001 IEEE Computer Society Conference on CVPR* Vol. 1, I-I.

48 Yoav Freund & Robert E. Schapire, 'A decision-theoretic generalization of on-line learning and an application to boosting' (1997) 55 *Journal of computer and system sciences*, 119.

49 Phillip I. Wilson & J. Fernandez, 'Facial feature detection using Haar classifiers' (2006) 21 *Journal of Computing Sciences in Colleges*, 127.

50 M. G. Krishna & A. Srinivasulu, 'Face detection system on AdaBoost algorithm using Haar classifiers' (2012) 2 *International Journal of Modern Engineering Research*, 3556.

- *Variable pose*. This is mainly observed when people are posing in front of the camera. They tend to assume different postures and thus the detection accuracy is usually affected. In our case, since guns are held by people, the orientation of the guns follows the posture of the people holding them. This, as was expected, equally affects the detection accuracy as will be seen in the experiments.
- *Illumination*. Another factor that may influence detection accuracy is lighting. Lighting depends on the weather conditions or on the time of the day. When inside, the artificial light may correspondingly affect the detection accuracy either positively, when it makes the objects sharper, or negatively when it cast shadows on parts of the image.
- *Camera Specifications*. Camera resolution is another important factor that influences detection accuracy. A good camera that is able to take high resolution images provides better detection results, since the quality of images is better. Taking images with a high-resolution camera provides images with many details and as a result better detection accuracy.
- *Occlusion*. Sometimes, clothes or other objects may interfere in the image and hide part of the gun, and as a consequence affect the detection accuracy.

4.3 *Weapon Detection Based on the Classifiers*

The experimental process involved collecting a custom dataset of more than 500 photos with a specific type of a weapon shown in different angles, weather conditions, time of day, etc. It was decided to select a specific type of weapon in order to improve the chances for obtaining higher detection rates. As expected, identifying different type of guns can be very difficult, since different types of guns have different features, such as size, magazines, barrel length, etc. We also collected a large number of photos with objects that resemble weapons, such as water pistols, bows, broomsticks, etc.

Then two people classified the photos as positive or negative in order to be able to measure the accuracy of the algorithm later. Following that, we used different compilations of the images creating different image sets in order to identify the detection accuracy of the algorithm.

Different image sets were used to train the algorithm in different configurations (Haar Training). Then, using the classifiers that were created, we run the Adaboost algorithm to check the testing image set and decide whether there was a weapon in it or not. Based on the results a number of different parameters were calculated. More specifically:

- Accuracy; which is the fraction of all predictions that were correct
- Misclassification rate; the rate of the predictions that failed
- True positive; the correctly identified images containing weapons

- False positive; the images falsely identified as having weapons when there was not such an object
- Specificity; the fraction of all negatives in the population we were able to keep away
- Precision; the quality of positive predictions which is calculated as the rate of the true positive images against those that were predicted as positives
- Prevalence; the rate of positive detection against the total number of images.

As described in the following section, the experiment with different image sets provided interesting results that are analytically discussed.

4.4 *Experiments Results*

As can be seen in Table 6.1, different numbers of photos were used to train the classifier. Thus, sets of 10, 40, 100, 140 and 200 photos were used.

More specifically, the set with the 40 photos included only photos with weapons against a white background, in an effort to examine the extent to which occlusion affects the results and whether the selection of photos with the same background can increase the precision of the program. In the set of 140 photos, the training of the classifier was made with multiple, individual pieces of the image such as the area where the trigger was visible, or the arm, the barrel, the magazine, etc. to see if selecting parts of the object would help to increase detection accuracy.

As will be shown in the results, the multi-point selection of the image did not help the detection process, but it led to an increase in the false detection index. In all the remaining photosets the training was performed by selecting the entire weapon.

In each experiment, a different number of photos was used in order to examine which combination of positive and negative images provided better results.

Table 6.2 summarizes all the metrics calculated for all the above-mentioned experiments. As can be seen, the highest accuracy was achieved in experiment 12 with an accuracy rate of 82% while in other experiments the accuracy was very low 0%–8% depending on the training procedure and the photoset used.

In Figure 6.2 and 6.3 the accuracy and misclassification rates per experiment are presented.

Based on the experimental process and our analysis, we were able to draw some conclusions that could help improving the overall detection phase of such a classification algorithm.

More specifically, training the classifier with photos that present the object in question – i.e., the weapon – in a precise and clear area improves the accuracy rate. Training the classifier with different subparts of a weapon does not

TABLE 6.1 Experiment Description and results

	Training		Samples	Positive	Negative	True positive	False positive	True negative	False negative
Experiment 1	10/0	Positive	21	10	11	5	2	9	5
Experiment 2	100/0	Positive	50	0	50	0	0	12	38
Experiment3	100/0	Positive	50	0	50	0	46	4	0
Experiment 4	200/0	Positive	40	40	0	0	40	0	0
Experiment5	140/0	Positive	40	40	0	40	0	0	0
Experiment6	100/0	Positive	40	40	0	40	0	0	0
Experiment7	200/0	Positive	700	200	500	36	62	438	164
Experiment8	140/0	Positive	639	139	500	139	498	2	0
Experiment9	40/0	Positive	239	39	200	3	24	176	36
Experiment 10	100/0	Positive	696	196	500	123	78	422	73
Experiment 11	40/0	Positive	541	41	500	24	209	291	17
Experiment 12	100/0	Positive	600	100	500	73	78	422	27

TABLE 6.2 The overall results of the experiments

	Experiment 1	Experiment 2	Experiment3	Experiment 4	Experiment5	Experiment6	Experiment7	Experiment8	Experiment9	Experiment 10	Experiment 11	Experiment 12
ACCURACY:	0.66	0.24	0,08	0	1	1	0.68	0.23	0.75	0.78	0.59	0.82
MISCLASSIFICATIONI RATE:	0.33	0.76	0 92	1	0	0	0.32	0.7	0.25	0.22	0.41	0.17
TRUE POSITIVE RATE:	0.5	0	0	0	1	1	0.18	1	0.07	0.63	0.58	0.73
FALSE POSITIVE RATE:	0.18	0	0,92	1	0	0	0.12	0.99	0.12	0.15	0.41	0.15
SPECIFICITY:	0.81	1	0,08	0	0	0	0.87	0.004	0.88	0.84	0.58	0.84
PRECISION:	0.71	0	0	0	1	1	0.87	0.22	0.11	0.61	0.10	0.48
PREVALENCE:	0.47	0.76	0	0	0	0	0.29	0.22	0.16	0.28	0.07	0.16

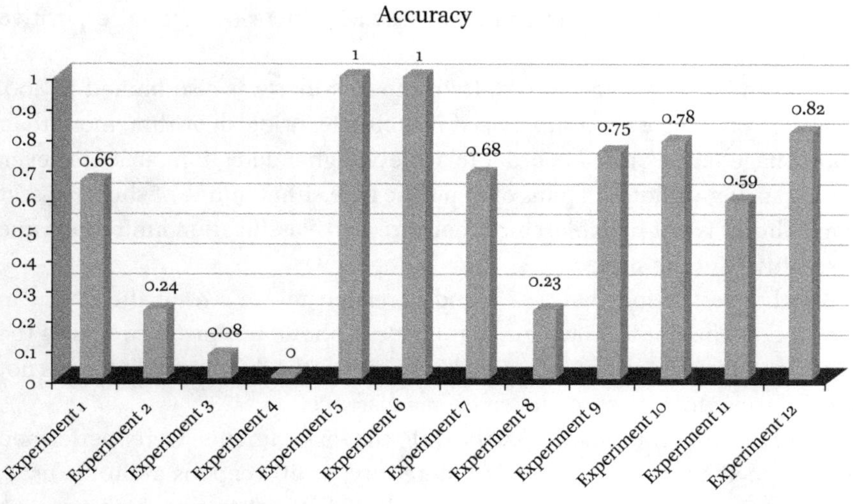

FIGURE 6.2 The accuracy rate per experiment

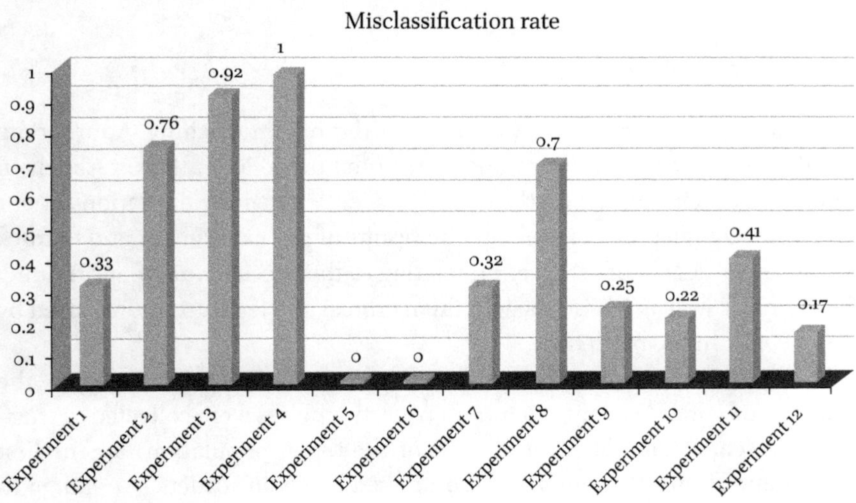

FIGURE 6.3 Misclassification rate per experiment

improve the results. On the contrary, it heavily increases the false positive detection rates.

The number of photos used to train the classifier was also limited to 400. Ideally, in order to train a supervised machine-learning algorithm, more than 4,000 images are required in order to achieve higher detection rates. However, finding so many photos of guns of a specific type either online or shooting that many photos is not possible, since there are also classification limitations due to sensitivity of the subject.

Another restriction that was found is related to the size of the object in question in the photo. Having a gun inside a photo at a distance makes the detection process less accurate, which means that the decision for action is not safe if it uses video or photo taken from a distance.

Another important point is that all the experiments were performed with a specific type of weapon. If different types of weapons are to be used, then a more complex training process should be followed which requires more advanced infrastructure than a common computer as was used in our experiments.

5 Discussing the Findings

After the experimental phase was over, we did one more thing. Appropriate questionnaires were developed and distributed to 3rd and 4th year Cadets in order to ask their opinion on the use of AI agents, given the limitations of our algorithm. Our goal was to evaluate the results of our experiment and to track down cadets' degree of satisfaction relating to the success rate of our training algorithm, as well as to discuss with them ethical and legal questions posed by the use of AI in the battlefield.

The questionnaires were distributed among cadets who study at the Hellenic Air Force Academy. In total, 73 questionnaires were collected (a trustworthy research sample covering 85% of the target population) for the first assessment of our experiment, all completed by senior cadets (34 and 39 in their third and fourth year of study respectively; 6 female and 67 male cadets in total). A briefing explaining some details of the experiment and the goal of the survey was initially held for the cadets, and then they were asked to fill out the questionnaire. In the following paragraphs the results from this survey are presented and briefly discussed.

In relation to the goal of our experiment, only 16% of the cadets were extremely satisfied with the option of introducing AI to the battlefield, while 39% stated that, according to their opinion, AI technology is currently too immature for military applications that could end up using lethal force. Only 7% of the cadets thought that programming and training algorithms can solve technological limitations and minimize possible collateral damage to civilians and their property. As far as the morality of the missions under consideration goes, while they reacted positively to the idea of replacing humans with AI agents in risky environments (56%), they also stated that ethical (42%) and legal (66%) aspects of the use of AI agents in real military operations should be treated beforehand.

At this point, we asked the cadets to recognize and state the most important challenges that relate to the introduction and use of AI in the battlefield. As far as the ethical and legal challenges are concerned, a very important issue that needs to be addressed is who will be considered responsible for any damage (intentional or unintentional) caused by a robot: the designer, the manufacturer, the procurement officer, the controller/supervisor, the field commander, the robot itself, or all of those just mentioned? Also, we need to define the person/agent who will be held responsible for the information gathered, accessed, analyzed and used as data from an AI agent in order for it to act. If the robot refuses to obey an order based on that data, who will be responsible for the decision-making and the following actions? Finally, military personnel should agree upon and consent to working with robots as there is an increased risk due to systems malfunction.

Technological challenges are also present and, usually, refer to discrimination issues among targets (combatants-noncombatants-insurgents who appear as noncombatants until the very last moment). First generation problems have to do mainly with accidents that may occur due to malfunction, errors, or bugs that inevitably exist, and are expected to be corrected in the next generation of the technology. At this moment, it is impossible to certify that a given robot is error free. Also, there is the possibility that robots may disengage from whatever they are programmed to do due to malfunction, programming error, or even hacking; therefore procedural and systemic safeguards should be developed. As far as the ethical and legal issues are concerned, we have to both build a framework, clear in ethical and legal rules, and the method to embed those rules into a machine that will have the ability to effectively network with other AI machines and systems, but also with humans as well. Last but not least, AI agents should have enough energy & power, so as to complete their missions, and this parameter poses a unique challenge since AI agents have an autonomy of both thought and action (therefore, given the complexity of the military environment, it is very difficult calculate in detail the needed amount of systemic autonomy).

According to the cadets,

- the main just war challenges concerning the military use of AI were:
  - attack decisions (45%),
  - lower barriers for war (16%), and,
  - collateral damage (26%);
- the main legal challenges were:
  - to whom one should assign blame for improper conduct and unauthorized harms caused by AI agents (37%),
  - what happens if an AI agent refuses to obey an order (21%), and,
  - the issue of consent by soldiers to increased risks when they run an operation along with AI agents (11%);
- the main technological challenges were:
  - Discriminating among targets (26%),
  - First generation problems (18%),
  - Robots running amok (12%),
  - Unauthorized overrides & Hacking (14%),
  - Competing ethical frameworks (13%), and,
  - Energy & Power issues (7%).

In relation to the cost of war, cadets proved to be more concerned (44%) with the legal aspects of the military operations and the cost after the end of war (as a means of inflicting punishment upon wrongdoing), than with lowering the cost of operating by the use of AI and autonomous means of fighting (23%). Cadets were also extremely concerned with issues of attributing the blame for misconduct within the chain of command (78%), while they were also annoyed (29%) by the fact that people not related to the military (such as manufacturing companies, programmers, etc.) were responsible to an extent for the success or not of a military operation.

In relation to the factors that influence cadets' opinion on the matter, we got the following answers: moral inhibitions (20%), the legal aspects of the mission (27%), any special circumstances (11%), and the necessity (8%) of each mission, the doctrine of the country with regards to justifying war, and the means of fighting the enemy (18%). A large percentage of the sample (38%) stated that moral and cultural factors influence their views of introducing AI in war – while 14% think that is not the case and a 17% did not want to even answer the question.

Overall, according to the cadets' answers (upon completion of the course on Philosophy of War), 57% said that the experiment and its results (especially those results that could lead to major failures) made them think of the commander's responsibility for deciding on the target and the means of executing the operation, as well as their responsibility to protect the innocent (37%) (something that happened only for 22% of the cadets when they were asked upon completion of the theoretical part of the course alone; i.e., the theory and discussion on Just War).

Cadets (82%) admitted that their understanding of the complexity of the modern operations environment and the introduction of AI was improved after the presentation of the results of our experiment and the discussions that followed on the ethical and legal concerns, as well as on the difficulties of observing principles and rules of justice and ethics during war in general.

6 Conclusion

Concluding, we can argue that if the current AI technology and its combined use with high precision weapon systems should prove a viable possibility, it could be used on the battlefield. At the same time, law should regulate any issues of responsibility, accountability, and liability, in case something goes wrong with the observation of the principles of distinction and proportionality: humans, organizations, and AI agents should fit into the scheme with a full range of responsibilities and measures for the victims of immoral and illegal attacks (whether they were the results of human mistake or AI).

As stated earlier, in our experiment, our best success rate in recognizing targets that were holding weapons was 82%. 82% definitely cannot be considered an efficient success rate that could allow us to use AI in military operations – especially with the task of deciding whom to target. In our minds, creating autonomous military robots that could act *at least as* ethically as human soldiers is perhaps a sensible goal, but we need to improve success rates, if use is intended for real life. Given the technical limitations, such as programming an AI agent with the ability to sufficiently discriminate between valid and invalid targets, we can expect that accidents will continue to occur, so it is important to raise and discuss throughout the questions of moral responsibility and legal accountability and liability.

We can argue that so far, the ethical and legal debate, as well as the technological development, which relates to the advancement, test, and uses of future military technology, appears to be supportive of our efforts to adhere to the principles of just war theory and the demands of International Humanitarian Law governing the conduct of just military operations. And it is vital that we adhere to these principles, as in all types of military operations our attention should focus on protecting and respecting human rights.

We need to keep reminding ourselves, however, that AI agents are nonhumans, that technologically they have advantages and disadvantages, and we need to be extra cautious in terms of when, how, and to what extent we can use them. For example, the fact that AI agents can replace human agents and complete extremely dangerous (and even life-threatening tasks) should not make us accept their currently given technological inability to discern between right and wrong as a secondary problem and use this as a pretense to 'legalize' accidental attacks against civilian targets that should not be under attack (as they are protected by international legislation). Accepting this argument could also be a step towards 'legalizing' the violation of the principles of distinction and proportionality, thus lowering our moral or legal standards. Collaboration is, therefore, needed among policymakers and analysts, roboticists, ethicists, sociologists, and psychologists. Because the use of military robots represents a new era in warfare, all aspects of their use should be equally covered.

7 Future Work

Our experiment is under development, so as to cover new areas and dilemmas related to the introduction of AI on the battlefield. In our ongoing and future tests, we have decided to add different types of tasks and operations that will also be included in discussions on the role of AI in military environments.

Therefore, in our preliminary discussions and initial testing with the cadets and officers of our Academy we focused on cases that are about:

- distinguishing and verifying targets while engaged in irregular fighting/skirmishes, especially in situations when the enemy dresses like the local population as a means of camouflage,
- collecting and using data to decide and execute effectively a preemptive strike while protecting civilians at the same time,
- collecting data and keeping areas or terrorist suspects under surveillance for future operations,
- using collected data to consider them along with possible risks and operational/tactical challenges for cases that would allow us to consider a preemptive war as a just possibility,
- gathering data, detecting and identifying targets during humanitarian intervention missions, where the protection of civilians is crucial if the intervention seeks to adhere to its humanitarian purpose.

We are also working on defining the system specifications and the rules that should be applied in the development and construction of AI agents/systems in order to meet operational requirements without violating the legal framework for the conduct of war.

We have incorporated the experiment described in this paper into the Philosophy of War module (via presentation, once the introductory lectures are completed) and we also use the discussions that follow the presentation as one of the tools for evaluating the trainees on aspects related to technological ethics, military ethics, and the conduct of operations. The schedule is to incorporate more experiments to be explored by the cadets themselves and not just be presented by the faculty. The cases we discussed just above, extended with a variety of factors, will form the basis of our new experiments on the ethical use of AI in war operations in HAFA's War Games Lab for the next two or three years.

In order for a full ethical/technological/legal discussion of the experiments to happen, further work needs to be done:

- First of all, we need to define exhaustively the ethical and legal framework of the experiments. Given the fact that new cases/scenarios are added, we need to analytically describe the parameters under investigation within a specific ethical and legal framework that will cover the full spectrum of our research.
- Following that, we shall work closely with senior officers, so as to further identify and analyze the factors that need to be evaluated/tested. Apart from the ethical and legal aspect concerning the use of AI agents with lethal power, we need to (at least) take into consideration:
  - the operational/tactical advantages and disadvantages of using AI systems,
  - the use of AI agents for non-lethal missions, and,
  - the ways that AI and complex computer algorithms shape our understanding of war and, at the same time, create new patterns and changes that need to be regulated. The ultimate goal is to investigate how we can regulate the design, development and use of AI technologies and systems in a way such that they will effectively serve International Humanitarian Law related to war, as well as Human Rights.
- Finally, we expect that the actual experimental phase should take a year or so, due to the different levels of work that will be accomplished partially by researchers assigned to our Lab and partially by cadets as case-studies as part of the Philosophy of War Module.

We expect to use the experiment as part of the War Game Lab for the final year cadets in the academic year of 2023/24.

References

Allen, Colin and Wendel Wallach, 'Moral machines: Contradition in terms of abdication of human responsibility?' in Patrick Lin, Keith Abney, and George A. Bekey (eds), *Robot ethics: The ethical and social implications of robotics* (MIT Press 2011).

Allen, Colin, Gary Varner, and Jason Zinser, 'Prolegomena to Any Future Artificial Moral Agent' (2000) 12 *Journal of Experimental & Theoretical Artificial Intelligence.*

Amoroso, Daniele and Guglielmo Tamburrini 'The Ethical and Legal Case Against Autonomy in Weapons Systems' *Global Jurist 18.1* (2017).

Arnold, Roberta, 'The Legal Implications of the Use of Systems With Autonomous Capabilities in Military Operations' (2015) *Issues for Defence Policymakers.*

Asaro, Peter M., 'How just could a robot war be?' (2008) *Current issues in computing and philosophy*, 50–64.

Asaro, Peter M., 'What should we want from a robot ethic?' (2006) 6 *International Review of Information Ethics*, 9–16.

Bekey, George, *Autonomous Robots: From Biological Inspiration to Implementation and Control* (MIT Press, Cambridge MA 2005).

Bird, Eleanor, Jasmin Fox-Skelly, Nicola Jenner, Ruth Larbey, Emma Weitkamp and Alan Winfield, 'The ethics of artificial intelligence: Issues and initiatives' (2020) *European Parliamentary Research Service*, March 2020 <https://www.europarl.europa.eu/RegData/etudes/STUD/2020/634452/EPRS_STU(2020)634452_EN.pdf> accessed 11 November 2020.

Boothby, William H., *New technologies and the law in war and peace* (Cambridge University Press 2019).

Bradski, Gary, 'The OpenCV Library' (2000) 25 *Dr. Dobb's Journal: Software Tools for the Professional Programmer.*

Brown, Gary D. 'Proportionality and Just War' (2003) 2 *Journal of Military Ethics.*

Cornock, Marc, 'Legal definitions of responsibility, accountability and liability' (2011) 23 *Nursing Children and Young People.*

Duff, R. A., *Answering for Crime. Responsibility and Liability in the Criminal Law* (Hart Publishing 2007).

Durhin, Nathalie, 'Protecting Civilians in Urban Areas: A Military Perspective on the Application of International Humanitarian Law' (2016) 98 *International Review of the Red Cross.*

Ebers, Martin, Susana Navas, *Algorithms and Law* (Cambridge University Press 2020).

Ford, Christopher M., 'Personal Self-Defence and the Standing Rules of Engagement' in Winston S. Williams and Christopher M. Ford (eds) *Complex Battlespaces: The Law of Armed Conflict and the Dynamics of Modern Warfare* (OUP 2018).

Fotion, Nicholas, 'Who, What, When and How to Attack' [Paper presented at the Joint Services Conference on Professional Ethics (JSCOPE): 1996] <http://isme.tamu.edu/JSCOPE96/fotion96.html> accessed 11 November 2020.

Freund, Yoav and Robert E. Schapire, 'A decision-theoretic generalization of on-line learning and an application to boosting' (1997) 55 *Journal of computer and system sciences.*

Galliott, Jai, *Military Robots: mapping the moral landscape* (Ashgate 2015).

Geneva Convention (I) for the Amelioration of the Condition of the Wounded and Sick in Armed Forces in the Field of 12 August 1949.

Geneva Convention (II) for the Amelioration of the Condition of the Wounded, Sick and Shipwrecked Members of Armed Forces at Sea of 12 August 1949.

Geneva Convention (IV) relative to the Protection of Civilian Persons in Time of War of 12 August 1949.

Gross, Emanuel, 'Self-defense against Terrorism-What Does It Mean? The Israeli Perspective' (2002) 1 *Journal of Military Ethics.*

Guldahl Cooper, Camilla, *'Introduction' in NATO Rules of Engagement* (Brill/Nijhoff 2019).

Hew, Patrick, 'Autonomous Situation Awareness: Implications for Future Warfighting' (2007) *Australian Defence Force Journal.*

Hibbard, Bill, 'Avoiding unintended AI behaviors' (2012) *Artificial General Intelligence.*

Holmes, Robert L., *On War and Morality* (Princeton University Press 1989).

Johnson, James Turner, *Morality and Contemporary Warfare* (Yale University Press 1999).

Kaempf, Sebastian, *Saving Soldiers or Civilians?: Casualty-Aversion versus Civilian Protection in Asymmetric Conflicts* (Cambridge University Press 2018).

Krishna, M. G. and A. Srinivasulu, 'Face detection system on AdaBoost algorithm using Haar classifiers' (2012) 2 *International Journal of Modern Engineering Research.*

Lekea, Joanne, 'Missile Strike Carried Out With Yemeni Cooperation' – The War Against Terrorism: A Different Kind of War? (2003) 2 *Journal of Military Ethics.*

Lin, Patrick, Georg Bekey and Keith Abney, *Autonomous military robotics: Risk, ethics, and design* (California Polytechnic State University 2008).

Lucas Jr, George R., 'Industrial challenges of military robotics' (2011) 10 *Journal of Military Ethics.*

Mapel, David R., 'Realism and the Ethics of War and Peace' in Terry Nardin (ed), *The Ethics of War and Peace. Secular and Religious Perspectives* (Princeton University Press 1996) 54–77.

Müller, Vincent C., 'Autonomous Killer Robots Are Probably Good News' in Ezio Di Nucci and Filippo Santoni de Sio (eds) *Drones and Responsibility: Legal, Philosophical and Socio-Technical Perspectives on the Use of Remotely Controlled Weapons* (Ashgate 2016).

Pagallo, Ugo, Pompeu Casanovas and Robert Madelin, 'The middle-out approach: assessing models of legal governance in data protection, artificial intelligence, and the Web of Data' (2019) 7 *The Theory and Practice of Legislation.*

Predelli, Stefano, 'Some Comments on Double Effect and Harmful Involvement' (2004) 3 *Journal of Military Ethics.*

Regan, Richard J., *Just War, Principles and Cases* (The Catholic University of America Press 1996).

Rhead, M., R. Gurney, S. Ramalingam and N. Cohen, 'Accuracy of automatic number plate recognition (ANPR) and real world UK number plate problems' (2012) in *2012 IEEE International Carnahan Conference on Security Technology* (*ICCST*).

Robinson, Darryl, 'A Justification of Command Responsibility' (2017) 28 *Criminal Law Forum*.

Robinson, Darryl, 'How command responsibility got so complicated: A culpability contradiction, its obfuscation, and a simple solution' (2012) 13 *Melbourne Journal of International Law*.

Roff, Heather M. 'Responsibility, liability, and lethal autonomous robots' in Allhoff, Fritz, Evans, Nicholas G. and Henschke, Adam (eds), *Routledge Handbook of Ethics and War: Just War Theory in the 21st Century* (Routledge 2013).

Roff, Heather M., 'The Strategic Robot Problem: Lethal Autonomous Weapons in War' (2014) 13 *Journal of Military Ethics*.

Roy, Ankush and D. P. Ghoshal, 'Number Plate Recognition for use in different countries using an improved segmentation' (2011) in *2nd National Conference on Emerging Trends and Applications in Computer Science* (*NCETACS*).

Sambaluk, Nicholas Michael, *Conflict in the 21st Century: The Impact of Cyber Warfare, Social Media, and Technology* (ABC-CLIO 2019).

Scheutz, Matthias, 'The need for moral competency in autonomous agent architectures' in Vincent C. Müller (ed) *Fundamental Issues of Artificial Intelligence* (Springer 2016).

Schmitt, Michael N., 'Deconstructing Direct Participation in Hostilities: The Constitutive Elements' (2010) 42 *New York University International Law and Politics*.

Schmitt, Michael N., 'State-sponsored Assassination in International and Domestic Law' (1992) 17 *Yale Journal of International Law*, 609–685.

Smith, Thomas W., 'Protecting Civilians ... or Soldiers? Humanitarian Law and the Economy of Risk in Iraq' (2008) 9 *International Studies Perspectives*.

Takata, Shozo et al., 'Maintenance: changing role in life cycle management' (2004) 53 *CIRP Annals*.

Turner, Jacob and Robot Rules, *Regulating Artificial Intelligence* (Springer 2019).

Tzafestas, Spyros G., *Roboethics: A Navigating Overview* (Springer 2016).

Viola, Paul and Michael Jones, 'Rapid object detection using a boosted cascade of simple features. In Computer Vision and Pattern Recognition' (2001) in *Proceedings of the 2001 IEEE Computer Society Conference on CVPR* Vol. 1.

Vladeck, David C., 'Machines without Principals: Liability Rules and Artificial Intelligence' (2014) 89 *Washington Law Review*.

Wallach, Wendell, Colin Allen, and Iva Smit, 'Machine Morality: Bottom-up and Top-down Approaches for Modeling Human Moral Faculties' (2008) 22 *AI & Society*.

Wallach, Wendell, *Moral Machines: Teaching Robots Right from Wrong* (OUP 2008).
Walzer, Michael, *Just and Unjust Wars, A Moral Argument with Historical Illustration* (4th edn, Penguin Books 1984).
Wilson, Phillip I. and J. Fernandez, 'Facial feature detection using Haar classifiers' (2006) 21 *Journal of Computing Sciences in Colleges*.
Wynsberghe, A. Van and S. Robbins, 'Critiquing the Reasons for Making Artificial Moral Agents' (2019) 25 *Science and Engineering Ethics*.
Zohar, Noam, 'Risking and Protecting Lives. Soldiers and Opposing Civilians' in Helen Frowe and Gerald Lang (eds), *How we Fight: Ethics in War* (OUP 2014).

PART 3

Drones

CHAPTER 7

Are Public Concerns over the Use of Drone Operations Ethically Justified?

Pete Brunton

1 Drones and the Just War Tradition

Military operations conducted by Western powers are generally guided by the Just War tradition, which is used as a common framework to discuss and establish what is acceptable and unacceptable when engaging in armed conflict.[1] Bellamy describes how the Just War tradition justifies armed conflict, and the resulting taking of human life, providing that the ethical principles of *jus ad bellum,* on the initiation of conflict, *and jus in bello,* on the conduct of the conflict, are applied.[2] These sentiments are enshrined in British Army doctrine and reflected in the practise and regulations of professional militaries worldwide.[3]

In order to satisfy the requirements of *jus ad bellum,* the principles of just cause, right intention, legitimate authority, having a goal that is proportional to the wrong committed by your opponent, a reasonable prospect of success and the use of military force as a last resort must be adhered to.[4] The most obvious example of a just cause is when a state acts in self-defence, though Haines highlights how the use of force has been justified through a 'responsibility to protect' a minority group within another state on the grounds of a humanitarian intervention.[5] Right intention ensures that not only is the right thing being done in the form of the just cause, but that it is being done with the right intentions and not simply, for example, for territorial expansion.[6] The United Nations charter states that when a state is not acting in self-defence the

---

1 David Whetham, 'The Just War Tradition: A Pragmatic Compromise,' in David Whetham (ed), *Ethics, Law and Military Operations* (Palgrave Macmillan, Basingstoke 2010) 65–89, 65.

2 Alex J Bellamy, *Just Wars: From Cicero To Iraq* (Polity Press, Cambridge 2006) 121–126.

3 Army Doctrine Publication, *Vol 5, Soldiering, The Military Covenant* (Her Majesty's Stationary Office 2002).

4 Whetham, 'The Just War Tradition' (n 1) 76–77.

5 Steven Haines, 'Humanitarian Intervention: Genocide Crimes against Humanity and the Use of Force' in George Kassimeris and John Buckley (eds) *The Ashgate Research Companion to Modern Warfare* (Ashgate, Farnham 2010) 307–328.

6 Whetham, 'The Just War Tradition' (n 1) 77–78.

 | DOI:10.1163/9789004507951_009

use of military force requires the prior authorisation of the Security Council, but in practice powerful states often rely on their own internal political mechanisms, or even merely popular support for the cause, to approve military force.[7] In order to be justified, a conflict must be righting some wrong, as already described, but also the response must be proportionate to that wrong.[8] Finally there must be both a reasonable chance of success, and all other non-violent alternatives must have been tried and failed before military force is resorted to.[9]

Sometimes an event does not even have to have happened yet for there to be a just cause to act. For example, Crawford considers the case of pre-emption, where a state acts against an immediate and credible threat of grievous harm before it can materialise.[10] The argument says that, if left unhindered, the credible threat would manifest itself in offensive action and at that point a state would be justified in employing force in self-defence. Walzer argues that provided there is a 'justified fear of imminent attack, where the potential attacker has clear intent to cause injury, is actively preparing to do so, and when waiting until the threat is realised greatly increases the risk', then the use of force is acceptable under the same provisions of *jus ad bellum*.[11] As opposed to this, preventative war, where a state acts against a potential adversary before that adversary can gain military advantage and where the threat is not imminent, is considered illegal and is associated with aggression.[12]

The Just War tradition also covers conduct once operations have begun, or considerations of *jus in bello*. The two main principles here are discrimination and proportionality. Discrimination requires that every possible effort is made to distinguish between combatants and non-combatants and that military force should only be targeted at combatants. Proportionality seeks to make the 'the violence of war proportionate to the threat it is meant to overcome, and to make the unintended mistakes of war proportionate to their intended benefits'.[13] Coates expands on this concept to include a basic respect for the human

7 Whetham, 'The Just War Tradition' (n 1) 79.

8 A. J. Coates, *The Ethics of War* (Manchester University Press, 1997) 227.

9 Whetham, 'The Just War Tradition' (n 1) 79.

10 Neta C. Crawford, 'The Justice of Preemption and Preventive War Doctrines' in Mark Evans (ed), *Just War Theory: A Reappraisal* (Edinburgh University Press, Edinburgh 2005) 25–49.

11 Michael Walzer, *Just and Unjust Wars: A Moral Argument with Historical Illustrations* (2nd edn, Basic Books 1992) 85.

12 Walzer, *Just And Unjust Wars* (n 11) 74.

13 Kateri Carmola, 'The Concept of Proportionality: Old Questions and New Ambiguities' in Mark Evans (ed), *Just War Theory: A Reappraisal* (Edinburgh University Press, Edinburgh 2005) 93–113, 94.

life engaged in the conflict on both sides, requiring an economy in the use of the force with regard to both sides. For example, a state should not waste the lives of its own soldiers in pursuit of unattainable or trivial objectives, and they should also not inflict undue or unnecessary suffering on the enemy.[14]

Though the Just War tradition is primarily a Western construct, similar frameworks exist in other cultures and traditions. For example Robinson has noted the 'necessary war trajectory' in Russian thinking, and the concept that 'necessity makes the forbidden things permitted' within some Islamic teachings.[15] It would therefore appear that normative frameworks aiming to limit the use of and escalation of violence within armed conflict are common across most cultures.

How then do these traditions of thought relate to the emerging reality of drone warfare? Is it possible to reconcile such normative frameworks with an instrument of war that makes killing specific people 8,000 miles away an unexceptional activity, and appears to reduce war to a video game? Using the Just War Tradition to frame the analysis, this chapter will examine and test some of the arguments that seek to demonstrate that there is something unethical specifically about employing drones in contemporary conflicts.

In an article that captures many of the popular objections to the use of drones in war, Ahmad expresses his opinion that the use of drones is romanticised in the United States, and he quotes a law professor who declares that drones are 'fun' and argues 'against more transparency' in their use.[16] When the original source is examined in more detail, however, not only is the quote very selective, warping the intended meaning, but it is employed emotively in order to demonstrate the 'virtue-less' employment of drones. The individual quoted by Ahmad was Professor Thomas Nachbar speaking at conference on the ethical implications of the use of drones hosted by Arizona State University in 2011.[17] When referring to 'fun', Nachbar actually said 'drones are fun for law professors because changes like drones allow you to divorce rules from their context and challenge our assumptions', clearly referring to the academic challenges the scenario presented, rather than taking pleasure in the use of lethal force.[18] Nachbar's argument against further transparency was drawing parallels

14 Coates, *The Ethics Of War* (n 8) 227.

15 Paul Robinson, *Just War In Comparative Perspective* (Ashgate Publishing 2003) 4–5.

16 Muhammad Idrees Ahmad, 'The Virtue-Less War Of The "Nintendo Bomber"' (*Al Jazeera* 28 June 2011) <http://www.aljazeera.com/indepth/opinion/2011/06/20116268282542422 2.html> accessed 15 September 2020.

17 Email from Thomas Nachbar to author (28 September 2020).

18 Nachbar (n 17).

to military rules of engagement, where the public know that strict regulations are in place and enforced, but the exact details of those rules of engagement are not released into the public domain through security concerns.[19] Despite Ahmad's assertions, Nachbar is not proposing that drone operations be carried out under a veil of complete secrecy, rather that legitimacy and governance can be maintained without the full disclosure necessary for complete transparency. It is enough to know that rules are in place and enforced, without knowing exactly what those rules are.

Ahmad's view of the use of drones highlights not only the emotionally charged, but potentially misguided, views held by members of the public, but also how sources can be intentionally or inadvertently manipulated in order to provide supporting evidence for such a viewpoint. Kreps also discusses how portrayals of drones in popular media, including television, Hollywood films, and video games, are almost always negative, focusing on their use by corrupt and oppressive regimes, with many plot themes focusing on semi-autonomous systems either being captured by hackers or going rogue.[20] Whilst these media portrayals are obviously not authoritative or even firmly based in reality, they do contribute to a general feeling of unease over the use of drones and a mismatch between their public perception and reality. For example, regular protests take place at Royal Air Force Waddington, the home of UK drone operations.[21]

There are parallels between the selective or partial quoting of academic examinations of the ethical implications of drone operations and the phenomenon that Rachels describes, whereby religious scriptures or church tradition are interpreted to seemingly support a moral conclusion the religious individual has already reached.[22] In Ahmad's case, it could be suggested that he appears to have formed a moral conclusion on the use of drones and is subsequently interpreting academic work in order to support that preformed view, rather than forming a moral view based on the academic body of work. This does not necessarily render Ahmad's views incorrect, but it does suggest that the academic source he has selectively quoted does not support his argument.

19 Nachbar (n17).

20 Sarah E. Kreps, *Drones: What Everyone Needs To Know* (Oxford University Press 2016) 152–153.

21 Emily Norton, 'Over 100 Drones Protesters Heading To RAF Waddington This Weekend' (*the Lincolnite* 30 September 2015) <http://thelincolnite.co.uk/2015/09/around-100-drones-protestors-heading-to-raf-waddington-this-weekend/> accessed 15 September 2020.

22 James Rachels and Stuart Rachels, *The Elements Of Moral Philosophy* (7th edn, McGraw-Hill, New York 2012) 58–60.

One aspect of public concern over the use of drones is related to their perception as autonomous weapon systems, with garish headlines often referring to 'Killer Robots'.[23] Whilst some drones have autonomous features, such as the ability to fly from predefined waypoint to waypoint without human intervention, at present all weapons systems are remotely controlled by a human rather than controlled autonomously by the drone itself. But the image of self-aware robotic killers running amok, taking independent decisions to kill humans, is one that is often repeated in popular culture, as examined by Lucas.[24] This has led to a number of groups campaigning against research and development in this area.

The Campaign to Stop Killer Robots is one of the most vocal of such groups, publicising concerns about the potential for deployments of autonomous weapon systems in the future.[25] Lucas distinguishes between the true autonomy required for independent ethical decisions and what he refers to as "machine autonomy."[26] Machine autonomy enables a weapon system to operate in a complex environment without the need for continuous human oversight, allowing it independently to respond to and overcome the obstacles, issues, and unexpected circumstances it encounters. Cruise missile systems such as Tomahawk Land Attack Missiles are already capable of this level of machine autonomy and have been routinely deployed for several decades. These systems are not capable of unilaterally altering their targeting parameters or changing their mission in mid-course without direct human intervention. Despite the widespread employment of cruise missiles, often for missions similar to those currently carried out by drones, their use has not created the same public protests despite their having a greater level of autonomy than the drones. Indeed, the only public protests over the use of cruise missiles have been over arming them with nuclear rather than conventional warheads during the Cold War.[27] It can be argued that even the use of systems displaying

23 Toby Walsh, 'The Rise Of The Killer Robots – And Why We Need To Stop Them' (*CNN* 26 October 2015) <http://edition.cnn.com/2015/10/26/opinions/killer-robots-walsh/> accessed 15 September 2020.

24 George Lucas, 'Engineering, Ethics and Industry: The Moral Challenges of Lethal Autonomy', in Bradley Jay Strawser (ed), *Killing By Remote Control: The Ethics Of An Unmanned Military* (Oxford University Press, Oxford 2013) 217.

25 Campaign to stop Killer Robots, 'The threat of fully autonomous weapons. The Problem' <https://www.stopkillerrobots.org/learn/#problem> accessed 15 September 2020.

26 Lucas, 'Engineering, Ethics and Industry' (n 24) 218.

27 'Greenham Common Women's Peace Camp', *Wikipedia* (Wikimedia Foundation) <https://en.wikipedia.org/wiki/Greenham_Common_Women%27s_Peace_Camp> accessed 28 December 2020.

machine autonomy does not represent a changed ethical situation that such systems exceed the level of autonomy within current drones, and therefore the public concerns lack an ethical justification.

A possible reason for public concern may be the conflation of the potential for future issues over drone systems with full autonomy, with the reality of how systems are actually employed today. One concern with developing systems towards fuller autonomy is the potential to create so-called 'responsibility gaps'. Leveringhaus describes these occurring with technologies that do not allow responsibility for an unethical action to be associated with an individual who can be held to account for it.[28] In the event that an autonomous weapons system commits a war crime, the responsibility for the crime could be blurred between the individual that designed the system, the industry that created the system, the chain of command that decided to deploy it or the operator responsible for supervising it. Under these circumstances it could be impossible to attribute blame to an individual, ultimately leading to no-one being held accountable for war crime. Leveringhaus argues that where there is a potential for such responsibility gaps to be created, then such technologies should not be allowed to leave the research laboratory until the ethical challenges they raise have been successfully addressed.[29]

By contrast, Arkin outlines an ethical duty to deploy more autonomy in unmanned systems rather than less, arguing that compared to human operators the greater discretion possible with integrated sensors, examined in more detail later in this chapter, combined with a dispassionate machine intelligence is likely to benefit rather than threaten non-combatants. In essence, autonomous, computer-controlled weapon systems are less likely to commit a war crime compared to a human placed in the same stressful situation.[30]

The subject of autonomy could form a separate chapter in its own right and will not be considered further here. Needless to say there is a significant difference between the level of autonomy some members of the public believe drones currently to have, the very limited autonomy such systems actually display, the ethical implications of full autonomy, and the level of machine autonomy that military research and development is likely to be aiming for. This chapter will now consider the reality of current drone systems and how

---

28 Alex Leveringhaus, 'Assigning Responsibility in Enhanced Warfare', in Jai Galliott and Mianna Lotz (eds), *Super Soldiers: The Ethical, Legal and Social Implications* (Ashgate Publishing 2015).

29 Leveringhaus, 'Assigning Responsibility' (n 28) 151.

30 Ronald Arkin, 'Ethical Robots In Warfare' (2009) 28 IEEE Technology and Society Magazine.

they are employed, focusing on the *jus in bello* aspects of discrimination and proportionality.

It is of note that many Western militaries employing the technology prefer terms such as 'Remotely Piloted Air System', which more accurately describe the capability and how it is employed, rather than the potentially emotive term 'drone'. For the purposes of clarity and consistency, the term drone will continue to be used throughout this chapter, but without any intention to evoke emotive meaning.

The Royal Air Force describe the Reaper MQ9A drone as being designed for 'surveillance, reconnaissance and, if required, ground-attack missions', operated 'by crews of professional pilots, sensor operators and Mission Intelligence Co-ordinators from Ground Control Stations'.[31] The Reaper aircraft carries a multi-spectral targeting system which integrates electro-optical, infrared, laser designator and laser illuminator into a single sensor package.[32] Equivalent or identical systems are employed by other Western militaries and agencies, including the United States.

Kaag and Kreps point out that these sensor packages can provide the operator with much more information than would be available to alternative systems, such as ground based forces, in order to discriminate between a combatant and a civilian.[33] The use of precision weapons systems launched from the drone gives significant confidence that the target selected using the advanced sensor package will be struck, and low-yield warheads can greatly reduce the potential for collateral damage, death, or injury as a result.

Despite this, Kaag and Kreps conclude that as humans are still involved in the selection of targets, the technology available in the sensor suite cannot ensure that the selected target is legitimate and that conflict inevitably generates complex and ambiguous situations which technological solutions cannot eliminate.[34] While the risk of unintended collateral damage is reduced, there remains the significant chance that the wrong target will be intentionally struck with the full authority of the operator.

A study on behalf of the North Atlantic Treaty Organisation concludes that there are many advantages in the physical dislocation of the drone operators from the deployed theatre of operations, and from the use of drones in lieu of

31 Royal Air Force, *Aircraft And Weapons* (3rd edn, MOD 2014) <https://www.raf.mod.uk/what-we-do/centre-for-air-and-space-power-studies/documents1/royal-air-force-aircraft-weapons-fourth-edition-revised/> accessed 15 September 2020.

32 U. C. Jha, *Drone Wars: Ethical, Legal And Strategic Implications* (KW Publishers 2014) 22–23.

33 Sarah E. Kreps and John Kaag, *Drone Warfare* (Polity Press, Cambridge 2014) 133–135.

34 Kreps and Kaag, *Drone Warfare* (n 33) 134.

ground forces. Operators working remotely are potentially able to make more rational decisions due to experiencing decreased levels of stress, attributable to the lack of any physical threat to them, and have a reduced susceptibility to strong emotions that could otherwise cloud their judgement.[35] As drone operators are easily monitored, recorded, and their activities archived, accountability can be increased, though it is questionable whether security concerns would allow the accountability to be matched by full transparency. The same report highlights how the deployment of drone systems can often be in lieu of ground forces in a given conflict, potentially leading to fewer casualties and refugees, making the approach inherently more ethical.[36]

Considering discrimination, Kasher argues that drones represent a new or novel technology due to their potential variations in size, from insect-like to the equivalent of a small airliner, and for their ability to deploy new tactics such as swarming. He also suggests that these characteristics require a review of the current ethical guidelines over their use.[37] Plaw disputes this, pointing out that for many years guided missiles and smart weapons have had a similar variation in size, and have been employed in swarms or clouds, such as the multiple independent targeted re-entry vehicles used in nuclear weapon technology from the 1960s onwards.[38] Plaw therefore concludes that drones as a weapon system consist of an operator, a weapon, and a target, and that the physical dislocation between the operator and the other two components of the system has no direct bearing on ethical considerations of discrimination.

It has already been shown that drones have the potential to discriminate better and thereby significantly to reduce collateral damage, injury, and death. Just War tradition informs and supports the development of international law, and the latter can be seen as codified and formalised elements of the former. In order to satisfy Just War tradition collateral damage need not be eliminated altogether, and the Geneva Convention states that collateral damage should not 'be excessive in relation to the concrete and direct military advantage anticipated'.[39] At first glance it seems logical to suppose that greater discrimination

35 Pierre Claude Nolin, 'Unmanned Aerial Vehicles; Opportunities And Challenges For The Alliance. Special Report' (NATO Parliamentary Assembly: International Secretariat. November 2012) <https://www.tbmm.gov.tr/ul_kom/natopa/docs/raporlar_2012/b3.pdf> 15 September 2020.

36 Nolin, 'Unmanned Aerial Vehicles' (n 35).

37 Asa Kaser and Avery Plaw, 'Distinguishing Drones: An Exchange', in Bradley Jay Strawser, *Killing By Remote Control: The Ethics Of An Unmanned Military* (OUP, Oxford 2013) 52.

38 Kaser and Plaw, 'Distinguishing Drones' (n 37) 53–55.

39 'Protocol Additional To The Geneva Conventions Of 12 August 1949, And Relating To The Protection Of Victims Of International Armed Conflicts (Protocol I), 1125 U.N.T.S. 3,

linked with reduced potential for collateral damage should result in greater proportionality when employing drones over other systems.

However, Melzer points out that in times of war, militaries have a tendency to adjust the ends with the means available to them.[40] In expanding on this point, Kaag and Kreps use the analogy of a surgeon: when given a more precise scalpel, the surgeon will be more likely to perceive ever smaller targets as tumours deserving surgical removal.[41] When faced with an opportunity to carry out a strike using a conventional, non-drone, weapon system against an individual believed to be a legitimate target, which would potentially result in a number of collateral civilian deaths, an operator may choose not to act, considering the collateral damage disproportionate to the direct military advantage. Continuing the earlier surgical analogy, the instrument is relatively blunt and the potential for damaging healthy tissue as well as removing the tumour is too great.

But if by utilising a drone's capabilities a strike could be carried out that was so precise that only the intended target was struck, and virtually no chance of collateral civilian injury or death existed despite the proximity of non-combatants, then the drone operator may be more willing to carry out the strike, believing the precision of the sensors and weapon systems reduces the risk. If the target is correctly identified as legitimate, then the previous level of proportionality is maintained, as there is zero collateral injury or death. If, on the other hand, the operator has misidentified a non-combatant as a legitimate target despite the fact that only one individual has been struck, the collateral damage leaps to one hundred percent. By making militaries more likely to employ lethal force, even though the chance of collateral damage is reduced in each individual engagement and the opportunities for discrimination are increased, drones introduce the potential to actually increase collateral damage overall by precisely striking the incorrect target.

Though the contrast between these two scenarios is deliberately stark, it highlights that drones' ability to hit a target more precisely cannot necessarily be equated to drones' ability to minimise non-combatant casualties.[42] As Hallgarth states, in terms of *jus in bello*, the use of drones and other unmanned

Entered Into Force Dec. 7, 1978.' (*Hrlibrary.umn.edu*, 2018) <http://hrlibrary.umn.edu/instree/y5pagc.htm> accessed 17 September 2020.

40 Yehuda Melzer, *Concepts Of Just War* (AW Sijthoff, Leyden 1975) 58.

41 Kreps and Kaag, *Drone Warfare* (n 33) 99.

42 Kreps and Kaag, *Drone Warfare* (n 33) 113.

vehicles is only as good or as evil as the moral agents controlling them.[43] The sensors on a drone may enable the potential for greater discrimination between combatants and non-combatants, but the decision to use lethal force still rests with the human operator. The use of a particular technology in this case does not confer either legitimacy or illegitimacy, and the Just War principles of discrimination and proportionality are not compromised by it.

Ahmad also argues that the deployment of drones allows operators to kill with no more concern than if they were playing a computer game. He suggests that drone operators, operating remotely and insulated from any physical risk of harm in the operational theatre, do not feel any empathy for their targets and guilt from their actions. Ahmad concludes that this removes the humanity of the targets, resulting in what he describes as 'virtue-less war'.[44] Sparrow outlines a number of military virtues considered common to many professional armed forces worldwide, including moral and physical courage, loyalty, honour and mercy, and considers how the advent of drone operations has affected them.[45]

Many militaries emphasise physical courage, linking an ability to withstand discomfort, pain, and injury with a parallel ability to display moral courage in difficult situations. For those operating drones, there are few requirements for physical courage, as the operator is removed from any risk of physical injury. Though the techniques and weapons systems are very similar to a manned aircraft, there is no risk to the operator if the aircraft is shot down or suffers a mechanical failure.

But it can be argued that drone operators still require *moral* courage, perhaps in greater measure than those under direct physical threat. One operator described the sense of mental dislocation involved in stepping out of his mission module having made life and death decisions and employed lethal force, only to then rush home at the end of his shift to help his children with their homework where 'no one in my immediate environment is aware of anything that occurred'.[46]

---

43 Matthew W. Hallgarth, 'Just War Theory and Remote Military Technology: A Primer', in Bradley Jay Strawser (ed), *Killing By Remote Control: The Ethics Of An Unmanned Military* (Oxford University Press, Oxford 2013) 45–46.

44 Ahmad, 'Virtue-Less War' (n 16).

45 Robert Sparrow, 'War without Virtue?', in Bradley Jay Strawser (ed), *Killing By Remote Control: The Ethics Of An Unmanned Military* (Oxford University Press, Oxford 2013) 84.

46 Elisabeth Bumiller, 'A Day Job Waiting For A Kill Shot A World Away' *The New York Times* (New York, 29 July 2012) <https://www.nytimes.com/2012/07/30/us/drone-pilots-waiting-for-a-kill-shot-7000-miles-away.html> accessed 21 September 2020.

A United States Government report in 2011 found that nearly half of all drone pilots reported 'high operational stress', nearly a third reported suffering a 'burnout,' and 17% were 'clinically distressed'.[47] The same report found that long and irregular shifts prevented integration into the civilian patterns of life followed by friends and family. Though dislocated from the risk of physical harm, they were also mentally isolated from the emotional support of those they were living with by this disengagement with conventional civilian lifestyles.

Kirkpatrick takes this concept further, highlighting that a drone operator may be required to exercise an element of moral courage after an event, such as when an order to fire on a target justly and legally identified has been carried out, only for a rapid change in the scenario and context to cause a tragedy to occur. Kirkpatrick gives the example of a previously unseen child emerging near a legitimate target just as a precision guided munition strikes, destroying the target and most likely killing the child. Reporting such an event requires significant moral courage: doing so could present significant risks to career advancement, one's relationship with one's peers, and bring scrutiny from the media.[48]

Dislocation from colleagues in the battlespace also presents challenges to the development of loyalty between those colleagues and the drone operators. Sparrow describes how soldiers on the battlefield require loyalty from those they fight alongside, as, without loyalty, those individuals are less likely to risk their own lives either for the benefit of a single individual or for the collective military objective of the group.[49] Despite the long hours and shift patterns already described, drone operators are in no physical danger, making that sense of loyalty harder to develop. While there are parallels to other technologies, such as long-range guided weapons, Sparrow notes that the advent of widespread drone technology could represent the ultimate expression of this phenomenon, and highlights it as an area of future concern.[50]

It could be argued that the same context that creates the potential to diminish individual loyalty generates the conditions for drone operators to develop a

47 Rachel Martin, 'Report: High Levels Of 'Burnout' In U.S. Drone Pilots' (2011) <http://www.npr.org/2011/12/19/143926857/report-high-levels-of-burnout-in-u-s-drone-pilots> accessed 21 September 2020.

48 Jesse Kirkpatrick 'Drones and the Martial Virtue Courage' (2015) 14:3–4 *Journal of Military Ethics*, 202–219.

49 Zack Beauchamp and Julian Savulescu, 'Robot Guardians: Teleoperated Combat Vehicles in Humanitarian Military Intervention' in Bradley Jay Strawser (ed), *Killing By Remote Control: The Ethics Of An Unmanned Military* (Oxford University Press, Oxford 2013).

50 Beauchamp and Savulescu, 'Robot Guardians' (n 49).

heightened sense of institutional loyalty, perhaps even to the further detriment of their bond with those deployed forward and in danger of physical harm. For example, a drone operator may witness a transgression of rules of engagement or a violation of international conventions and feel more compelled to report it to the chain of command, in order to protect the institution; whereas a witness further forward and experiencing the same physical risks may not feel as compelled to do so. In this case institutional loyalty trumps individual loyalty, or a sense of sympathy for the situation the transgressors find themselves in, potentially resulting in a failure to investigate war crimes.

An example of this can be seen in the case of Sergeant Alexander Blackman, formerly a member of the Royal Marines. In September of 2011 a patrol base at Taalanda, in Southern Afghanistan, was attacked by Taliban insurgents. An Apache helicopter from Camp Bastion was tasked to respond and engaged the insurgents with 139 30mm rounds. The Taliban attack was defeated and, in the opinion of the crew of the Apache, the insurgents could not have survived.[51]

Subsequently a foot patrol from a patrol base at nearby Omar was tasked to confirm the effect of the helicopter's engagement and report any evidence of insurgent casualties. This patrol consisted of Sergeant Blackman, Corporal Watson, and Marine Hammond. The official report of the patrol stated that they had found the body of an insurgent along with his weapon system, and it was assumed that the insurgent had died of wounds inflicted by the Apache helicopter's 30mm rounds.

In September 2012, as part of an investigation into an unrelated matter, the military police discovered footage of the patrol captured on a privately owned helmet mounted camera that was being used by Corporal Watson. This footage showed the insurgent being discovered alive but seriously wounded. Rather than administering first aid, Sergeant Blackman ordered the insurgent to be dragged to an area that was not being observed by the Persistent Ground Surveillance System (PGSS), an aerostat balloon-mounted camera system used to identify insurgent movements in the area.

After ordering one of the Marines who was administering first aid to stop, Sergeant Blackman shot the wounded insurgent in the chest, killing him, and then calmly informed the rest of the patrol 'Obviously this doesn't go anywhere, fellas. I just broke the Geneva Convention.'[52] The Court Martial that convicted him of murder and the subsequent appeal of the sentence listed

51 *Regina v. Sergeant Alexander Wayne Blackman and Secretary of State for Defence* [2014] EWCA Crim 1029.

52 'Jailed Ex-Marine Loses Appeal Against Afghan Murder Conviction' (2014) *BBC UK* (22 May 2014) <http://www.bbc.co.uk/news/uk-27514493> accessed 23 September 2020.

Sergeant Blackman's decision to stop the administration of first aid, the order to move the wounded insurgent to an area that couldn't be observed by the PGSS, the decision to shoot the insurgent in the chest rather than the head (which would be more likely to be viewed suspiciously) and the instruction to the rest of the patrol not to disclose what had happened, as aggravating factors.

It is clear from the case the Sergeant Blackman was aware that his actions were in violation of the Geneva Conventions on the treatment of wounded combatants, and that he took several deliberate actions to avoid being discovered. It was also clear that the other, more junior, members of the patrol were equally aware that a war crime had been committed, and that is was their duty to report the incident, irrespective of the seniority of Sergeant Blackman in the chain of command relative to them. Following the Court Martial verdict, the Deputy Commandant of the Royal Marines described the incident as 'Not consistent with the ethos, values and standards of the Royal Marines' and said that 'It was a truly shocking and appalling aberration'.[53]

The fact that the incident wasn't reported and was only subsequently discovered by chance, gives an example of how individual loyalty between those members of the patrol who committed or witnessed the murder of the insurgent being committed trumped the institutional loyalty felt to the Unit, the Royal Marines, or to British Defence as a whole. It is also clear that Sergeant Blackman was aware that had his actions been witnessed by the PGSS, then the operator, likely to be further removed from his chain of command, would be more likely to report the incident.

This effect is likely to be magnified the further removed from the battlespace the operator of the surveillance system sits, with a drone operator in Creech or Waddington Air Force bases being, as earlier suggested by Sparrow, the ultimate expression of this phenomenon, and therefore likely to increase the chance of any suspected war crime being reported and, by extension, reducing the likelihood of one being committed in the first place.

With regards to the virtue of honour, the moral agent for the act of violence remains the operator who decides whether to fire or not, regardless of whether that decision is taken from a manned system above the battlefield or remotely from several thousand kilometres away. However, Sparrow notes that the same distance that isolates the remote operator from risk also isolates them from contact with enemy peers or the local civilian population, who could praise or condemn honourable or dishonourable acts.[54] A similar constraint exists to

53 'MOD: Truly Shocking And Appalling Aberration' (2013) *BBC UK* (8 November 2013) <http://www.bbc.co.uk/news/uk-24873039> accessed 23 September 2020.

54 Robert Sparrow, 'War without Virtue?' (n 45) 98.

displaying mercy, in that a local population or enemy peer is unlikely ever to be in a position to recognise when a drone operator has carried out a merciful act remotely.

Sparrow goes on to question whether there is something fundamentally dishonourable in killing via a drone, in that it requires no physical risk on the part of the operator and makes this task itself too easy.[55] Sparrow is unable to draw definitive conclusions, but highlights the area as one requiring further study as drone operations become more prevalent as stand-alone deployments, rather than in direct support of other conventional military operations.

In would appear then, that public concerns over the effect of drone warfare on warrior virtues have some ethical basis. Though some areas are unchanged by the introduction of remote technology, others do have the potential to raise new ethical challenges, either through a genuinely unique aspect of drone operations or through such operations representing the ultimate expression of challenges already present in other guided or semi-autonomous weapon systems. Ultimately, however, it would not appear that drone operations represent 'virtue-less warfare' as proposed by Ahmad; indeed some aspects would seem to require additional virtues compared to conventional operations, but some additional study is necessary.

The final concern raised in the Ahmad article is that the availability of armed drones has allowed America and her allies to sidestep the normal questions of legal jurisdiction, political approval, and humanitarian considerations. Ahmad argues that by not placing any American soldiers at risk, political constraints on the deployment of military force have been reduced, implying that operations in Pakistan and elsewhere do not satisfy the requirements of *Jus ad bellum*.

This chapter has already shown that drones themselves do not represent a technology that is inherently incompatible with *jus in bello* principles. However, though drones have been used extensively in a conventional context in support of other components of military forces, they have been increasingly used outside of this context, and not necessarily operated by military forces at all.

An example of this is the use of drone strikes in the Federally Administered Tribal Areas of Pakistan by the Central Intelligence Agency (CIA). The use of force in this manner was begun by the Bush administration post the 11 September 2001 attacks on the World Trade Centre and was both continued and escalated under the Obama administration. The attacks were authorised

---

55 Robert Sparrow, 'War without Virtue?' (n 45) 99–100.

by the US Congress three days after 9/11 in the Authorisation for the Use of Military Force (AUMF), with little or no dissent from politicians from either political party.[56]

As justification for the use of force, the US legislation chose to use the 'hostile status' of the Al Qaeda operatives in Pakistan, reasoning that as enemy combatants they are liable to be kinetically struck at any time, rather than using 'self-defence'.[57] Despite this, President Obama has described the actions as morally and legally justified acts of war, and as part of a war of self-defence.[58] The use of self-defence in this instance allows the drone strikes to satisfy the just cause element of *Jus ad bellum,* but also to side-step the requirement to seek prior authorisation for the use of force from the United Nations in order to obtain legitimate authority.

Van der Linden argues that the justification of self-defence could be considered appropriate immediately following on from 9/11 when the AUMF was passed, but continuing to rely on national rather than international legitimacy 15 years later could be seen at best as a convenient shortcut and at worst an attempt to subvert Just War tradition.[59] Whetham notes that it is not necessarily unusual for powerful states to rely on national political authorisation, or even public opinion, to lend legitimacy to the use of force,[60] though Van der Linden notes that the AUMF only gives authorisation for the use of *military* force, rather than giving it to the CIA, and allows only for those directly involved in 9/11 attacks to be targeted, rather than terrorist groups or members of Al Qaeda in general.[61]

One aspect of the CIA running the drone operations is that information regarding the number of strikes made and civilian casualties caused are not openly released. A number of Non-Governmental Organisations have estimated that from 2004 to 2013, between 2296 and 3719 casualties were caused by drone operations, and within that it estimates that between 416 and 957 non-hostile casualties were caused, potentially including up to 202 children, with between a further 1089 and 1639 civilians injured. Van der Linden argues

56 S.J.Res. 23 (107th): Authorization for Use of Military Force (2001–2002).

57 Harry van der Linden, 'Drone Warfare and Just War Theory' in Marjorie Cohn (ed), *Drones And Targeted Killing: Legal, Moral, And Geopolitical Issues* (Olive Branch Press 2014) 171.

58 Barack Obama, *Remarks By The President At The National Defense University* (2013) (National Defense University, Washington DC, 23 May 2013).

59 van der Linden, 'Drone Warfare' (n 57) 173.

60 Whetham, 'The Just War Tradition' (n 1) 79.

61 van der Linden, 'Drone Warfare' (n 57) 173.

that given that the benefits in terms of threat prevention are unknown, the proportionality of the tactic is questionable.[62]

A US Government fact sheet released by the Obama administration states that the use of force in drone operations is always a last resort and kinetic strikes will not take place unless capture is not feasible, and local authorities will not or cannot take effective measures to deal with the 'imminent threat to US persons'.[63] It is difficult to conceive of a threat that is of a type and magnitude sufficient to justify the use of a kinetic drone strike that also presents such an imminent threat to US citizens, undermining the legitimacy of the justification used. The lack of such imminence means the use of force begins to stray from legitimate self-defence or pre-emption, and towards the illegitimate use of preventative force, classified by Walzer as an act of aggression.[64] Van der Linden goes even further, suggesting that the use of force by the US is in order to punish, rather than to prevent further aggression or violence.[65]

The evidence would seem to suggest that public concern over lowering the threshold for the use of lethal force does have an ethical justification, and the use of drones by the CIA in Pakistan fails to comply with the Just War traditions of *jus ad bellum*. It is important to stress the distinction between a drone operation of that type being inherently unethical and drone operations in general. Ironically, despite being criticised by Ahmad in his article, one of the specific points that Nachbar raises is that in order to restore legitimacy, the drone operations should be transferred from CIA to military control, or even treated as purely a policing matter and transferred to the Federal Bureau of Investigation.[66] It does, however, appear that both the manner of the operation and the legislation used to authorise it have been selected in order to lower the threshold where the use of force is considered appropriate.

This chapter began by setting out the ethical frameworks that determine whether the use of force can be considered legitimate, namely the Just War traditions of *jus ad bellum* and *jus in bello,* as well as outlining the continuum between legitimate self-defence, legitimate pre-emption, and illegitimate preventative war. Public concerns regarding the use of armed drones have then been tested against these principles in order to determine whether such concerns are ethically justified. The popular view of drones, influenced by an incomplete understanding of the military realities and the depiction in

62 van der Linden, 'Drone Warfare' (n 57) 180.
63 van der Linden, 'Drone Warfare' (n 57) 173.
64 Walzer, *Just And Unjust Wars* (n 11) 81.
65 van der Linden, 'Drone Warfare' (n 57) 172.
66 Nachbar (n 17).

multiple media of drones as fully autonomous systems vulnerable to malevolent interference, was also touched upon. The potential for such misgivings to be based purely on human instinct, with ethical justification subsequently selectively applied to add credence to the misgivings, was also explored.

It has been demonstrated that the technology of armed drones is not such that it raises fundamentally new ethical challenges or questions, with parallels drawn to weapon systems such as precision weapons launched from manned aircraft or semi-autonomous cruise missiles, for which public concern has been directed at the use of nuclear warheads rather than at the fundamentals of the technology itself. Misgivings about future fully autonomous weapon systems have the potential to be ethically justified, particularly if 'responsibility gaps' could emerge, but current levels of autonomy do not appear to contradict any of the principles of *jus in bello*. Despite the technology, the moral agent remains the human operator controlling or committing the system to action.

The question of whether armed drones represent 'virtue-less' warfare, and diminish the ethical standing of the operators is less clear. While the requirement for physical courage is reduced with the remote operator separated from the battlespace and the risk of harm, the requirement for moral courage potentially increases, born out by the high incidences of stress, depression, and post-traumatic stress disorders among drone operators. Similarly, opportunities to develop individual loyalty are diminished by the physical separation, yet a higher level of institutional loyalty is both expected and required. A practical example of this can be seen through the case of Sergeant Blackman during operations in Afghanistan during 2011. Virtues such as honour and mercy are challenged by the remote nature of the technology, but the virtues are required and demonstrated still. The assertion that drone warfare is 'virtue-less' appears unfounded, but some virtues are challenged, and others are identified as areas for further consideration.

Though not inherently unethical in and of itself as a means, the technology of drone warfare does appear to offer the opportunity to circumvent, or at least undermine, the Just War principles of *jus ad bellum* regarding the resort to the use of those means in the first place. The ability to deploy such systems remotely and without physical risk to friendly troops does create scenarios where the use of force does appear more likely than when compared to conventional operations requiring significant deployed forces, and the public and international scrutiny that accompanies them. This lack of scrutiny, or even public awareness of what is happening, could undermine the perceived political necessity to adhere to the principles of just cause and legitimate authority, whereas the low cost of drone strikes compared to a policing-led counter-terrorist campaign, risks the undermining of the principle of the use of force as a genuine last resort as it relatively so easy to do. This ethical concern, arguably the most significant of the four considered in this chapter, does appear to be justified.

References

Ahmad, Muhammad Idrees, 'The Virtue-Less War Of The "Nintendo Bomber"' (*Al Jazeera* 28 June 2011) <http://www.aljazeera.com/indepth/opinion/2011/06/2011626 82825424222.html> accessed 15 September 2020.

Arkin, Ronald, 'Ethical Robots In Warfare' (2009) 28 *IEEE Technology and Society Magazine*.

Army Doctrine Publication, Vol 5, *Soldiering, The Military Covenant* (Her Majesty's Stationary Office 2002).

Beauchamp, Zack and Julian Savulescu, 'Robot Guardians: Teleoperated Combat Vehicles in Humanitarian Military Intervention' in Bradley Jay Strawser (ed), *Killing By Remote Control: The Ethics Of An Unmanned Military* (Oxford University Press, Oxford 2013).

Bellamy, Alex J., *Just Wars: From Cicero To Iraq* (Polity Press, Cambridge 2006).

Bumiller, Elisabeth, 'A Day Job Waiting For A Kill Shot A World Away' *The New York Times* (New York, 29 July 2012) <https://www.nytimes.com/2012/07/30/us/drone-pil ots-waiting-for-a-kill-shot-7000-miles-away.html> accessed 21 September 2020.

Campaign to stop Killer Robots, 'The threat of fully autonomous weapons. The Problem' <https://www.stopkillerrobots.org/learn/#problem> accessed 15 September 2020.

Carmola, Kateri, 'The Concept of Proportionality: Old Questions and New Ambiguities' in Mark Evans (ed), *Just War Theory: A Reappraisal* (Edinburgh University Press, Edinburgh 2005) 93–113.

Coates, A. J., *The Ethics of War* (Manchester University Press, 1997).

Crawford, Neta C., 'The Justice of Preemption and Preventive War Doctrines' in Mark Evans (ed), *Just War Theory: A Reappraisal* (Edinburgh University Press, Edinburgh 2005) 25–49.

'Greenham Common Women's Peace Camp', Wikipedia (Wikimedia Foundation) <https://en.wikipedia.org/wiki/Greenham_Common_Women%27s_Peace_Camp> accessed 28 December 2020.

'Jailed Ex-Marine Loses Appeal Against Afghan Murder Conviction' (2014) *BBC UK* (22 May 2014) <http://www.bbc.co.uk/news/uk-27514493> accessed 23 September 2020.

Haines, Steven, 'Humanitarian Intervention: Genocide Crimes against Humanity and the Use of Force' in George Kassimeris and John Buckley (eds) *The Ashgate Research Companion to Modern Warfare* (Ashgate, Farnham 2010) 307–328.

Hallgarth, Matthew W., 'Just War Theory and Remote Military Technology: A Primer', in Bradley Jay Strawser (ed), *Killing By Remote Control: The Ethics Of An Unmanned Military* (Oxford University Press, Oxford 2013).

Jha, U. C., *Drone Wars: Ethical, Legal And Strategic Implications* (KW Publishers 2014).

Kaser, Asa and Avery Plaw, 'Distinguishing Drones: An Exchange', in Bradley Jay Strawser, *Killing By Remote Control: The Ethics Of An Unmanned Military* (OUP, Oxford 2013).

Kirkpatrick, Jesse 'Drones and the Martial Virtue Courage' (2015) 14:3–4 *Journal of Military Ethics*, 202–219.

Kreps, Sarah E. and John Kaag, *Drone Warfare* (Polity Press, Cambridge 2014).

Kreps, Sarah E., *Drones: What Everyone Needs To Know* (Oxford University Press 2016).

Leveringhaus, Alex, 'Assigning Responsibility in Enhanced Warfare', in Jai Galliott and Mianna Lotz (eds), *Super Soldiers: The Ethical, Legal and Social Implications* (Ashgate Publishing 2015).

Lucas, George, 'Engineering, Ethics and Industry: The Moral Challenges of Lethal Autonomy', in Bradley Jay Strawser (ed), *Killing By Remote Control: The Ethics Of An Unmanned Military* (Oxford University Press, Oxford 2013).

Martin, Rachel, 'Report: High Levels Of 'Burnout' In U.S. Drone Pilots', (2011) *NPR* <http://www.npr.org/2011/12/19/143926857/report-high-levels-of-burnout-in-u-s-drone-pilots> accessed 21 September 2020.

Melzer, Yehuda, *Concepts Of Just War* (AW Sijthoff, Leyden 1975).

'MOD: Truly Shocking And Appalling Aberration' (2013) *BBC UK* (8 November 2013) <http://www.bbc.co.uk/news/uk-24873039> accessed 23 September 2020.

Nolin, Pierre Claude, 'Unmanned Aerial Vehicles; Opportunities And Challenges For The Alliance. Special Report' (*NATO Parliamentary Assembly*: International Secretariat. November 2012) <https://www.tbmm.gov.tr/ul_kom/natopa/docs/raporlar_2012/b3.pdf> 15 September 2020.

Norton, Emily, 'Over 100 Drones Protesters Heading To RAF Waddington This Weekend' (*the Lincolnite* 30 September 2015) <http://thelincolnite.co.uk/2015/09/around-100-drones-protestors-heading-to-raf-waddington-this-weekend/> accessed 15 September 2020.

Obama, Barack, *Remarks By The President At The National Defense University* (2013) (National Defense University, Washington DC, 23 May 2013).

'Protocol Additional To The Geneva Conventions Of 12 August 1949, And Relating To The Protection Of Victims Of International Armed Conflicts (Protocol I), 1125 U.N.T.S. 3, Entered Into Force Dec. 7, 1978.' (Hrlibrary.umn.edu, 2018) <http://hrlibrary.umn.edu/instree/y5pagc.htm> accessed 17 September 2020.

Rachels, James and Stuart Rachels, *The Elements Of Moral Philosophy* (7th edn, McGraw-Hill, New York 2012).

Regina v. Sergeant Alexander Wayne Blackman and Secretary of State for Defence [2014] EWCA Crim 1029.

Robinson, Paul, *Just War In Comparative Perspective* (Ashgate Publishing 2003).

Royal Air Force, Aircraft And Weapons (3rd edn, MOD 2014) <https://www.raf.mod.uk/what-we-do/centre-for-air-and-space-power-studies/documents1/royal-air-force-aircraft-weapons-fourth-edition-revised/> accessed 15 September 2020.

S.J.Res. 23 (107th): Authorization for Use of Military Force (2001–2002).

Sparrow, Robert, 'War without Virtue?', in Bradley Jay Strawser (ed), *Killing By Remote Control: The Ethics Of An Unmanned Military* (Oxford University Press, Oxford 2013).

van der Linden, Harry, 'Drone Warfare and Just War Theory' in Marjorie Cohn (ed), *Drones And Targeted Killing: Legal, Moral, And Geopolitical Issues* (Olive Branch Press 2014).

Walsh, Toby, 'The Rise Of The Killer Robots – And Why We Need To Stop Them' (*CNN* 26 October 2015) <http://edition.cnn.com/2015/10/26/opinions/killer-robots-walsh/> accessed 15 September 2020.

Walzer, Michael, *Just and Unjust Wars: A Moral Argument with Historical Illustrations* (2nd edn, Basic Books 1992).

Whetham, David, 'The Just War Tradition: A Pragmatic Compromise,' in David Whetham (ed), *Ethics, Law and Military Operations* (Palgrave Macmillan, Basingstoke 2010) 65–89.

CHAPTER 8

The Use of Drones in Armed Conflict – Ethical Aspects of Emerging Military Technology

Tamar Meisels

1 Introduction

The question of how to contend with terrorism in keeping with our pre-existing moral and legal commitments now challenges Europe as well as Israel and the United States: how do we apply Just War Theory and International Law to new weapons and methods of killing? Over the past few decades, the United States has adopted a clear policy of assassinating terrorist leaders and operatives. Israel, which had long resorted to this tactic, accelerated its use even further after the outbreak of the second Intifada.

Targeted killings can be carried out by ground forces or by conventional airplanes, and may involve the use of bullets, bombs, or poison.[1] Mostly though, at least in the American case, targeted killings are performed by "drones", operated from a distance. These are also the well-publicized cases of targeted killing, attracting the greatest public attention, not least because of the collateral damage they are reported to cause, and possibly due to the science fiction type images they invoke in the popular imagination.

My topic here is drones, *not* targeted killing, though in practice the two issues are closely intertwined. As Danny Statman notes, although there is no essential connection between the use of drones and targeted Killing, the two are contingently connected, so that the moral debate about drones is very much entangled with the debate about the morality and the legality of targeted killing.[2] Some disentangling is in order: I am not going to defend the practice of targeting identified combatants as opposed to conventional killing in war, though

1 As in Israel's failed targeting of Hamas leader Khaled Mashal in Jordan in 1997, when Mossad agents administered poison into Mashal's left ear. Israel was subsequently compelled to hand over the antidote.

2 Daniel Statman, 'Drones and Robots: On the Changing Practice of Warfare', in Helen Frowe and Seth Lazar (eds), *Oxford Handbook of the Ethics of War*, Oxford Handbooks Online (Oxford University Press, New York 2015), Chapter 22.

 | DOI:10.1163/9789004507951_010

I believe it is worth defending and I defend it elsewhere.[3] Instead, I focus narrowly on the technology used to carry out these killings, though drones are also used for other purposes.

The following offers some initial thoughts and comments regarding the specific use of remotely piloted aircrafts to carry out targeted killings, and addresses the various sources for discomfort with this practice, identified by Michael Walzer as well as others.

2 Drones Are Here to Stay

First and most obviously: regardless of academic debate, I think it is safe to assume that drones are here to stay. To quote the recent American film *Good Kill*: "Drones aren't going anywhere. In fact they're going everywhere".[4] Perhaps quite soon everyone will have them,[5] though the feasibility of non-state actors successfully operating drone programs in American or Israeli skies appears most unlikely.

3 Drones Are Asymmetrical

The second point about drones is this: they are essentially asymmetrical weapons favoring states, both morally and strategically. Arguably, this is actually one of their advantages. Running an effective drone program requires, among other things, sophisticated satellite systems, large infrastructure, and trained man-power, where state-level air superiority is already established and working in cooperation with the drone operations. Drones offer a built in advantage to powerful states that are capable of operating such large scale schemes. Despite the remote control imagery, Michael Walzer explains, "drones are actually flown from bases fairly near their targets and it requires some 170 people to maintain the drones and get them into the air."[6]

3 Tamar Meisels, 'Targeting Terror' (2004) 30 (3) *Social Theory and Practice*, 297; Tamar Meisels, *The Trouble with Terror* (Cambridge University Press, 2008), Chapter 5.

4 Niccol, Andrew, *Good Kill* (Voltage Pictures, Sobini Films 2014) <http://www.imdb.com/title/tt3297330/> accessed 27 January 2020.

5 Michael Walzer, 'Targeted Killing and Drone Warfare', Dissent Magazine, 11 January 2013 <http://www.dissentmagazine.org/online_articles/targeted-killing-and-drone-warfare> accessed 27 January 2020.

6 Michael Walzer, 'Just & Unjust Targeted Killing & Drone Warfare' (2016) 145 (4) *Daedalus* 12, 15.

Given the expense and complexity of running an effectively lethal drone-system, as well as the anti-aircraft defenses operated in Israel and the U.S., drones are going to be far less effective in the hands of individuals or terrorist organizations flying over countries with anti-aircraft capability.[7]

Notwithstanding, there is a growing concern among military experts, as well as scholars, that smaller, less sophisticated off-the shelf drones that are rapidly becoming readily available, may be used by terrorist organizations to carry out indiscriminate attacks. Walzer cautions us to "imagine a world, in which we will soon be living, where everybody has drones."[8] A recent article in the NY Times quotes J. D. Johnson, a retired general who previously commanded the threat-defeat agency, warning that terrorist drones constitute a very real danger: pointing out that, "these things are really small and hard to detect, and if they swarm in groups, they can overload our ability to knock them all down".[9]

There have been numerous articles to this effect in the Israeli and American press.[10] At the start of 2018, a *Washington Post* headline warned that "Drones keep entering no-fly zones over Washington, raising security concerns."[11] The

---

7 Bradley J. Strawser explains: "Many speak of drones not as individual weapons, but more as 'drone systems'. Each drone flight involves the drone itself (or drones, usually many drones working in tandem), but also involves the integrated satellite systems that navigate them and communicate with them anywhere on the planet, the ground uplink stations themselves that send and receive this communication, as well as sophisticated secondary satellite systems the piloting teams draw upon for navigation. It is this – the large infrastructure that is required for even minimally successful drone operations – that is only plausible for states to possess; and far out of the reach of even the most well-funded non-state actor groups. Additionally, without state-level air superiority, drones are incredibly ineffective. They are slow, lumbering planes that can **easily** be shot down by even the most basic anti-aircraft defenses. They would be like shooting down a slow moving, low flying Cessna, or even easier. The only reason they are effective where we use them is because we use them in places where complete air superiority is already established and working in cooperation with the drone operations. Non-state actors almost never have this. As such, even if they somehow COULD co-opt the massive infrastructure needed for an effective drone program (which I don't think they could), their drones would be pathetically and easily shot down out of the sky almost instantly." In an email, quoted with Bradley J. Strawser's permission.

8 Walzer, 'Just & Unjust Targeted Killing' (n 6) 18.

9 Eric Schmitt, 'Pentagon Tests Lasers and Nets to Combat a Vexing Foe: ISIS Drones' *The New York Times* (New York, 23 September 2017).

10 Yossi Melman, 'Hamas Increases its efforts to develop unmanned aerial vehicles' (Hebrew) *Maariv* (Tel Aviv 20 Januar 2018) <http://www.maariv.co.il/journalists/Article-618572> accessed 28 January 2020.

11 Michael Laris, 'Drones keep entering no-fly zones over Washington, raising security concerns' *The Washington Post* (Washington, D.C. 13 January 2018) <https://www.washingtonpost.com/local/trafficandcommuting/drones-keep-entering-no-fly-zones-over-washington-raising-security-concerns-and-illustrating-larger-problems/2018/01/13/1030159a-db7d-11e7-b1a8-62589434a581_story.html?undefined=&utm_term=.4b7f42cc03fc&wpisrc=nl_headlines&wpmm=1> accessed 28 January 2020.

low cost, low operational skill requirement, and off-the-shelf availability may make airborne I.E.D. (improvised explosive devices) an ideal weapon for terrorists. This seems to be the opinion of the Pentagon, which sent technical specialists to Iraq, Syria, and Afghanistan to protect US and local troops from ISIS drones.[12]

Nevertheless, the basic point about asymmetry holds: while terroristic drone attacks pose a potential threat, the asymmetry in capabilities will probably remain. A distinction needs to be drawn here between highly advanced US and Israeli military drones and satellite-operated drones systems, versus airborne improvised explosive devices. Moreover, drones are particularly effective where complete air superiority is established, as is the case with the US drone program in Afghanistan, Pakistan, and Yemen. Non-State actors don't have this. While a cause for concern, terrorist drones are likely to be far less efficient than a massive drone program run by a super-power like the United States, or a regional super-power such as Israel. However effective they ultimately become, terrorists with drones will be least effective over U.S. and Israeli skies, well protected by anti-aircraft defenses. Moreover, as terrorist capabilities improve (if they do improve), so most likely will our technology for detecting them and shooting them down.

I do not wish to belabor this point about strategic asymmetry because I am no expert on emerging technologies, and I have already strayed irresponsibly into the realm of predictions. More importantly, I cannot figure out how imagining what may come to pass when everyone has drones affects the ethical debate over targeted killing with drones in the present. Terrorists will do what they can, with whatever means at their disposal, totally irrespective of what we do or do not do with drones.

As for moral asymmetry, drones are not only currently weapons of state, but particularly useful to law-abiding states aspiring to distinguish combatants from civilians. Asymmetry may seem unfair, but it is actually a moral point in favor of killing with UAVs. Drones are precision weapons, offering the possibility of careful compliance with the laws of war, to those who wish to comply. In terms of upholding traditional *jus in bello*, drones are useful to the "good guys", though we know that good states will not always act well. Drones offer a built-in advantage to states that try to distinguish between combatants and civilians, over murderous terrorist organizations that kill indiscriminately.

---

12 Schmitt, 'Pentagon Tests Lasers' (n 9).

To recap: at present, drones favor powerful states that wish to minimize collateral damage and should be used to that effect. It is possible that in the foreseeable future, less sophisticated drones, requiring lower construction and operational costs, could inflict terroristic destruction, but I deny this has any normative bearing on what we ought to do in our struggle with terrorism today. Terrorists may soon be able to harness drone technology effectively for their fiendish purposes of carrying out indiscriminate, murderous attacks. I cannot predict the extent to which we might be capable of refining our anti-aircraft defenses to contend with this threat. But I fail to see the connection between these warnings and our ethical questions about whether and how to use drones right now. ISIS is not likely to refrain from drone technology if only we would do the same.

4 How Should We Use Drones?

Given these two previous points (drones are not going away, and they currently favor (relatively) law abiding states), the relevant question is how – not whether – to use them. The laws and customs of war supply the answer: aim narrowly at identified combatants, sparing civilians whenever possible. Drones have this capacity to refine, rather than dull, our moral sensibilities, and enhance compliance with the laws about distinction and proportionality, minimizing collateral damage. If they are not used to this end, then humans are at fault, not the machines they employ.

5 Collateral Damage

What about collateral harm and the resentment caused by drone warfare, as well as further objections directed at the use of unmanned aerial vehicles, "killing by remote control"?[13] Statman poses and answers the appropriate question: "Are civilians put at higher risk of harm by the use of drones than by the use of alternative measures?"[14] Recall, we are assuming armed conflict:

13 Bradley Jay Strawser (ed), *Killing by Remote Control – The Ethics of an Unmanned Military* (Oxford University Press, New York 2013).

14 Statman, 'Drones and Robots' (n 2) 2; Daniel Statman, 'Drones, Robots and the Ethics of War' (2014) 1 *Zebis Ethics and Armed Forces. Controversies in Peace Ethics & Security Policy* 41 <http://www.ethikundmilitaer.de/fileadmin/inhalt-medizinethik/Full_issue_2014_1_Anonymous_Killing_by_new_Technologies_The_Soldier_between_Conscience_and_Machine.pdf> accessed 28 January 2020.

> The crucial point to remember here is that the alternative to the use of drones is not the avoidance of violence altogether, which would entail zero-risk to civilians but the use of other, more conventional, lower-tech measures, such as tanks, helicopters, and so on. (Of course, if the use of force were not necessary, there would be no justification for using force even when no harm to civilians was to be expected). But such imprecise measures would almost certainly lead to more civilian casualties rather than to fewer.[15]

More critical of drone warfare generally, Jeff McMahan nonetheless concedes that the advantage of remotely controlled weapons is their ability to be highly discriminating in the targets they destroy:

> What differentiates the newer models of remotely controlled *weapons* from traditional long-range precision-guided munitions is that they allow their operators to monitor the target area for lengthy periods before deciding whether, when, and where to strike. These are capacities that better enable the weapons operators to make morally informed decisions about the use of their weapons.[16]

Similarly, Walzer notes, drones "combine the capacity for surveillance with the capacity for precise attack".[17]

(Note the variety of scholars from conflicting just war traditions making this moral point in favor of drones and their precision capabilities. A rare moment of agreement between Michael Walzer and Jeff McMahan, and between Just War Theory and the revisionist morality of war.)

Solving one moral problem, however, may in this case entail another. Drones that hover above for lengthy periods of time enable better informed moral decisions; but what about the psychological collateral harms they inflict, as the costs of increased precision is offloaded onto surrounding civilians "Living under Drones"?[18]

---

15 Statman, 'Drones and Robots' (n 2) 2; Statman, 'Drones, Robots and the Ethics of War' (n 14) 42.

16 Jeff McMahan, 'Foreword to *Killing by Remote Control*' in Bradley Jay Strawser (ed), *Killing by Remote Control: The Ethics of an Unmanned Military* (Oxford University Press 2013) ix <http://jeffersonmcmahan.com/wp-content/uploads/2012/11/Foreword-Killing-by-Remote-Control1.pdf> accessed 28 January 2020.

17 Walzer, 'Targeted Killing and Drone Warfare' (n 5).

18 International Human Rights and Conflict Resolution Clinic (Stanford Law School) and Global Justice Clinic (NYU School of Law), 'Living under Drones: Death, Injury, and Trauma to Civilians from US Drone Practices in Pakistan' (New York, September

6 Living under Drones

The undoubtedly terrifying experience of daily life under the continuous buzzing of circling predator drones overhead, monitoring their target area for lengthy periods of time, is by now well documented, as well as quite easily imaginable.[19] Israelis, in particular, cannot be impervious to this argument that counts psychological harm to civilians in wartime proportionality calculations. This type of damage to civilians has been repeatedly appealed to by Israel in justifying massive military incursions into the Gaza strip, in response to relatively few casualties on the Israeli side. Both in 2008–9 and more recently, Israel has effectively suggested that its proportionality calculus accounts not only for the physical costs inflicted by Hamas, but also the psychological implications to its southern population living under the continuous threat of Hamas rocket attacks. Advocating for Israel in these matters commonly involves reference to the devastating, life-disrupting, emotionally traumatic, and economic costs to terrorized civilians, rather than merely to the number of actual fatalities on the ground.[20] And what is true when making 'the case for Israel', must apply with even greater force to civilians under drones in Pakistan and elsewhere.

I have no experience of living under drones, and only short-term experience of living under ineffective Hamas rocket attacks (as well as Scud missiles from Saddam Hussein's Iraq in 1991). Despite the statistically low risk, shrieking rockets (not to mention buzzing drones) imminently threatening sudden death or injury from the skies, is admittedly quite an unsettling and unnerving experience, most notably for children. All the more so, I can only imagine, in the case of effective lethal aerial vehicles circling in the sky for extended stretches of time, threatening to strike at any moment.[21] Jeremy Waldron is quite right to point out that the relevant perspective for assessing the terrorizing effects

---

2012) <https://chrgj.org/wp-content/uploads/2016/09/Living-Under-Drones.pdf> accessed 29 January 2020.

19 International Human Rights and Conflict Resolution Clinic, 'Living under Drones' (n 18) Chapter 3, 59–101; This is the core section of the report, including firsthand accounts describing the emotional trauma, as well as the total disruption of every aspect of private and social life, caused by drone attacks in Pakistan. See also the testimony in Appendix A.

20 Alan Dershowitz, 'Israel's Policy is Perfectly Proportionate' *The Wall Street Journal*, (New York, 2 January 2009).

21 See: International Human Rights and Conflict Resolution Clinic, 'Living under Drones' (n 18) 81, where one man recounts this harrowing experience, describing the reaction to the sound of the drones as "a wave of terror" coming over the community: "Children, grown-up people, women, they are terrified. ... They scream in terror."

of drones is that of the people who actually endure them, rather than professional risk assessments.[22]

Terror on the ground (far more so in Pakistan than in Tel-Aviv) must be accounted for in any proportionality calculation, whether *ad bellum* (as in the Israeli case) or *in bello*, when the US chooses its weapons for combating terror. Nevertheless, psychological harm to civilians, just like any other collateral damage in war, has to be balanced alongside, and against, other considerations, such as military objectives and the costs of alternative weapons.

One significant factor in comparing terrorized populations with the terrifying effects of drones is the question of intent. Is the harm to civilians intentional, or is it a side effect of a legitimate objective? In the case of terror bombings, civilian casualties are intended directly, providing a just cause for war, as are the additionally terrorizing effects of these murderous attacks. Similarly (though not entirely equivalently), drones ought not to be deployed deliberately to "hover visibly and audibly precisely in order to terrify the villagers, so that they expel Taliban militants hiding among them".[23] In the case of drones, psychological harm is justifiable to the extent that it is incurred sincerely as an undesirable side-effect of the war on terror. Moreover, unlike physical collateral damage, justifiable solely with reference to military objectives, the frightening effects of drones are primarily the by-product of their surveillance capacity, focusing their aim and minimizing concrete harm to civilians.

Consider the following important point by Michael Walzer in response to Stanford/NYU Clinics' reports. Notwithstanding clear evidence of constant fear and buzzing drones, Walzer notes that

> ... the very effectiveness of drone attacks raises questions about these accounts of the fear they provoke. Attacking drones must hover at such high altitudes that they can't be seen or heard. If they didn't do that, the intended targets, who presumably know they are targets, would simply stay out of sight.[24]

Walzer adds:

22 Jeremy Waldron, 'Death Squads and Death Lists: Targeted Killing and the Character of the State'(2016) 23 *Constellations* 292, 296.

23 Walzer, 'Just & Unjust Targeted Killing' (n 6) 16.

24 Ibid.

> Even the most nuanced accounts are contradictory: Gusterson quotes reporters who liken the sound of drones to "lawnmowers in the sky", but then describes a successful killing that happened "without warning".[25]

Undeniably, reconnaissance drones hover (and hum) at lower (visible and audible) altitudes. But they do so precisely in order to allow for accurate targeting of a particular individual or target. So while, "The buzz of a distant propeller is a constant reminder of imminent death",[26] it should also serve as a reminder of our attempt to spare civilians.

7 Killing by Remote Control[27]

Is there nonetheless something about killing at a distance that makes drones particularly objectionable or prone to misuse? Historically, hurling flying cannon balls, tearing people apart across the battlefield, must also have seemed like terrifying remotely controlled weapons in their time. "The crossbow, when it was introduced, was considered a terrible and indiscriminate weapon, 'hateful to God and unfit for Christians', because it could penetrate the armor of knights".[28] Pierre Terrail, seignior de Bayard (1473 -1527), 'le Chevalier sans peur et sans reproche' is said never to have given quarter to a musketeer. (Ultimately, "le bon Chevalier" was mortally wounded on an Italian battlefield by an arquebus ball).[29]

Defending the usefulness of artillery in the 16th century, Machiavelli contests, "the universal opinion of many" in his time "that by means of artillery, men cannot show their virtue as they could in antiquity."[30]

---

25 Walzer, 'Just & Unjust Targeted Killing' (n 6) (Walzer's note 10), with reference to Hugh Gusterson, *Drone: Remote Control Warfare* (MIT Press 2016).

26 Jeremy Waldron, 'Death Squads', 296, 305 note 43 citing firsthand report by David Rohde, 'Reuters Magazine: The Drone Wars' (2012) *Reuters* 26 January 2012.

27 Strawser, *Killing by Remote Control* (n 13).

28 Eugene Davidson, *The Nuremberg Fallacy* (University of Missouri Press 1998) 284.

29 Davidson, *Nuremberg Fallacy* (n 28); I am grateful to Azar Gat for this, and other, historical examples, as well as for the below references to Machiavelli.

30 Niccolo Machiavelli, *Discourses on Livy* (trs by Harvey C. Mansfield and Nathan Tarcov), (The University Of Chicago Press, Chicago & London 1996) book II, Chapter 17: "How Much Artillery Should Be Esteemed by Armies in the Present Time; and Whether the Opinion Universally Held of It Is True", 163–168. In the *Discourses*, Machiavelli also notes the asymmetry of artillery warfare, favoring those who take the offensive over the defending army, 163–165. Finally, he addresses the concern "that war will in time be reduced to artillery", a 16th century version of Walzer's futuristic warning about drones: imagine a world in which hand to hand combat will be obsolete, and "war will be conducted

Unmanned Aerial Vehicles, however, are entirely distant from the battlefield and offer their operators (though not necessarily everyone involved in maintaining the drones and getting them airborne)[31] the advantage of risk-free combat. Various writers have suggested that riskless warfare is bad in itself, either because it renders one's opponent non-threatening and therefore non-liable to attack in self-defense,[32] or else because it is dishonorable, unfair, and (again) lacking in military valor.[33] Many of these arguments are close relatives, or modern descendants, of the objections raised by Machiavelli's 16th century contemporaries to the use of artillery.

Some objections to drone strikes – those concerning asymmetrical warfare, distant engagement, the loss of old fashioned military virtues and defenseless targets facing a faceless death – apply equally to long range missiles[34] and, though perhaps to some lesser degree, also to aerial bombardment by manned aircrafts.

Several answers have been put forward to these objections, most notably by B. J. Strawser and Danny Statman. Drones are economical: morally, they have the capacity to minimize casualties among civilians and combatants; financially, they are relatively cost-effective for states to produce and deploy in relation to inhabited planes carrying out similar missions, freeing shared resources for welfare expenditure.[35] Consequently, Strawser argues for a moral duty to employ UAVs as opposed to exposing soldiers to unnecessary risk, contending "that in certain contexts UAV employment is not only ethically permissible, but is, in fact, ethically obligatory".[36] Statman points to the motivational benefits

altogether by artillery", 166. For further debate on the use of artillery, see also Niccolo Machiavelli, *The Art of War* (trs, ed, and with commentary by Christopher Lynch, The University of Chicago Press, London & Chicago 2003), book 2–3 (esp. the battle scene described in book 3), 33–83.

31 Walzer, 'Just & Unjust Targeted Killing' (n 6) 15.

32 Paul Kahn, 'The Paradox of Riskless Warfare' (2002) 22 *Philosophy & Public Policy Quarterly* 2, 3. For discussion of this argument, see: Jeff McMahan, 'Foreword to *Killing by Remote Control*' (n 16) xi-xii; and Statman, 'Drones and Robots' (n 2) 4; Statman, 'Drones, Robots and the Ethics of War' (n 14) 44.

33 Statman, 'Drones and Robots' (n 2), 5; Statman, 'Drones, Robots and the Ethics of War' (n 14) 43–44.

34 See Statman, 'Drones and Robots' (n 2) 4, 8; Statman, 'Drones, Robots and the Ethics of War' (n 14) 44.

35 Bradley Jay Strawser, 'Moral Predators: The Duty to Employ Uninhabited Aerial Vehicles' (2010) 9 *Journal of Military Ethics* 342, 344 <http://www.tandfonline.com/doi/abs/10.1080/15027570.2010.536403> accessed 31 January 2020; Statman, 'Drones and Robots' (n 2) 2–3; Statman, 'Drones, Robots and the Ethics of War' (n 14) 42–43.

36 Strawser, 'Moral Predators' (n 35) 344. See also Strawser, *Killing by Remote Control* (n 13) 3–24, 17–20.

of safe warfare in enlisting risk-averse nations to take part in humanitarian military interventions.[37]

8 Zero Risk Warfare

In "Targeted Killing and Drone Warfare", however, Walzer worries that this capacity for riskless warfare makes drones dangerously tempting. The ability to kill the enemy without risking our soldiers makes killing too easy, leading to a relaxation of the targeting rules and actually increasing general unfocused warfare.[38] Moreover, unlike soldiers in conventional wars, drones and their remote operators cannot demonstrate "due care" for civilians by assuming risks on their behalf.[39] Walzer invites "us to imagine a war in which there won't be any casualties (on our side), no veterans who spend years in VA hospitals, no funerals. The easiness of fighting with drones should make us uneasy. This is a dangerously tempting technology".[40] This diagnosis appears painfully plausible – zero risk warfare encourages trigger happiness.

The appropriate remedy is less clear, bearing in mind the images of war paraplegics and body bags invoked by Walzer's comment. It seems entirely preposterous, even slightly grotesque and obscene, to place our young soldiers, and probably also enemy civilians, in greater physical danger by reverting to lower tech weapons. Walzer does not suggest this. In fact, the only appropriate response in keeping with *jus in bello* is actually more targeted warfare: using drone capacity to focus the aim as narrowly as humanly and technologically possible, attempting to hit the enemy-target and preferably no one else. Any other use of drones is clearly unacceptable, as is any other use of a sling shot, or a bow and arrow. Complaints about the misuse and over-use of drones,[41] intentionally or negligently terrorizing populations,[42] ought rightly to be aimed at particular policies and policy makers, rather than at the technology.

---

37 Statman, 'Drones and Robots' (n 2) 3; Statman, 'Drones, Robots and the Ethics of War' (n 14) 42–43.

38 Walzer, 'Targeted Killing and Drone Warfare' (n 5).

39 On "due care" for civilians and Walzer's requirement that soldiers take demonstrative risks in order to prevent excessive harm to civilians, see Michael Walzer, *Just and Unjust Wars: A Moral Argument with Historical Illustrations* (Basic Books, New York 1977), 155–156, and Michael Walzer and Avishai Margalit, 'Israel: Civilians & Combatants' (2009) 56 (8) *The New York Review of Books* 6.

40 Walzer, 'Just & Unjust Targeted Killing' (n 6) 15.

41 Walzer, 'Targeted Killing and Drone Warfare' (n 5).

42 Waldron, 'Death Squads' (n 22) 14.

9 Concluding Remarks

The surgical killing of identified enemy combatants is as good as war gets, certainly compared to the common practice of killing young conscripts in battle and incurring large scale collateral damage. Unmanned aerial vehicles have the capacity to perform this task at a distance, focusing lethal harm at a liable target while minimizing collateral deaths, provided of course that we program them to do just this. If we do not, the fault is not in our drones, but in ourselves.

Unlike many conventional weapons (though not unlike long-range missiles and aerial bombing), drones pose no danger to their operators. Some count this as a point in their favor, while others worry about the dangers of riskless warfare. This dispute is largely academic. Either way, no state in its right mind would give up the strategic superiority offered by drones. Not only are drones safe to use, but we also need not worry too much about their proliferation. Drones are primarily weapons of powerful states. While it is true that a single predator may not be all that expensive, running a drone program requires a huge, complicated, massive infrastructure around it. Additionally, drones are far more effective where complete air superiority is established.

Moreover, drones are not only weapons of states, but especially useful in the hands of those states that care about complying with discrimination and proportionality, since drones are very good at that. This type of asymmetry or double standard – enabling law-abiding states to fight safely against terrorists who cannot respond in kind – is a good thing.

References

Davidson, Eugene, *The Nuremberg Fallacy* (University of Missouri Press 1998) 284.

Dershowitz, Alan, 'Israel's Policy is Perfectly Proportionate' *The Wall Street Journal*, (New York, 2 January 2009).

Gusterson, Hugh, *Drone: Remote Control Warfare* (MIT Press 2016).

International Human Rights and Conflict Resolution Clinic (Stanford Law School) and Global Justice Clinic (NYU School of Law), 'Living under Drones: Death, Injury, and Trauma to Civilians from US Drone Practices in Pakistan' (New York, September 2012) <https://chrgj.org/wp-content/uploads/2016/09/Living-Under-Drones.pdf> accessed 29 January 2020.

Kahn, Paul, 'The Paradox of Riskless Warfare' (2002) 22 *Philosophy & Public Policy Quarterly* 2, 3.

Laris, Michael, 'Drones keep entering no-fly zones over Washington, raising security concerns' The Washington Post (Washington, D.C. 13 January 2018) <https://www.washingtonpost.com/local/trafficandcommuting/drones-keep-entering-no-fly-zones-over-washington-raising-security-concerns-and-illustrating-larger-problems/2018/01/13/1030159a-db7d-11e7-b1a8-62589434a581_story.html?undefined=&utm_term=.4b7f42cc03fc&wpisrc=nl_headlines&wpmm=1> accessed 28 January 2020.

Machiavelli, Niccolo, *Discourses on Livy* (trs by Harvey C. Mansfield and Nathan Tarcov), (The University Of Chicago Press, Chicago & London 1996) book II, Chapter 17.

Machiavelli, Niccolo, *The Art of War* (trs, ed, and with commentary by Christopher Lynch, The University of Chicago Press, London & Chicago 2003), book 2-3 (esp. the battle scene described in book 3), 33–83.

McMahan, Jeff, 'Foreword to *Killing by Remote Control*' in Bradley Jay Strawser (ed), *Killing by Remote Control: The Ethics of an Unmanned Military* (Oxford University Press 2013) ix <http://jeffersonmcmahan.com/wp-content/uploads/2012/11/Foreword-Killing-by-Remote-Control1.pdf> accessed 28 January 2020.

Meisels, Tamar, 'Targeting Terror' (2004) 30 (3) *Social Theory and Practice,* 297; Tamar Meisels, *The Trouble with Terror* (Cambridge University Press, 2008), Chapter 5.

Melman, Yossi, 'Hamas Increases its efforts to develop unmanned aerial vehicles' (Hebrew) *Maariv* (Tel Aviv 20 Januar 2018) <http://www.maariv.co.il/journalists/Article-618572> accessed 28 January 2020.

Niccol, Andrew, *Good Kill* (Voltage Pictures, Sobini Films 2014) <http://www.imdb.com/title/tt3297330/> accessed 27 January 2020.

Rohde, David, 'Reuters Magazine: The Drone Wars' (2012) *Reuters* 26 January 2012.

Schmitt, Eric, 'Pentagon Tests Lasers and Nets to Combat a Vexing Foe: ISIS Drones' *The New York Times* (New York, 23 September 2017).

Statman, Daniel, 'Drones and Robots: On the Changing Practice of Warfare', in Helen Frowe and Seth Lazar (eds), *Oxford Handbook of the Ethics of War*, Oxford Handbooks Online (Oxford University Press, New York 2015), Chapter 22.

Statman, Daniel, 'Drones, Robots and the Ethics of War' (2014) 1 *Zebis Ethics and Armed Forces. Controversies in Peace Ethics & Security Policy* 41 <http://www.ethikundmilitaer.de/fileadmin/inhalt-medizinethik/Full_issue_2014_1_Anonymous_Killing_by_new_Technologies_The_Soldier_between_Conscience_and_Machine.pdf> accessed 28 January 2020.

Strawser, Bradley Jay (ed), *Killing by Remote Control – The Ethics of an Unmanned Military* (Oxford University Press, New York 2013).

Strawser, Bradley Jay, 'Moral Predators: The Duty to Employ Uninhabited Aerial Vehicles' (2010) 9 *Journal of Military Ethics* 342, 344 <http://www.tandfonline.com/doi/abs/10.1080/15027570.2010.536403> accessed 31 January 2020.

Waldron, Jeremy, 'Death Squads and Death Lists: Targeted Killing and the Character of the State' (2016) 23 *Constellations* 292, 296.

Walzer, Michael and Avishai Margalit, 'Israel: Civilians & Combatants' (2009) 56 (8) *The New York Review of Books* 6.

Walzer, Michael, 'Just & Unjust Targeted Killing & Drone Warfare' (2016) 145 (4) *Daedalus* 12, 15.

Walzer, Michael, 'Targeted Killing and Drone Warfare', Dissent Magazine, 11 January 2013 <http://www.dissentmagazine.org/online_articles/targeted-killing-and-drone-warfare> accessed 27 January 2020.

Walzer, Michael, *Just and Unjust Wars: A Moral Argument with Historical Illustrations* (Basic Books, New York 1977), 155–156.

CHAPTER 9

The Loss of Innocence in the Age of Drones

Redefining the Notion of Innocence in the Context of Drone Warfare

Dragan Stanar

1 Introduction

The prominent American psychologist, Abraham Maslow, famous for his hierarchy of needs,[1] places security[2] at the top of the list of essential human needs. Our need to be safe is second only to our physiological needs – to breathe, sleep, eat, drink, etc. Unfortunately, many people have recognized that when our security, or the security of our loved ones, is jeopardized, even the most fundamental human needs like eating and sleeping seem insignificant and secondary. Human obsession with safety is completely justified, as being safe is a prerequisite for any type of a normal life – we must be able to predict, with a minimal amount of certainty, and plan, at least our near future. Therefore, all human cultures and civilizations have invested tremendous efforts in increasing their level of security, and enabling people to have a minimal level of predictability and certainty in their lives, necessary for everyday life. Our attempts to maximize our security are fully epitomized in our perpetual endeavor to enhance and perfect our weapons: to make our weapons more reliable, more powerful, more lethal. This human quest for security has led from primordial stone weapons to modern day scientific and technological wonders – high-end weapons of mass destruction. It truly is curious to observe that we invest all of our civilizational achievements into creating weapons capable of eradicating all civilization. The eternal paradox of man.

At this point in our historical journey, we are capable of fighting, killing and destroying our enemies in all corners of our planet – on land, in air, on and under water. We are not far from being able to fight even outside of our planet, and talk of 'space forces', 'outer-space conflicts', and 'orbit wars' is

1 Abraham Maslow identifies five categories of basic human needs – Physiological needs, safety, love, esteem and self-actualization. See more in: Abraham Maslow, 'A Theory of Human Motivation' (1943) 50 *Psychological Review* 370.

2 In Maslow's classification, *Safety needs* include personal security, employment, resources, health and property.

 | DOI:10.1163/9789004507951_011

becoming increasingly common. We, as humanity, are at a moment in our historical development in which we must ask ourselves a crucial question – has the development of our weapons outpaced the development of our culture and civilization? Are our modern super-weapons 'compatible' with who we are, with humanity? Naturally, as ethicists we are primarily concerned with ethical implications and challenges presented by modern weapons and their use. These ethical challenges are plentiful, complex, and controversial, and we must all strive to provide our modest contributions to moral discourses and discussions on the topic, especially because "the literature on the ethics of lethal drones, and the discussion of remote killing more broadly, is still in its infancy."[3]

This chapter aims to investigate moral dilemmas shadowing the use of Unmanned Aerial Vehicles, or drones. More precisely, we wish to examine the notion of innocence in war, and determine whether drone warfare can be compatible with the notion of innocence in the Just War Theory. Our claim is that the complete elimination of risk in drone warfare represents a qualitative shift in the nature of war, making drone warfare incompatible with the existing Just War Theory, and perhaps even common morality itself.

2 What Are Drones and Why Everybody Wants Them?

The notion of drone refers to different things, from small inexpensive gadgets used for bird's-eye filming to complex weapons systems. In this paper, we will use the word drone to signify Armed Unmanned Aerial Vehicles (AUAVS), used by armies as powerful lethal weapons. There are numerous different terms found in the literature, that all refer to armed drones – Unmanned Military Systems (UMS),[4] Remotely Piloted Vehicles (RPVS),[5] Uninhabited Aerial Vehicles (UAVS),[6] Armed Uninhabited Combat Aerial Vehicles (UCAVS),[7] etc. All these terms are used by different authors to signify those military drones that are used to kill enemy combatants or other targets. Regardless of how they

3 Bradley Jay Strawser, 'Introduction: The Moral Landscape of Unmanned Weapons' in Bradley Jay Strawser (ed), *Killing by Remote Control: The Ethics of an Unmanned Military* (OUP 2013) 4.

4 Robert Sparrow, 'War without Virtue?' in Bradley Jay Strawser (ed), *Killing by Remote Control: The Ethics of an Unmanned Military* (OUP 2013) 86.

5 Sparrow, 'War without Virtue?' (n 4) 87.

6 Robert Sparrow, 'Drones, Courage, and Military Culture' in George Lucas (ed), *Routledge Handbook of Military Ethics* (Routledge 2015) 380.

7 Sparrow, 'Drones, Courage, and Military Culture' (n 6).

refer to them, practically all experts concur that drones represent the present and the future of war, and are predicting "a greatly increased role for unmanned systems in the future of the armed services".[8] Drones were introduced to the battlefield at the beginning of the century, i.e., in the early 2000s. Interestingly, it was the CIA, not the military, that used drones for the first time – more precisely a Predator drone used for targeted killing. Since that time, drones have become increasingly popular, not only in western armies. Some studies done in Washington indicate that "at least 11 countries are using 56 different types of unmanned aerial vehicles (UAVs)".[9] A paper published in 2017 shows that only "the U.S. has 8,000 drones"[10] – these are not all armed combat drones, and the number includes various types of drones in use. Nevertheless, the fact remains that armed combat drones are being widely introduced in all armies of the world that can afford to have them. The most popular, and most used, drones are General Atomics MQ-1 'Predator' and General Atomics MQ-9 'Reaper', also known as 'Predator B'.[11] It was precisely the use of these two types of drones in "Afghanistan that has led to a massive influx of funding from governments all around the world for research on military robots",[12] and that irreversibly altered the nature of warfare. Obviously, drones have proven their practical military worth.

But why are drones so appealing to armies around the world? Simply, they provide numerous practical advantages for the side using them; they are unique assets that ensure that their operators will have the upper hand – "they function without risk to their operator, can be highly discriminating in the targets they destroy, and can be used in places that are inaccessible to soldiers or prohibitively dangerous for their deployment."[13] The most obvious and crucial advantage of drones is the opportunity to fight and kill from a safe distance. They allow us to strike without any previous warning, without ever being heard or seen. All officers and soldiers who have experienced war know very well the overwhelming effect of surprise attacks and stealth strikes. High-end drones are equipped with state-of-the-art technology, enabling them to

8 Sparrow, 'War without Virtue?' (n 4) 88.

9 Mary Manjikian, *A Typology of Arguments about Drone Ethics* (Strategic Studies Institute and U.S. Army War College Press 2017) 1.

10 Anne Hopkins, 'The Ethical Debate on Drones', *Ethics Essay Contest* (2017).

11 The 'Avenger' drone, or 'Predator C', represents the latest addition to the General Atomics' drone fleet.

12 Robert Sparrow, 'Just Say No to Drones' (2012) 31 *IEEE Technology and Society Magazine* 56, 57.

13 Jeff McMahan, 'Foreword' in Bradley Jay Strawser (ed), *Killing by Remote Control: The Ethics of an Unmanned Military* (OUP 2013) ix.

track, monitor and strike their targets with increased precision. Powerful optical and digital solutions allow drone operators to literally peek through the windows or zoom in on faces and license plates of their targets, introducing unparalleled accuracy even in densely populated areas. Accordingly, Israeli Rafael Armament Development Authority claims that their new missiles used by drones can achieve "urban warfare precision", something that was previously impossible. All these reasons make a strong case for us to "believe that teleoperated weapons will play an increasingly central role in wars over the coming decades."[14] Being unnoticeable and invisible, drones can stay above their target for extended periods of time, enabling their operators to wait as long as necessary for the perfect opportunity for action. This 'extended loitering period', as experts call it, in combination with extreme precision, can in theory increase effectiveness to its maximum, meaning that drones could, again in theory, ensure full respect of the *Jus in Bello* principles of proportionality and discrimination. Unfortunately, it is extremely hard, perhaps even impossible, to accurately estimate the effectiveness of drone strikes, in regard to the *in Bello* principles, in practice, because of some wildly problematic interpretations of the category of combatants. It has been reported that the U.S. treats "all military-age males in strike zone as combatants ... unless there is explicit intelligence posthumously proving them innocent."[15] By the same token, Guiora and Shelton claim that the current U.S. interpretation of legitimacy of targets in their war against terrorism is "broadly defined, potentially without reliance on criteria, standards, and limits."[16] Empirical data regarding the efficiency of drones is contradictory – some studies show that they are "ineffective and even counterproductive"[17] while others report the opposite.[18] When it comes to ethical problems of drone use, there are authors who even assert that "UAV employment is not only ethically permissible, but is, in fact, ethically obligatory,"[19] as every commander of any army has a duty to eliminate

14 Sparrow, 'Drones, Courage, and Military Culture' (n 6) 381.

15 Jo Becker and Scott Shane, 'Secret 'Kill List' Proves a Test of Obama's Principles and Will' *The New York Times* (New York, 29 May 2012).

16 Amos Guiora and Jason Shelton, 'Drones and Targeted Killing: Facing the Challenges of Unlimited Executive Power' in George Lucas (ed), *Routledge Handbook of Military Ethics* (Routledge 2015) 369.

17 Christian Enemark, 'Unmanned Drones and the Ethics of War' in Fritz Allhoff, Nicholas G. Evans and Adam Henschke (eds), *Routledge Handbook of Ethics and War* (Routledge 2013) 331.

18 Enemark, 'Unmanned Drones and the Ethics of War' (n 17) 331.

19 Bradley Jay Strawser, 'Moral Predators: The Duty to Employ Uninhabited Aerial Vehicles' (2010) 9 *Journal of Military Ethics* 342, 344.

all unnecessary risk.[20] Many others strongly disagree, and find drone warfare to be extremely morally problematic.

3 Objections to Drone Warfare

Despite all the advantages just mentioned, there are numerous authors who firmly object to the use of armed drones in military operations. Perhaps the greatest advantage that drones provide – riskless killing – is the source of much controversy and the aspect of drone warfare deemed most problematic. The opportunity to wage war without taking any risk may have stark consequences, not just on the very manner of fighting, but also in regards to the decision to start a war. The *Jus ad Bellum* element of the Just War Theory presents us with various strict conditions, six of them to be precise, that must be met in order for a war to be just. As Orend points out, the Just War Theory "insists that *all six* criteria must be met in order to justify a declaration of war",[21] meaning that all criteria are equally important. One of these criteria demands that the aim of war must be proportional to the suffering inflicted by war, simply put – that our war is worth the sacrifice. If we do not have to sacrifice our men in war, or put them in any type of danger, then it may seem that virtually every war, if it satisfies the remaining *Jus ad Bellum* criteria, would be just. Another criterion demands that war, due to its destructiveness and costliness, must be our last resort, our last option when resolving a conflict. But, if we eliminate risk for our soldiers and our citizens, war could become much more appealing, and less costly than non-military means of conflict. This may "render governments more willing to go to war, lower the threshold of conflict, trigger accidental wars, and thus ultimately lead to more death and destruction."[22] Other authors agree that drones lower "the *Jus ad Bellum* threshold such that more unjust wars might be conducted because the risk of war to a nation-state could become so minimal".[23] Kahn argues that "Riskless warfare … may take the destructive power of war outside of the boundaries of democratic legitimacy, because we are far more willing to delegate the power to use force without risk

20 Under The Principle of Unnecessary Risk (PUR).

21 Брајан Оренд, 'Рат' in Драгана Дулић и Бранко Ромчевић (eds), *Етика рата – хрестоматија*, (Факултет безбедности 2010) 269.

22 Sparrow, 'Just Say No to Drones' (n 12) 60.

23 Strawser, 'Moral Predators' (n 19) 358.

to the president than we are a power to commit the nation to the sacrifice of its citizens."[24]

The asymmetry created by the elimination of risk for one side in war may also encourage the other side to resort to other means of fighting. If one side is left with absolutely no option to defend itself, then there is a high probability that it will turn to the most criminal and unjust manners of retribution, including terrorism. Some authors assert that aggressive asymmetric warfare "provides the weaker side with a valid justification to engage in terrorism"[25] and that "asymmetry may become an invitation to … terrorism".[26] Some authors, like Chomsky and Dalziel go as far as to claim that "drones … are synonymous with terrorism …" and even that "drone strikes are a form of terrorism … and that those who engage in it are terrorists."[27] Another issue is being raised in discussions about drones and the effect they have on the very nature of war. If all risk to drone operators is eliminated, how are they to be treated – as warriors or simply as some particular type of IT experts or even gamers? Throughout history, warriors have been respected and admired as virtuous and laudable, considered to be fighters who live by the warrior's code.[28] There has always been a huge essential difference between murderers and warriors, despite the fact that they both kill. Moreover, military organization embodies virtues of honor, courage, loyalty, sacrifice, etc. Even today, the military community represents "one of the most powerful and most cohesive moral communities in modern society, precisely because its members as individuals identify primarily as members of an army. Military virtues are a part of these personal identities …"[29] If there is no personal risk involved in killing, can we still speak of warriors and martial virtues? The virtue of courage has been inherent to warriors, signifying their "willingness to face fear and overcome it",[30] and regardless of the era, "any account of the nature of a good warrior must begin with courage,

---

24 Paul W. Kahn, 'The Paradox of Riskless Warfare' (2002) 22 *Philosophy and Public Policy Quarterly* 2, 4.

25 Uwe Steinhoff, 'Killing Them Safely: Extreme Asymmetry and Its Discontents' in Bradley Jay Strawser (ed), *Killing by Remote Control: The Ethics of an Unmanned Military* (OUP 2013) 197.

26 Kahn (n 24) 6.

27 Manjikian (n 9) 42.

28 Shannon French provides a deep historical insight into the warrior's code. See more in: Shannon E. French, *The Code of the Warrior: Exploring Warrior Values Past and Present* (Rowman and Littlefield 2003).

29 Александар Фатић, 'Савремена технологија ратовања у светлу хришћанског морала: наоржани дронови' in Борислав Гроздић (ed), *Православље и рат* (МЦ Одбрана 2017) 120.

30 Sparrow, 'War without Virtue' (n 4) 89.

which is the martial virtue par excellence."[31] But, if one is to be courageous, there must be some type of physical risk included, as by definition, courage requires overcoming of fear and preparedness to risk one's life for his comrades and his country. Drone operators do not engage in combat, and do not have the opportunity to "demonstrate courage by risking physical injury or death"[32] in combat. Other martial virtues are also closely linked with combat and risk. Loyalty, for example, "involves a willingness to bear risk and make sacrifices for the sake of that to which one is loyal",[33] meaning that warriors require risk to prove their loyalty. For many authors, "the mentality of drone operators is incompatible with the honor of military profession."[34] Within the military itself, there is a difference in perception between those who are exposed to risk and those who are not. When U.S. Defense Secretary Leon Panetta wished to award drone operators with Distinguished Warfare Medals,[35] there were those in the U.S. military who considered drone operators not really to be warriors, and argued that they simply do not "deserve the honor accorded to those who risk their lives in the service of their nation."[36] It truly seems that preparedness to take risk and to sacrifice for your country is inextricably and profoundly entangled with our perception of a warrior. The introduction of drones "may have profound implications for the culture of the armed forces",[37] paving the way for a new age of post-heroic militaries.[38]

4 From the Sling to the Predator

In our perpetual quest to better our weapons, we have not only made them more reliable, powerful, and lethal, as we already mentioned, but we have also increased their range, thus making us much safer in our process of killing. This aspiration to fight from a distance is not unnatural; on the contrary, it is "instinctive in man ... From the first day he has worked to this end, and he continues

31 Sparrow, 'Drones, Courage, and Military Culture' (n 6) 383.
32 Sparrow, 'Drones, Courage, and Military Culture' (n 6) 382.
33 Sparrow, 'War without Virtue' (n 4) 90.
34 Фатић, 'Савремена технологија ратовања у светлу хришћанског морала' (n 29).
35 Distinguished Warfare Medals outrank prestigious combat medals of the U.S. army, such as the Bronze Star and the Purple Heart.
36 Sparrow, 'Drones, Courage, and Military Culture' (n 6) 380.
37 Sparrow, 'Drones, Courage, and Military Culture' (n 6) 389.
38 Sparrow coined a remarkably adequate term: "post-heroic military".

to do so."[39] In that regard, drones are not unprecedented – from the invention of the sling and crossbow until today, our goal has been to create a weapon that allows us to kill our enemy from a distance. And with every innovation, with every new technology of killing that extended the range of our weapons, always came new moral dilemmas, new arguments against such "perversions and diabolical contraptions" that enabled the weak to kill the strong. Sparrow brilliantly observes that the argument that "new weapons render war immoral by making it too easy to make the decision to take human life is hardly new. Indeed, it is at least as old as the crossbow – which was condemned for making it possible for peasants to kill armored knights – and perhaps even as old as the sling."[40] Indeed, the range of a weapon is inversely proportional to the combat risk for its operator. From the sling, across spears, bows and arrows, and crossbows to modern day artillery weapons, snipers, and stealth bombers, man's ability to kill from a distance and to distance "himself both physically and psychologically from his prey"[41] has improved drastically. So, does this mean that our concerns and objections to armed combat drones are, though historically necessary, ephemeral and futile; or is there something peculiar and distinctive about drones that separates them from all previous cases? We believe that there is. Admittedly, all the aforementioned weapons have reduced the risk to their operators in one way, but they have also increased the risk in another way. For example, using a crossbow provides us with an advantage when facing an opponent armed with a sword or an axe. But, if our opponent gets within arm's reach of us, our choice of weapon is disadvantageous and our risk drastically increases. A soldier firing a sniper rifle is able to kill without being noticed, but if he is noticed and discovered, his enemies armed with automatic weapons are in a much better position, especially as they get closer to him. Artillery weapons can always malfunction and endanger the lives of their operators, much more than an assault rifle can. Pilots of stealth bombers are always at risk of being shot down, regardless of their stealth characteristics. The best example of this possibility is the shootdown of the "invisible" Nighthawk F-117A over Serbia, when Yugoslav Air Defense managed to hit the aircraft with the old and obsolete S-125 Neva system. Even if not hit by air defense missiles, pilots are always at risk of their aircraft malfunctioning. In these cases, even if the pilot catapults himself over enemy territory, he is at enormous risk, parachuting down behind enemy lines, usually armed only with his sidearm. We firmly

---

39 Ardant du Picq, quoted in Dave Grossman, *On Killing: The Psychological Cost of Learning to Kill in War and Society* (Back Bay Books 1996) 107.

40 Sparrow, 'War without Virtue' (n 4) 88.

41 Manjikian, *A Typology of Arguments about Drone Ethics* (n 9) 34.

believe that all previously mentioned weapons represented a quantitative leap in military technology, increasingly reducing the risk for their operators, while drones represent an unprecedented qualitative leap. Drones have managed to remove "the operators from the theatre of operations entirely, allowing them to 'fight' wars in complete safety";[42] not with lesser or even minimal risk, but without any risk at all, thus marking a "qualitative change in the nature of military combat".[43] Unlike with all those other weapons, with the emergence of drones we have effectively crossed the minimal threshold of risk, necessary for justification of killing. The risk of being a drone operator is far less than that of being a coal miner, an electrician, a taxi driver, a construction worker, etc.[44] Furthermore, their command modules are located inside of highly secured and guarded military bases in their own territory, surrounded by their compatriots, equipped with medical facilities, doctors and surgeons, their food and water are regularly controlled and monitored for quality and sanitary safety, etc. One can even argue that being a drone operator is one of the most risk-free occupations there is! But why is risk so imperatively important for the military profession?

5 What Justifies Killing in War?

Simply put, risk allows us to kill in war. Let us now elaborate on that claim. It has been said numerous times by numerous people that war is hell and that it represents a state in which laws are suspended and in which the future is unpredictable. The *differentia specifica* of war is the nature and quantity of killing that happens before returning to the state of peace. Killing in war is profoundly different than killing in peace, but not all killing in war is equal. Despite war being hell, it is in fact a hell with its own rules and laws, and one of the most important rules of war is that only certain people can be targeted and killed. The *Jus in Bello* element of the Just War Theory demands that all actors of war respect the principle of selection or discrimination; i.e., that only combatants can be targeted and killed, while non-combatants retain the same immunity we all enjoy in peace. In the Just War Theory discourse, non-combatants are innocent and combatants are non-innocent. As we all know, we cannot kill innocent people, neither in peace nor in war, as "deliberate killing of

---

42 Sparrow, 'War without Virtue' (n 4) 88.

43 Sparrow, 'War without Virtue' (n 4) 85.

44 Sparrow argues that risk to drone operators is "lower than that faced by ordinary U.S. citizens". Sparrow, 'Drones, Courage, and Military Culture' (n 6) 385.

the innocent is murder, and in warfare the role of innocent is filled by noncombatants."[45] Before we continue with our argumentation, we must first define the notion of innocence in war, because, as Nagel remarked, misunderstandings often derive from "the connotation of the word 'innocence'."[46] In peace, innocent means not guilty or not culpable for something, not breaking any legal[47] or moral norms. But, in war innocence and guilt are "emptied of moral content and become simply synonymous with the roles of war",[48] i.e. roles of combatants and noncombatants. This means that in war the notion of guilt, or non-innocence, refers not to personal responsibility and moral culpability, but something else – it refers to posing risk. Therefore, the element that separates innocent and non-innocent in war is not moral culpability, or the absence of it, it is risk or harm. Those who pose a risk and who are harming are non-innocent and thus legitimate targets, and those who do not pose a risk and who are not harming are innocent and thus are not legitimate targets. As McMahan explained in his seminal work, *Killing in War*, the meaning of the notion of innocence in the Just War Theory is "solidly grounded in the etymology of the term. 'Innocent' derives from the Latin word *nocentes* which refers to those who are injurious or threatening."[49] Anscombe and Nagel agree that the only difference between innocents and non-innocents in war is the fact that the innocents are "currently harmless"[50] and "not harming"[51] while non-innocents are those who are "engaged in an attempt to destroy us".[52] This 'engagement in an attempt to destroy us' means that combatants, or the non-innocent, are legitimate targets not only and exclusively in the moment of their attack and violence, but also during the entire period of war in which they are combatants, i.e., harming – when they are deep behind the lines, when they are having breakfast, even when they are sleeping. They forfeited their 'innocence' and non-harming character when they took up arms and became a legitimate threat in war, or, as Michael Walzer formulated it, the innocence and right not to be attacked "is lost by those who bear arms 'effectively' because they

45 Thomas Nagel, *Mortal Questions* (CUP 1979) 70.

46 Nagel, *Mortal Questions* (n 45) 70.

47 "Legally, a man is innocent if he is not guilty, i.e. if he has not engaged in conduct explicitly prohibited by rules of the criminal law" – Jeffrey Murphy, 'The Killing of the Innocent' (1973) 57 *The Monist* 527, 529.

48 Gabriel Palmer-Fernandez, 'Innocence in War' (2000) 14 *International Journal of Applied Philosophy* 161, 164.

49 Jeff McMahan, *Killing in War* (Clarendon Press 2009) 11.

50 Nagel, *Mortal Questions* (n 45) 70.

51 McMahan, *Killing in War* (n 49).

52 Murphy (n 47) 532.

pose a danger to other people".[53] To conclude, we are permitted to kill in war only those who pose a threat, because they have lost their innocence and right not to be attacked by being involved in harming, while the innocents "have done nothing … that entails the loss of their rights",[54] specifically the right not to be attacked and killed. Soldiers enjoy an equal right to kill, in Walzerian terms, due to the "mutual threat that soldiers in a conflict pose toward one another",[55] and this relationship of reciprocity is sustainable "as long as they stand in a relationship of mutual risk."[56] But, if we cross the mentioned necessary minimal threshold of risk, i.e. if we eliminate risk entirely for one side, and given the fact that the non-innocent in war have not lost their innocence by being morally and legally culpable and guilty, we must ask ourselves "what is the moral basis for injuring the morally innocent?"[57] The 'paradox of riskless warfare' as Kahn named it, "arises when the pursuit of asymmetry undermines reciprocity"[58] that represents the basis for the moral justification for killing in war. We are confident that drones eliminate risk entirely for their operators, leaving them without any moral basis for killing their enemies; i.e., rendering all enemies innocent, and "for men to kill the innocent as a means to their ends is always murder, and murder is one of the worst of human actions."[59] In classical warfare, as soon as the enemy ceases to pose a threat – i.e., if he or she surrenders – "they become in this sense innocent and so may not be maltreated or killed",[60] as killing prisoners of war would be considered murder. Accordingly, if we allow drone operators to kill enemies who pose no threat, we must also allow soldiers to kill enemies who surrender and cease to pose any risk or threat – additionally, we would also be forced to allow drone operators to kill combat medics, army doctors, chaplains, etc. Hopefully, no reasonable human being would agree.

Before continuing, we are obliged to allow another possibility – that drone operators are allowed to kill enemies because their enemies are waging an unjust war. Unlike the classical interpretation of the basis for moral justification of killing in war, the revisionists claim that only those who fight on the just side are justified in killing their enemies, because their enemies are

---

53 Michael Walzer, *Just and Unjust Wars* (4th ed. Basic Books 2006) 145.
54 Walzer, *Just and Unjust Wars* (n 53) 146.
55 Strawser, 'Introduction: The Moral Landscape of Unmanned Weapons' (n 3) 6.
56 Kahn (n 24) 3.
57 Kahn (n 24) 2.
58 Kahn (n 24) 2.
59 G. E. M. Anscombe, Mr. Truman's Degree (Pamphlet published by the author 1958) 2.
60 Anscombe, Mr. Truman's Degree (n 59) 5.

contributing to an unjust cause, and accordingly, that the riskless nature of drones "makes them unambiguously good in hands of just combatants."[61] The perspective of these authors is that the notion of innocence is not emptied of moral content, as they maintain "a connection between innocence and the absence of moral culpability"[62] as unjust combatants are perhaps not guilty for war, but they are morally responsible for "fighting such a war."[63] At this point, we shall not go any further in explaining the difference between the classical and revisionist understanding of the moral symmetry of combatants in war, their responsibility for war and the capability of soldiers to know whether or not their war is just, and the implications of these considerations for the basis of the moral justification of killing in war, as it requires a much longer discussion. What we will do, in regards to revisionism, is to explore the compatibility of riskless drone warfare with the revisionist understanding of the moral justification for killing in war. Immediately we can notice that this perspective allows for much more room for drones in war, as the moral basis for killing is not the risk posed by the enemy, but rather the unjust cause the enemy is contributing to. However, there are some problematic implications of riskless warfare even in this approach. If we accept that drone operators on the just side are morally justified in killing enemy combatants because of their contribution to an unjust cause, even if they are not posing any risk or threat, then we must ask ourselves: why limit drone operators only to killing enemy combatants? If contribution to an unjust cause forfeits one's right not to be attacked – i.e., their innocence in war – then all those who contribute to this unjust effort must be legitimate targets of drone strikes. As Anscombe wrote in her protest against Truman being awarded an honorary Oxford degree, "The military strength of a nation includes its whole economic and social strength. Therefore, the distinction between the people engaged in prosecuting the war and the population at large is unreal."[64] If the media, political elites, public figures, wealthy industrialists, rich merchants, and other parts of a society unequivocally support an unjust regime in its pursuit of an unjust cause, why not simply kill all of them? Classical Just War Theory would say that we are not allowed to target them because they are innocent; i.e., they are not posing a threat. Kahn asks the same question when he writes about many social groups that supported Saddam Hussein – "Why not target his bankers or his oil

61 McMahan, 'Foreword' (n 13) 10.

62 Lionel K. McPherson, 'Innocence and Responsibility in War' (2004) 34 *Canadian Journal of Philosophy* 458, 486.

63 McPherson, 'Innocence and Responsibility in War' (n 62) 502.

64 Anscombe, Mr. Truman's Degree (n 59).

resources?"[65] Jeffrey Murphy provides an even more compelling example from World War II, when he opens the possibility that a civilian, "an avid supporter of Hitler's war effort (one who pays taxes gladly, supports warmongering political rallies, etc.)"[66] contributes more to the war effort, and is even more morally guilty, than "the poor, frightened, pacifist frontline soldier who is only where he is because of duress and who intends always to fire over the heads of the enemy."[67] In conclusion, if, as revisionists, we allow just drone operators to kill unjust enemy combatants from the safety and comfort of their air-conditioned modules, we must also allow them to kill all non-combatants who contribute to the unjust cause. Again, hopefully, no reasonable human being would agree.

6 Is There Such a Thing as Riskless War?

The explained reciprocity of risk is one of the fundamental characteristics of war as we know it, an inherent quality of war. Perhaps with the elimination of risk we can no longer speak about the evolution of *war*, as its essential feature is no longer present. Perhaps the process of riskless killing cannot fall under the notion of war, and is better described by some other notion. As Kahn noticed, "without the imposition of mutual risk, warfare is not war at all ... It most resembles police enforcement."[68] Policing implies that one side is justified in its use of force against the other side, a side that is legally (and morally) culpable for something. The guilty side, being a criminal side, has no right to violence and force, not even in self-defense, as it forfeited its right not to be attacked by breaking some law and must be held accountable for its misdeeds. In this case, there is absolutely no need for the police to incur any risk; moreover, complete elimination of risk for the police would represent a perfect situation, as their justification for the application of force and possible killing is based on the criminal behavior of their opponents, not the risk they pose to them. Armed drones would make an ideal weapon for policing. Steinhoff claims, and we agree, that it would "not only be justified but ... also morally quite unproblematic"[69] to use drones and completely eliminate risk in a one-global-state world, against "dangerous, unjust and unjustified criminals ...".[70]

65 Kahn (n 24) 5.
66 Murphy (n 47) 531.
67 Murphy (n 47) 532.
68 Kahn (n 24) 4.
69 Steinhoff (n 25) 207.
70 Steinhoff (n 25) 207.

We shall leave the discussions about the current possibilities of global policing, using military forces for police-like actions, the (il)legitimacy of such actions, and similar topics for another, much more voluminous paper. Steinhoff compares riskless warfare to pest control,[71] and we would add that it also shares more similarity with hunting with modern technology than with war. In this regard, it is quite interesting to notice that the popular MQ-9 Reaper drone is referred to as a 'hunter-killer' system, that allows tracking its 'prey' for extended periods of time, and then killing it from high altitude.

7 Is There a Place for Drones in War?

Our main argument in previous sections of this paper is that the elimination of risk for the drone operator cancels his or her 'license to kill' in war, that in the absence of risk, he or she is no longer morally justified in killing enemies. But we are not claiming that drones are inherently evil or bad. We are not even claiming that there can be no place for sophisticated unmanned armed aerial vehicles in war. What we are claiming is that there is no justified killing in war, as a matter of fact that there is no war, without risk. If we introduce risk into the drone equation, then drones become just as acceptable as cannons or aircraft. As Martin van Creveld said, "War does not begin when some people kill others; instead, it starts at the point where they themselves risk being killed in return",[72] meaning that, in order to use drones in war, we must allow our drone operators to be at risk, to be legitimate targets, regardless of where they are. This would imply that the side using drones must be prepared to recognize the killing of its drone operator as a legitimate act of war, not an act of terrorism. If an operator is a combatant in war, and he most certainly is, he is a legitimate target as long as he is harming; i.e., as long as he is engaged in an attempt to destroy his enemies – in the command module inside of a base, in a bus or taxi driving him from and to work, in his home, his front yard, etc. It does not seem reasonable to expect that the U.S. government, for example, would treat killing a U.S. drone operator in Nevada, on his porch drinking a beer with his wife, as a legitimate act of war, for which the attacker cannot be put to trial as a criminal. Especially if members of his family become collateral damage of the attack. But the same operator that killed an enemy combatant in his home, perhaps injuring his family or neighbors in the process, would not be

71 Steinhoff (n 25) 207.

72 Martin van Creveld, *The Transformation of War* (The Free Press 1991) 110.

considered a criminal, as he killed a legitimate target in war. David Whetham provides a great analogy between two similar situations – a man, a civilian, drives his brother to plant an IED device and thus becomes a legitimate target, or at least acceptable collateral damage, for a drone operator monitoring him from the sky; but are we willing to accept that the husband of a drone operator, driving her to work can be targeted too, or at least treated as acceptable collateral damage?[73] Would we call a hostile drone operator, who targets and kills our own soldiers in our own territory, while playing football or sleeping, a courageous warrior? Not likely. But how can we then call our own drone operators heroes and warriors? We shall conclude with Whetham's wise words – "a norm that works only as long as the other side cannot or will not adopt it doesn't seem to be a very sustainable one, nor does it seem to be a morally correct one on even the most basic notions of moral reciprocity."[74]

8 Conclusion

Drones represent an unprecedented change in the very nature of war, not because they are the stealthiest, the most powerful, or the most lethal weapon in history, but because they eliminate risk entirely for their operators. Throughout history, man has increased the range of his weapons, lowering the risk for their operators; but until now, he never succeeded in completely eliminating risk. If a conflict is created in which one side is unable to pose any risk and is unable to 'reach' its enemies, then a riskless conflict is created – a conflict that cannot be called war. Riskless war is an oxymoron, as war inherently implies mutual risk, and it is precisely this risk that morally justifies the killing of certain people in war – in Walzer's words "You can't kill unless you are prepared to die."[75] If no ordinary[76] enemy citizen is posing a risk or is harming, and no ordinary enemy citizen is responsible for war, then they are all innocent and thus cannot be killed. Therefore, in order to allow armed drones to be used in war, we must either redefine the notion of innocence in the context of Just War Theory and redefine the notion of war itself, or allow drone operators to be legitimate targets, and thus at risk of enemy actions. Drones are definitely

73 David Whetham, 'Drones and Targeted Killing: Angels or Assassins' in Bradley Jay Strawser (ed), *Killing by Remote Control: The Ethics of an Unmanned Military* (OUP 2013) 75.

74 Whetham, 'Drones and Targeted Killing' (n 73) 79.

75 Michael Walzer, *Arguing about War* (YUP 2004) 101.

76 "Ordinary," meaning not a top-tier political decision maker; i.e., all those who do not make the decision to go to war.

here to stay, and we must act quickly, as "riskless warfare may be a prescription for short-term success and long-term disaster."[77]

References

Anscombe, G. E. M., Mr. Truman's Degree (Pamphlet published by the author 1958) 2.

Becker, Jo and Scott Shane, 'Secret 'Kill List' Proves a Test of Obama's Principles and Will' *The New York Times* (New York, 29 May 2012).

Enemark, Christian, 'Unmanned Drones and the Ethics of War' in Fritz Allhoff, Nicholas G. Evans and Adam Henschke (eds), *Routledge Handbook of Ethics and War* (Routledge 2013) 331.

French, Shannon E., The Code of the Warrior: Exploring Warrior Values Past and Present (Rowman and Littlefield 2003).

Grossman, Dave, On Killing: The Psychological Cost of Learning to Kill in War and Society (Back Bay Books 1996).

Guiora, Amos and Jason Shelton, 'Drones and Targeted Killing: Facing the Challenges of Unlimited Executive Power' in George Lucas (ed), *Routledge Handbook of Military Ethics* (Routledge 2015) 369.

Hopkins, Anne, 'The Ethical Debate on Drones', *Ethics Essay Contest* (2017).

Kahn, Paul W., 'The Paradox of Riskless Warfare' (2002) 22 *Philosophy and Public Policy Quarterly* 2.

Manjikian, Mary, *A Typology of Arguments about Drone Ethics* (Strategic Studies Institute and U.S. Army War College Press 2017) 1.

Maslow, Abraham, 'A Theory of Human Motivation' (1943) 50 *Psychological Review* 370.

McMahan, Jeff, 'Foreword' in Bradley Jay Strawser (ed), *Killing by Remote Control: The Ethics of an Unmanned Military* (OUP 2013) ix.

McMahan, Jeff, *Killing in War* (Clarendon Press 2009).

McPherson, Lionel K., 'Innocence and Responsibility in War' (2004) 34 *Canadian Journal of Philosophy* 458.

Murphy, Jeffrey, 'The Killing of the Innocent' (1973) 57 *The Monist* 527.

Nagel, Thomas, *Mortal Questions* (CUP 1979).

Palmer-Fernandez, Gabriel, 'Innocence in War' (2000) 14 *International Journal of Applied Philosophy* 161.

Sparrow, Robert, 'Drones, Courage, and Military Culture' in George Lucas (ed), *Routledge Handbook of Military Ethics* (Routledge 2015) 380.

---

77 Kahn (n 24) 7.

Sparrow, Robert, 'Just Say No to Drones' (2012) 31 *IEEE Technology and Society Magazine* 56.

Sparrow, Robert, 'War without Virtue?' in Bradley Jay Strawser (ed), *Killing by Remote Control: The Ethics of an Unmanned Military* (OUP 2013) 86.

Steinhoff, Uwe, 'Killing Them Safely: Extreme Asymmetry and Its Discontents' in Bradley Jay Strawser (ed), *Killing by Remote Control: The Ethics of an Unmanned Military* (OUP 2013) 197.

Strawser, Bradley Jay, 'Introduction: The Moral Landscape of Unmanned Weapons' in Bradley Jay Strawser (ed), *Killing by Remote Control: The Ethics of an Unmanned Military* (OUP 2013) 4.

Strawser, Bradley Jay, 'Moral Predators: The Duty to Employ Uninhabited Aerial Vehicles' (2010) 9 *Journal of Military Ethics* 342.

van Creveld, Martin, *The Transformation of War* (The Free Press 1991).

Walzer, Michael, *Arguing about War* (YUP 2004).

Walzer, Michael, *Just and Unjust Wars* (4th ed. Basic Books 2006) 145.

Whetham, David, 'Drones and Targeted Killing: Angels or Assassins' in Bradley Jay Strawser (ed), *Killing by Remote Control: The Ethics of an Unmanned Military* (OUP 2013) 75.

Оренд, Брајан, 'Рат' in Драгана Дулић и Бранко Ромчевић (eds), *Етика рата – хрестоматија*, (Факултет безбедности 2010) 269.

Фатић, Александар, 'Савремена технологија ратовања у светлу хришћанског морала: наоржани дронови' in Борислав Гроздић (ed), *Православље и рат* (МЦ Одбрана 2017) 120.

CHAPTER 10

Technology, Justice and the Return of Humanitarian Terrorism

Boris Kashnikov

> I love humanity but … the more I love humanity in general the less I love men in particular … I became an enemy of people the moment they come close to me. But … the more I hated men individually, the more ardent became my love for humanity at large
>
> DOSTOYEVSKY, "*The Possessed*"

1 The Idea of Humanitarian Terrorism[1]

"Humanitarian terrorism" is not a contradiction in terms. Terrorism is humanitarian par excellence. It is the very nature and the very logic of terrorism, which drives it in search humanity.[2] Humanitarian terrorism is, so to say, a mature terrorism, a terrorism of moral standing, striving to inhabit the sphere of universal moral justice. Terrorism is called so, because it is supposed to reach its goals by inflicting fear and trembling on its opponents. The terror becomes immeasurably more profound and all-embracing if it is imposed in the name of God, and terrorists usually believe they act as the messengers of either God or Humanity, or both. It means that the regime of terror must be imposed by moral authority, or someone representing the moral authority. The humanitarian terrorist is the one who is engaged in moralistic violence; more than anything else he needs a lofty humanitarian pedestal. Besides, the precision of terror strikes has a substantial terrorizing effect in its own right. The greatest of all terrors is the terror of almighty God delivering to everyone his or her due. If

1 This research has been carried out in terms of the research project "Applied Ethics" funded by the National Research University "Higher School of Economics".

2 See: Faisal Devji, *The Terrorist in Search of Humanity: Militant Islam and Global Politics* (Columbia University Press 2008).

 | DOI:10.1163/9789004507951_012

we compare two possible terrorisms – a terrorism of indiscriminate attacks on civilians and a terrorism of personalized strikes – the second is much more terrorizing. But precision strikes are in need of advanced technology, affordable only to the few, which is why indiscriminate terrorism more often than not is simply the terrorism of necessity, whilst precision terrorism is a terrorism of choice. In both cases, for a terrorist it is not enough simply to kill the enemy. The killing must be rightful and degrading, preferably precise – that is exactly what makes it terrorizing. The terrorists are not only keen to monopolize the power of moral judgment; they are no less keen to carry on exclusively 'rightful' executions and to do it precisely and scrupulously. In this regard, humanitarian terrorism is the summit of just war theory. Not only the proclaimed course of humanitarian terrorists is perfectly just. The means tend to be almost absolutely proportional and distinctive. The terrorists kill the culpable few, if at all, and terrorize all the rest into submission.

It should come as no surprise that humanitarian terrorism also constitutes the summit of absolute war. When Clausewitz explicated the logic of war as escalation without limit and a transformation into absolute war, he predicted the emergence of terrorism. What makes terrorism different from war is that terrorism is a case of absolute war and absolute war invariably merges into terrorism. Public war is usually waged without any enmity between combatants. On the contrary, it is compatible with respect and even admiration of the foe. Terrorism of indiscriminate attacks is based on enmity, but this is still imperfect, impersonal enmity. Even if a terrorist plants a bomb in a public place, he may wish that the bomb went off without killing anyone, not only because he usually harbors no personal hatred against his enemies, but also because he does not need to kill anyone. He needs to send a message: that he is about to kill and will continue doing so if the message is not apprehended. If it is apprehended without resorting to explosive devices, it is even better. When it comes to the humanitarian terrorist, he wants to kill or maim a particular and definite individual. Hatred, as well as love, raises to its heights only if it is individualized hatred of a particular individual or individuals with proper names and postal address. Absolute war arises when public politics give way and the combatants switch to personal hatred. The personal becomes the political and vice-versa. For this very reason, absolute war knows no compromise or reconciliation. There can be no truce with the damned. The damned must be wiped from the face of earth, like a contagious disease. At this point politics seizes to exist, according to Clausewitz, because politics is all about compromise and negotiations. What remains is pure hatred and enmity, and even if the killings are still carried out quite rationally and consistently, it has little to do with political rationality. It is not an absence of a moral compass which propels absolute war; on the contrary, it is the morality of the absolute uncompromised annihilation of the opponent, which substitutes for the morality of peace and cooperation. Moral indignation is compatible with constrained means and sublime goals. Humanitarian niceties do not make terrorism less 'terroristic'. On the contrary, terroristic absolute war is the logical end to which just war considerations usually drive war.

Strictly speaking, terrorism is a theory and practice of violent action that works by the production of overall terror. By means of a series of well-placed killings, the terrorist transmits a message. As a trueborn child of modernity, the terrorist is engaged in communicative action. The terror must reverberate. The enemy must be cognizant of our murderous zeal; we must know that he knows and he must know that we know that he is terrified. This kind of game-theoretical reverberation only becomes possible with the invention of mass media, the emergence of the autonomous Kantian individual, and democracy. There are thus two sides to terrorism of which we have to be aware. One is an objective factual side. In its factual sense (which existed at all times), terrorism is about systematically inflicting terror on the opponent. But that is not enough for terrorism proper, the terrorism of modernity. The true terror and the true meaning of terrorism may only emerge when the opponent knows that we are truly terrorizing him and we know that he knows that. It only becomes possible when terrorism colonizes the subjective, moral and humanitarian sphere. True terrorism is a subjective, evaluative phenomenon. The full-fledged humanitarian terrorist not only does not conceal, but brags about his subjective (real or faked) terrorizing motives, means, and goals, which are represented as the summit of moral reason. Three things make our subjective mood truly terrifying to others. First is that our motives are seemingly imprudent, from the point of view of the opponent. The motives may even seem irrational or like they stem from some kind of supreme moral rationality, unattainable to ordinary reason. Second, the means must be truly frightful, but not only frightful in the ordinary sense of the term; they must carry on what I would call *terroristic depersonalization*. The means which we employ are humiliating, hubristic, and depersonalizing, in addition to being terrorizing. In fact, when we employ terrorism, we degrade the opponent, so that it is not even just the fear of death, which the victim experiences. It is the fear of degrading and humiliating death. The terrorists are broadcasting a message through their acts of terror that the opponents of the regime are less than human beings and must be subjected to terroristic depersonalization by means of most degrading violence.

> In that register violence aims not only to injure but to degrade and not simply to degrade the immediate victim, but also all those who see in the victim's actions an expression of their own political beliefs.[3]

The third subjective component of terrorism is its goal, also broadcast by means of terror. This is the goal of absolute enmity, of total annihilation of all the culpable individuals without reservation. As Carl Schmitt puts it, such is the logic of a war of pure *justa causa* in the absence of a *justus hostis* (just enemy).[4] It is by presenting this disturbing performance that humanitarian terrorism works. The traditional respect for the enemy does not exist at the level of absolute enmity, where humanitarian terrorism belongs.

2 Jacobin Revolutionary Terrorism

Not only is there no logical contradiction between terrorism and humanitarianism, the original meaning of the term 'terrorism' as well as 'enemy of humanity' was first and foremost humanitarian to the very core. "Terror" was the generic name of the period extending from September 1793 to July 1794, during which the Jacobins made 'terror the order of the day' by suppressing their political opponents. Jacobin rhetoric positioned terrorism as an indispensable mechanism of progress, promoting highly humanistic values of the enlightenment: equality, liberty, fraternity and justice for all. The enemies of the revolution were tarred as the enemies of humanity and were to be crushed completely, without delay. To crush the enemies of humanity, total and absolute war must be waged against them, war unprecedented in human history, simply because that was the greatest, decisive, and final, truly eschatological battle, which would finally eliminate the forces of evil and the enemies of humanity. To be crushed completely, the enemies of humanity should have been not only defeated, but also degraded. Terrorism thus exceeds terror. Human history is rife with terror, but terrorism, especially the humanitarian kind, is the product of modernity. It is not simply about inflicting terror, but inflicting degrading and moralistic terror, meaningful terror, and communicative terror. The revolutionaries were transmitting a message through their deeds, containing statements about their motives, means, and goals. The motives were supposed to be

3 See: Paul Kahn, *Sacred Violence. Torture, Terror and Sovereignty* (The University of Michigan Press 2008).

4 Carl Schmitt, *The 'Nomos' of the Earth in the International Law of the 'Jus Publicum Europaeum'* (Telos Press 2003) 26.

apprehended as rational (totally irrational from the point of view of the reactionaries), the means degrading, and the goals absolute. The reactionaries were supposed to be subjected to the mythologized condition of pre-modernity, the condition of terror and torture (which is also a myth, since modernity is much more violent than pre-modernity). The terrorists acted in accordance with the imposed revolutionary law, which was promulgated as the summit of natural law. The terror itself was promoted by a revolutionary state and was based on a seemingly legal monopoly of violence. But the law was in fact highly improper and simplistic, not to say "sadistic". It allowed violations of many if not all of the formal judicial procedures. "Millions of devils of hell called terrorists have been let loose on the world," observed Edmund Burke at the time. These words are recognizable in the title of a seminal Dostoyevsky novel devoted to Russian terrorists: "The Devils", sometimes translated as "The Possessed". The word 'terrorism' originally referred to actions by a political state of a terroristic political regime, and not to illegal actions of a group of radicals. It is much later that terrorism was perceived above all as an illegal form of activism conducted against a state.

3 Russian Individual Terrorism of the Late 19th to the Early 20th Century

Revolutionaries all over Europe continued the course of French revolutionary terrorism. The only difference was that it was a terrorism of groups of radicals engaged in targeted assassinations of the reactionaries. The most paradigmatic form of this activism was Russian terrorism of groups like Zemlya I Volya (Society of Land and Liberty) and the Narodnaya Volya (People's Will). These two groups were in program and in action terror organizations, which were promoting the transformation of Russian society by the assassination of government officials. Governmental violence was to be met with popular violence, and terror became an integral part of the Russian societal process. The formation of the Socialist-Revolutionary Party in the last decade of the nineteenth century helped to institutionalize assassination as political instrument.[5] In many ways Russian revolutionary terrorism was a replica of French revolutionary terrorism, only the other way around: it was terrorism of small groups fighting the legitimate government. The revolutionaries could not inflict mass

5 See: Robert A. Friedlander, 'The Origins of International Terrorism' in Yonah Alexander and Seymour Maxwell Finger (eds), *Terrorism. Interdisciplinary Perspectives* (McGraw-Hill Book Company 1977).

purges on the elite but they could commit summary executions of the most notorious and vicious functionaries of the state apparatus and paralyze the state. These killings to no small extent were possible due to the technological advancements of the time.

> Another factor, which contributed significantly to the intensification of violence in the empire, was the fact that scientific progress and technical innovations had greatly simplified the production of terrorist's weapons and basic explosive devices.[6]

Among them were dynamite, the revolver, the telegraph, the railroad and aviation. More than that, the drone was already dreamed about as the perfect weapon:

> The fantasies on the subject frequently involved farfetched schemes, including the construction of the flying apparatus to drop explosives in the Winter Palace.[7]

These innovations could render all the giant advantage of the government moot, especially if we take into consideration that outdated considerations of honor prevented the nobles from taking the necessary precautions.

Like their Jacobin brethren, these terrorists were "in search of humanity". Not only did they proclaim the highest moral cause, they restrained themselves to targeted killings only. They were confident in their right of pronouncing death sentences and appropriated the highest of all rights – "the right to humiliate".[8] The killings were indeed causing paralyzing terror among the officials and since the public was very often sympathetic to terrorists, this was also degrading terror. This made the terroristic performance rather theatrical. The terror effect was produced not by fear of death alone. It was mostly the fear of public disgrace and humiliation. The death at the hands of terrorists was a matter of disgrace, not only because the bombs physically and symbolically were mingling ruptured bodies with mud, but also because it was scornfully reminiscent of a death sentence, promulgated by a quasi-legitimate authority.

---

6 Anna Geifman, *Thou Shalt Kill. Revolutionary Terrorism in Russia, 1894–1917* (Princeton University Press 1993) 16.

7 Geifman, *Thou Shalt Kill* (n 5) 17.

8 In Dostoyevsky's novel, one of the terrorists mentions in passing that the highest revolutionary right is the right to humiliate. See Fyodor Dostoyevsky, *The Possessed. The Devils.* Translated by Constance Garnett (The Floating Press 2011).

It was the greatest factor of terror and highly humanitarian terror not only from the point of view of goals, but means also. One of the terrorists, Nikolay Morozov wrote:

> The massive revolutionary movements, where people fight each other bluntly, where people slaughter their own children, at the time when the enemies are looking at their deaths, from the safe havens, – it substitutes by a series of separate, but always efficient and well targeted political assassinations. It executes only those who are truly guilty of the continuous evil. Terrorist Revolution should be regarded as the most just of all possible revolutions.[9]

The humanitarian constraints were taken seriously, even to the extent of putting the success of the operation in danger. At the same time, the revolutionaries were still the same 'devils' of the French revolutionary terrorism, and it was Dostoevsky who clearly depicted the demoniac nature of this kind of humanitarian activism. The most notorious of the moral drawbacks of the terrorists was a total disregard for human life. In "The Devils" Dostoyevsky depicted the murder of the student Shakhov by the terrorists. The murder was carried out on a personal whim of the head of the group and for no other reason but to bind the rest of the group with blood. Dostoyevsky made it clear, that the terrorists had no moral right to kill. They did not represent anyone and were driven by vicious spite. It was only their subjective and immoral hubris which was propelling their activity. They did not even have any quasi legitimacy of revolutionary justice behind them, as was the case with the Jacobins, and there are clear indications that many revolutionaries felt some kind of remorse, since the killings they were perpetrating were still nothing but murders. This moral predicament was resolved to some extent by the conception of redemption, which revolutionaries developed as part of their ethical code. Since the revolutionaries were supposed eventually to fall in the struggle, they are morally redeemed by the very fact of their self-sacrifice.

9 Nikolay Morozov, *Terroristicheskaya Borba* (London: Russkaya Tipografia 1880) 7–8. It is interesting to admit the usage of the term "justice". It was only in the lexicon of terrorists that this word was used in relation to violence in Russia.

4 American Killer Drones Campaign

American drone warfare should be regarded as a clear-cut case of humanitarian terrorism. It continues the legacy of French revolutionary terrorism and is a product of modernity. It blends the features of French and Russian revolutionary terrorisms, but drops both: the conception of redemption of the Russian terrorism and the quasi-legitimacy of the French terrorism.[10] Like French revolutionary terrorism, it is a state terrorism. Like Russian individual terrorism, it is a terrorism of targeted executions. Drones are weapons that can find and strike a single target, often a single individual, via remote control. The small lethal machine can accomplish what the traditional military operation cannot and it is a dream weapon of terror. The first known killing by armed drones occurred in November 2001, when a Predator targeted Mohammed Atef, a top al-Qaeda military commander, in Afghanistan. Later, the drone campaign was made the linchpin of the Obama administration's counterterrorism strategy in Central Asia. Anyone who is familiar with the history of terrorism, cannot help noticing its striking similarities with revolutionary terrorism of the past. Nick Hewlett holds:

> Drone warfare is one of the latest examples of state terrorism, where 'suspected terrorists' are killed in some cases without evidence that they have in fact engaged in violent acts, let alone been put on trial; moreover, unknown associates of those people are killed at the same time in what is euphemistically termed 'collateral damage', meaning deaths of – by any definition – innocent men, women and children.[11]

Civilian casualties in such precision strikes may be rather significant, but even if the precision was perfect, it is still terrorism and a case of absolute war. Two features make this terrorism humanitarian. First, it presumably is based on a self-proclaimed just cause, which has very little to do with what we ordinary understand by self-defense. Even if it is self-defense, it is self-defense of America as an exceptional power, the guarantor of the sense of world order, assured of its propriety. The American mission is about bringing the promise of democracy to the whole world. In this vein, America continues the Enlightenment mission of the French revolution.

10 I mean the legitimacy in terms of Westphalian doctrine.

11 Nick Hewlett, *Blood and Progress. Violence in Pursuit of Emancipation* (Edinburg University Press 2016) 147.

Targeted killings are not only the summit of asymmetric, casualty-free warfare (for the powerful, of course). The pilots of the drones leveling the attacks on the targets beneath them do not suffer any personal danger and are more executioners than they are military pilots. They are assassins, and the violence they prosecute is not warfare. Drone terrorism is a paradigmatic terrorism growing out of drone warfare. War may only be considered as such if it contains at least some risk of life and limb for the perpetrators, at least some chivalry. This war cannot be victorious, not because it cannot be successful, but because it is not a war. Like the Jacobin terrorism, this terrorism is based on the presumed legitimacy of the ethical state. However, there is even less due process than in the case of French revolutionary justice, and no moral right to pronounce death sentences on particular individuals. Like Russian revolutionary terrorism, this terrorism is engaged in assassinations, not legal executions. This drone terrorism is a unique combination of subjective motives, means, and goals. It brings together the perception of this set by the victims and its reproduction by the agents of terrorism. The motives of this terrorism are unclear to the victims and are regarded by others as unreasonable revengeful cruelty or sadism. These motives are the display of sovereign hubris on the part of America in its goal of global sovereignty. The means are degrading, depersonalizing, and humiliating, especially given the traditional code of honor of the people against whom the terror war is waged. The supposed terrorists are chased like wild animals and annihilated like poisonous insects, and that is the most important message. The goals are the goals of absolute enmity and perpetual war. I may agree with Ross:

> The War on Terror is formulated as a potentially endless struggle against an infinitely extended enemy, that permeates all borders, and that may inhabit any sphere. The new situation is essentially militarized, the sovereignty of individual states less important than a coordinated and integrated system of "security." Such a system may be centralized in the Unites States, but nevertheless implies the creation of planetary security arrangements that transcend any particular state. The development of such a system of security produces its own means, logic and autonomy, unlimited by the concept of state sovereignty.[12]

It was made evident that the goals are not to be compromised; as is usually the case in any interstate war, the goal is the complete elimination of the

12 Daniel Ross, *Violent Democracy* (CUP 2004) 2.

opponent. As a result, those living under drones have to face the constant worry that a deadly strike may be fired at any moment, and the knowledge that they are powerless. In addition, the US practice of striking one area multiple times, and evidence that it has killed rescuers, makes both community members and humanitarian workers afraid or unwilling to assist injured victims. Some community members shy away from gathering in groups, including important tribal dispute resolution bodies, out of feat that they may attract the attention of drone operators.[13]

The humanitarian terrorism in any of its three incarnations is immoral, not because it is not sufficiently just, but because it is absolute war. But our third paradigmatic case reaches the summit of immorality possible for humanitarian terrorism. It triggers lawlessness and in the long run becomes the norm rather than an exception. Kreps and Kaag draw an important distinction:

> Advanced technology has allowed states to limit the unintended damage of targeted violence, but the ability to undertake more precise, targeted strikes should not be confused with the determination of legal or ethical legitimacy.[14]

Legal and ethical legitimacy is exactly what is missing in any act of terrorism, including those with the help of UAVs. It devalues the people who are subject to the attacks, denying them their human dignity. The corresponding rhetoric is telling. For example, in 2001, President George W. Bush declared that "I have faith in our military. And we have got a job to do – just like the farmers and ranchers and business owners and factory workers have a job to do … we will rid the world of evil doers."[15] The eradication of evil from the world is exactly the vague and terrifying goal characteristic of terrorism. Even the nuclear bombing of Hiroshima was not exactly terrorism, because the motivation was to win the war, not to obliterate evil and it was not, of course, based on personal enmity. For the French, Russian, and contemporary American terrorists, it is exactly the eradication of evil, represented by individuals – so to say, possessed by evil – which drives them and that is a major character trait of absolute war. The war of drones undermines the possibility of compromise and postulates itself as perpetual war. The list of moral drawbacks may be continued. In fact,

---

13 See: Noam Chomsky and Andre Vlitchek, *On Western Terrorism. From Hiroshima to Drone Warfare* (Pluto Press 2017).

14 Sarah Kreps and John Kaag, 'Unmanned Aerial Vehicles in Contemporary Conflict. A Legal and Ethical Analysis' (2012) 44 (2) *Polity* 276, DOI: 10.1057/pol.2012.2.

15 Kreps and Kaag, 'Unmanned Aerial Vehicles' (n 13) 277.

all the ills of absolute enmity are also in place for this kind of drone warfare, because it is absolute war. It is an absolute war and as such deserves all the curses and maledictions people can pour out. Besides, American drone warfare is a unique case of humanitarian terrorism without redemption. It arouses resentment, which tends to multiply the number of determined terrorists, rather than reduce their number. The way terrorism is fought produces more future terrorists than it is able to eliminate. Reconciliation and compromise become less and less attainable. This kind of terrorism more than anything else is a case of absolute war.

5 Conclusion: The Advancement of Military Technology and the Clash of Humanitarian Terrorisms

Humanitarian terrorism is morally wrong not because it is humanitarian, but because it is terrorism. I will outline three major moral drawbacks of humanitarian terrorism. First and foremost, it is a case of absolute war. It is morally problematic for the same reason the use of assassins during war should be avoided. Kant holds that it must be avoided because it "makes mutual confidence in the subsequent peace impossible".[16] Strictly speaking, the use of assassins or targeted killing drags us into the quagmire of absolute war. If war is not firmly moored to political sphere, it can be easily blown out of proportion and never be resolved by peace negotiations. Humanitarian terrorism plunges the world into a state of perpetual war and it is destructive, since it does not lead to compromise and reconciliation. A conventional, modernistic, state-centered war is an enterprise resembling a chess game. It could be resolved by political maneuver rather than killing. Even a straightforward terrorism of impersonal attacks is morally superior in a way, whatever the number of victims, because it does not presuppose personal hatred. We shift away from the concept of human rights and due process towards the self-justification of violent means. In the concept of humanitarian terrorism, liberal states are discovering a new potentiality for violence and are granting themselves a new right to act on it.

Secondly, we have to bear in mind that enmity is not only a socially destructive feeling, but also a resourceful and creative feeling. It is capable of professing the normative conceptions which suit its purpose and serve as justifications, by perpetrating war without end. In this sense, the particular theories of

16 For Kant this is one of the preliminary articles for perpetual peace among states. See Immanuel Kant, *To perpetual peace: a philosophical sketch* (Hackett Publishing, 2003).

justice and even just war theory in general, may be regarded as the product of vicious spite, more than anything else. The result is the creation of what Marx called 'false consciousness', the consciousness serving as the justification of war and proclaiming it as objectively valid. The just war theory itself may be stemming from 'false consciousness'. It serves no other reason but that of perpetrating war in global terms and by means of creating the myth of the just war. Each and every war in particular, in the same vein, creates its own special justificatory myth about our unalienable right to kill and the existence of an inherently just cause for doing so. Justice of war both in general and in particular is a myth supported by nothing else but pathological atavisms of human enmity. Thirdly, humanitarian terrorism, although the summit of the just war, is still terrorism. In this capacity it is totally deprived of all the major prerogatives of war, especially of those which makes it, in a Kantian sense, 'sublime'.[17] At the level of absolute war, or – which is the same – humanitarian terrorism, war links with its less honorable brethren: terrorism, genocide and criminal violence. The distinctive features and birthmarks of terrorism are the lack of chivalry, valor and the impossibility of victory. There can be no victorious terrorism, as there can be no victorious genocide, simply because we do not use this term to qualify the base deeds, as with murder. War presupposes personal risk, courage, and honor, and that makes it possibly victorious. Although terrorists may to a certain extent demonstrate at least some military virtues, the level hardly meets the necessary threshold. Terrorism, especially a humanitarian one, is hallmarked without reservation as a murder. More than that, it is the most disgusting murder, which Leo Tolstoy qualified as the murder in cold blood of a particular defenseless individual. In the case that humanitarian terrorism substitutes for war proper and becomes "the only game in town", humanity will be immeasurably degraded.

There is a possibility that the further transformation of war will leave us with no alternative to humanitarian (more or less) terrorism. In this case, future wars will be nothing but the clash of terrorisms. We have to understand that humanitarian terrorism is a matter of degree. In the same way that there can be more or less terrorism, there can be more or less humanitarianism, or justice. The complete humanitarian terrorism is affordable only to the few and only to the overdogs of contemporary asymmetric warfare. In the long run, we may predict the emergence of military technology, which will enable the overdogs to wipe from the face of earth each and every particular individual

17 In the "Critique of Judgment" Kant mentions that war is often sublime activity. This qualification is hardly applicable to terrorism, even if it is humanitarian.

they do not want. Perhaps it will be done by dialing his or her genetic code on a special keyboard and pressing a button. The underdogs will be left, and already are left, with no alternative but to respond in kind. The only option left to them will be to resort to some less humanitarian and more straightforward terrorism of indiscriminate attacks on the civilians of the opposing side. In this case, their actions should be regarded as a case of 'supreme emergency'[18] and thus perfectly just. The vicious circle of humanitarian terrorisms may so arise. Absolute war turns into the global clash of terrorisms.

References

Chomsky, Noam and Andre Vltchek, *On Western Terrorism. From Hiroshima to Drone Warfare* (Pluto Press 2017).

Devji, Faisal, *The Terrorist in Search of Humanity: Militant Islam and Global Politics* (Columbia University Press 2008).

Dostoyevsky, Fyodor, *The Possessed. The Devils*. Translated by Constance Garnett (The Floating Press 2011).

Friedlander, Robert A, 'The Origins of International Terrorism' in Yonah Alexander and Seymour Maxwell Finger (eds), *Terrorism. Interdisciplinary Perspectives* (McGraw-Hill Book Company 1977).

Geifman, Anna, *Thou Shalt Kill. Revolutionary Terrorism in Russia, 1894–1917* (Princeton University Press 1993).

Hewlett, Nick, *Blood and Progress. Violence in Pursuit of Emancipation* (Edinburg University Press 2016).

Kahn, Paul, *Sacred Violence. Torture, Terror and Sovereignty* (The University of Michigan Press 2008).

Kant, Immanuel, *To perpetual peace: a philosophical sketch* (Hackett Publishing, 2003).

Kreps, Sarah and , JohnKaag , 'Unmanned Aerial Vehicles in Contemporary Conflict. A Legal and Ethical Analysis' (2012) 44 (2) *Polity* 276, DOI: 10.1057/pol.2012.2.

Morozov, Nikolay, *Terroristicheskaya Borba* (Russkaya Tipografia, London 1880).

Ross, Daniel, *Violent Democracy* (CUP 2004).

Schmitt,Carl, *The 'Nomos' of the Earth in the International Law of the 'Jus Publicum Europaeum'* (Telos Press 2003).

Walzer, Michael, *Just and Unjust Wars* (3rd edn Basic Books, 2000).

18 See Michael Walzer, *Just and Unjust Wars* (3rd edn Basic Books, 2000). According to Walzer, a 'supreme emergency', allows a state to drop all moral constraints on means. The terrorists may follow this advice. In fact, terrorism is always the case of supreme emergency.

PART 4

Enhancement

CHAPTER 11

The Enhanced Soldier: Ethical Issues

Gérard de Boisboissel

1 Introduction

Probably almost as old as humanity is the desire for a soldier to be able to exceed his biological limits or to rise above his condition as a mere mortal. He dreams of breaking free from his physical and physiological limits, by an improvement of his equipment, advanced training, a strong psychological action to increase his aggressiveness and his moral force, and by the acquisition of an *esprit de corps* that can be fed by an ideological or religious background.

This aspiration to improvement also takes on a new dimension if we consider that war is becoming so complicated and fast that soldiers in their unchanged state cannot adequately keep up with its pace and demands, as discussed by Professor Ryan Tonkens.[1]

At the same time, the topic of human performance enhancement is now becoming widespread, because of the emergence of new technologies that can be directly applied to the man and not just to his armament or his combat tactics, as was done in the past. This can be explained by recent advances in research, particularly in the fields of Nanotechnologies, Biotechnologies, Informatics, and Cognitive Sciences (NBIC), as well as advances in the medical and pharmaceutical sectors and the neurosciences.[2]

Indeed, Nanotechnology offers techniques operating at the atomic or molecular level, Biotechnology can rely on epigenetics that studies the impact of the environment on the functioning of cells, Computer Science will offer new ways of processing information such as the quantum computer or artificial intelligence (AI), and the cognitive sciences aim at fully understand the functioning of the human brain.

In a desire to anticipate the different military challenges and issues posed by the appearance of these new technologies and their effect on humans, the

1 Ryan Tonkens, 'Morally Enhanced soldiers: Beyond Military Necessity', in Jai Galliott and Mianna Lotz (eds), *Super Soldiers: The Ethical, Legal and Social Implications* (*Emerging Technologies, Ethics and International Affairs*) (Ashgate, Farnham, United Kingdom 2015).

2 Pierre-Yves Cusset, 'Améliorer les capacités humaines: actualité d'un vieux rêve' (2015) 45 *DSI Hors-série Le soldat augmenté, repousser les limites pour s'adapter*, Décembre 2015, 8.

 | DOI:10.1163/9789004507951_013

CREC Saint-Cyr started a research program on the "enhanced soldier" in 2015, with the support of military officials, the Defense Health Service, Defense companies, and researchers. It published a book in French on "Le soldat augmenté" in December 2017, and is currently continuing its researches by focusing on finer themes.[3] Ethics is one of them, and in 2018 the CREC requested the support of EuroIsme, in order to develop a common European position about ethical questions on this subject, which will become a major stake of the society.

An international conference has been organized in Paris by the CReC Saint-Cyr and EuroIsme on the 16th October 2019 on the theme "Enhancing soldiers: a European ethical approach". The proceedings of the conference have been published and are available at https://www.euroisme.eu/index.php/en/publications/other-publications. This publication has enriched the work carried out on the subject by the France's Defence Ethics Committee, created in 2020.

This article attempts to present a summary of some of the issues already addressed by the previous developments that the CREC has performed, and list the major ethical issues that are still to be addressed in the context of the work to be done with EuroIsme.

2 How to Translate Major Issues Raised by Enhancement into Questions?

Several fundamental questions arise when we talk about enhancement:

1. Which enhancement methods can be made available or even imposed on a combatant: Is there an ethics of means?
2. Straightforwardly, as the soldier may risk his life in the extreme cases he can be confronted with, would it be permissible to impose potential medical or sociological effects on his person, through the use of augmentation procedures, if in return it reduces the operational risks or provides greater operational efficiency? Is there an ethics of military necessity?
3. Until now, the grandeur of the military profession has consisted in a soldier accepting risk to his life and putting himself in danger to protect the Nation. With the possibility of enhancement, a new question is raised about potentially accepting a measured risk to his health, within the framework that the enhancement can bring a significant advantage and a better operational efficiency. Can we move from an ethics of the sacrifice of one's life to an ethics of the sacrifice of one's health for a soldier?

3 Please contact Gérard de Boisboissel for more details about this program: gerard.de-boisboissel@st-cyr.terre-net.defense.gouv.fr.

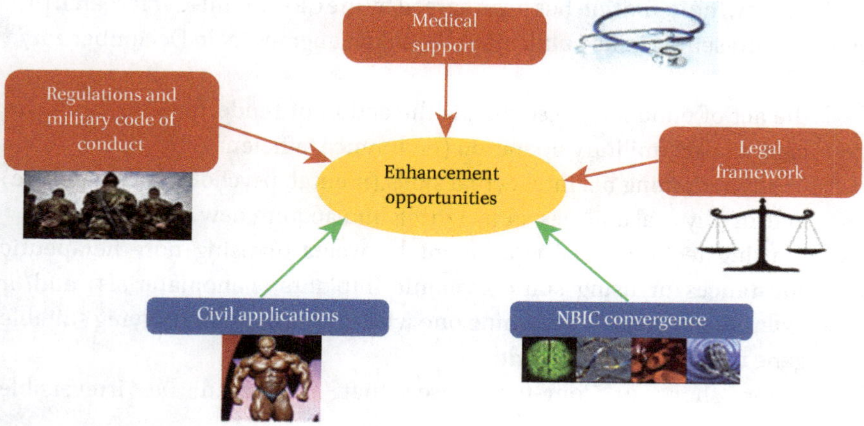

FIGURE 11.1 Enhancement and Constraints

Enhancement opportunities for a combatant are also to be considered in a broader context than that of the individual himself. Indeed, if the possibilities offered by new societal uses and civilian applications are in full development, driven by the new NBIC technologies and their convergence, they must be filtered through the various normative and legal constraints imposed by the medical, civil, and military worlds.

Figure 11.1 below illustrates various enhancement opportunities and their related constraints that should be considered before approval.

Eventually, we may then foresee an imperative to write a Code of Soldier Enhancement, based on the Code of Ethics and Behaviour in the military profession, in order to accompany and guide enhanced soldiers and military leaders.

In very practical terms, how should human performance enhancement be used in a way that enhances capability while still respecting the ethical and legal implications that stem from French military traditions and the respect of our nations' rules and regulations in terms of the demanding profession of a soldier?

To do that, we will need to define and propose rules for potential developments where there are lines that must not be crossed.

3 Definition of an Enhanced Soldier

But what do we mean by enhancing a soldier?

The following definition has been agreed by the CREC Saint-Cyr research program and presented in its publication "Le soldat augmenté" in December 2017.[4]

> the act of enhancing a soldier, is the action of rendering him more efficient in each military operation (endurance, efficiency) by:
> strengthening his intellectual skills (mental, psychological, cognitive) and/or physical abilities, or by letting him acquire new ones;
> using technological equipment he wears or using non-therapeutic substances or using static dynamic implants (nanomaterials) and/or external prostheses, becoming one with his body, or by applying suitable gene therapeutic treatment;
> for short or long-term use, that can even be irreversible (anthropotechnics).

Furthermore, any enhancement should in theory be agreed upon without any negative physiological impact on the soldier.

The definition given above is intentionally broad in scope and unrestrictive to encompass enhanced performance derived from NBICs and technological equipment worn by the combatant. It determines various enhancement possibilities following two key aspects:

> The first one relates to the enhancement of the soldier by the equipment worn by him (non-invasive); the second relates to enhancing the soldier with various means that have a direct impact on the human body, with reversible or irreversible consequences (invasive).

This definition must be passed through the prism of acceptability by the armed forces, because the latter guarantee the respect of human rights and therefore the rights of their own fighters, but also are prescribers of behaviours and uses that are reference models for the entire society.

Ethical guidelines stemming from this definition are developed hereafter, derived from previous work done by the CREC Saint-Cyr.

We will now consider the different ethical questions raised by the increase in performance of the soldier, by addressing them through various approaches centered on (1) the individual, (2) the new societal practices, (3) the social and

4 'Le soldat augmenté – Les besoins et les perspectives de l'augmentation des capacités du combattant' (2017) *Les cahiers de la Revue de la Défense Nationale* (Décembre 2017) <https://iatranshumanisme.com/2018/02/28/le-soldat-augmente-cahier-de-la-rdn/> accessed 22 March 2020.

military environmental factors to consider, (4) the roles and responsibilities and more widely (5) the soldier's place in the military systems of the future.

4 Section 1: On the Individual Level

4.1 *Recruiting Soldiers*

As an introductory remark, we should bear in mind that the options offered in enhancing the performance of an individual arise as soon as he embraces the military profession (recruitment, selection process), throughout his career (depending on the positions held and primarily during military operations), healing potential injuries associated with possible enhancements, and on his return to civilian life (eventual after-effects, psycho-social support, family reintegration).

Moreover, before knocking at the door of the recruitment office, the young soldier is a boy or a girl with a civil society background having often adapted to its habits.

In this regard, we should consider the various stages contributing to enhancement: at the initial recruitment stage, when recruiting for a specific mission, during operations, fitting back to civilian life, etc.

If the prohibition of discrimination and the principle of equality must be respected when recruiting soldiers, objective factors may lead to a legal differentiation: the sex of the person, the specific operational needs and the aptitude to exercise them; thus, the physical or intellectual level desired for the selection. What happens to these rules once we introduce the notion of possible enhancement?

Professor Henri Hude has already addressed this topic.[5] According to him, if enhancement is taken into account in the recruitment process, it necessarily requires the recruiters to choose the "future best", without knowing who can really become such, nor who will be able to remain such, or whether those who could have become such with specific techniques will be the same ones who could have become such with other techniques. In a word, any objective rule may disappear and we risk being thrown into complete arbitrariness, at the very moment when these techniques will be able to considerably increase natural inequality.

To go further, extra study is nonetheless required through a debate on:

5 Henri Hude, 'Quelle éthique du recrutement?' (2015) 45 *DSI Hors-série Le soldat augmenté, repousser les limites pour s'adapter*, Décembre 2015, 84.

- The intangible principle for selection by the Armed Forces has always involved physical fitness. However, even if a prosthesis won't fix a disability but is only intended to offset such ailments, can the same be said of irreversible enhancement techniques such as anthropotechnics? This technique raises the question whether individuals having made changes to their bodies can join the army. For instance, there is a growing trend practiced by some Asians in lengthening their legs to improve their aesthetic appearance. Undergoing such an operation would enable them to pass selection procedures which they would otherwise have failed, notably in meeting minimum size limits. If the frailty of this type of surgery is currently unacceptable for military operations, it is worth mentioning that certain practices are irreversible and severely disrupt the body. Yet, such practices are not considered as affecting a candidate's aptitude (transgender surgery, for instance). Accordingly, will the Armies be able to detect physical changes and discriminate between the acceptable and unacceptable?
- Normal recruitment procedures may well have to be reviewed with an upward adjustment of the current SIGYCOP selection process.[6] Would simple eye operations increasing visual acuity to 12/10th become the norm for selected special units? Note that some elite military units throughout the world already seem to be practicing unnecessary medical enhancements.
- Extensive genetic testing to avoid the development of certain pathologies, excluding soldiers' injuries (e.g. cancer). If testing is currently prohibited by French law, notably due to its discriminatory nature, it is nonetheless authorised on the human embryo for detecting specific anomalies. Considering the great ease in performing genetic tests, there is little doubt that significant public pressure will be made to obtain such tests. There is also a growing tendency in accepting the detection of certain pathologies that will prevent access to certain professions (allergies, claustrophobia, etc.) or pose serious medical risks (the risk of stroke or heart attack). Consequently, will an army doctor reject a soldier attempting to join the forces, alleging that his or her genome indicates a 60% risk of developing cancer before the age of 50?
- Legal issue: As of now, the medical and biographical questionnaire requested in the first stage of the selection process is not enforceable

6 SIGYCOP is a medical profile determining whether a candidate has the capacity of joining the French Army.

by law. Yet individuals can very well conceal several pathologies and/or risks which could adversely affect the recruiting body. Such is the case, for instance, with the police where, once a candidate has been selected, they cannot renege on the agreement. Do we need further legislation on the matter?

It should be noted that enhancing performance does not call for the revocation of existing medical fitness standards, as the army does not expect every individual to meet military requisites. It selects those it deems fit, following well established State norms.

It should also be noted that military doctors do not take any risks nowadays. Their standpoint, however, rests on the crisis level a nation finds itself in. This may very well change under exceptional circumstances (preparing for a general mobilisation, for example, just as the Germans did during the end of the Second World War with the *Volksstum* with recruitment procedures ignoring the age limits and the usual standards of medical profile to join the German army).

4.2 *Enhancement Acceptance*

When affected by enhancement, the respect of a soldier's fundamental rights is governed by a wide-ranging and protective legal corpus requiring his voluntary and free consent.[7]

If the individual agrees to risk his life in the difficult and demanding profession of soldier, the military institution in exchange undertakes to respect him as he is, namely in the dignity of his integrity.

Therefore, no medical act nor treatment cannot be practiced without the free and enlightened consent of a person, which may be withdrawn at any time.

Therefore, questions that can be posed thereon touch on the soldier's acceptance of enhancement, given that his or her rights should be respected:

- Must it necessarily be done on a one-to-one basis, the decision being made by the person him- or herself?
- Could it potentially be done collectively, the decision being made by a military leader in the collective best interest or in the interest of the mission?

7 Sandrine Turgis, 'L'augmentation du soldat à la croisée des droits de l'homme et du droit des conflits armés' (2017) Les cahiers de la Revue de la Défense Nationale (Décembre 2017) 171 <https://iatranshumanisme.com/2018/02/28/le-soldat-augmente-cahier-de-la-rdn/> accessed 22 March 2020.

- Can a proposal be made, or can an order be given by a military leader with prior consent from the medical corps, where extreme or exceptional circumstances require such?

To answer these questions, we have to keep in mind that there are differences between civilian and military ethical frameworks. Soldiers do not have the opportunity to disobey orders, unless they do not respect International Humanitarian Law.

Consent is not always adapted to the military world. The safety of soldiers goes through that of their fellow soldiers. A moral reason may justify not resorting to the soldier's consent,[8] for if a soldier refuses to be enhanced, it then may become a risk for all.

The example of the vaccine is therefore revealing, as it points out the necessity of maximum vaccination of soldiers to ensure the success of the mission in the long term. Let us remember that in the colonial era of the 19th and 20th centuries, soldiers died far more often from diseases than from war. And a sick soldier drastically reduces the operational efficiency of his unit.

We can mention here the individual responsibility to the service of the military community.

A red line could be that, subject to the respect for the inviolability of human dignity, the soldier must accept enhancements for the good of all if the success of the mission is at stake – as long as this doesn't affect the discerning abilities of the fighter and preserves his moral integrity.[9]

5 Section 2: New Societal Practices

5.1 *Societal Practices*

The perception by civil society of enhancement techniques is currently variable and contradictory. Sport is eloquent in this respect. Let's take the example of the Tour de France, an internationally renowned competition, followed by millions of viewers, and where cyclists are asked to eschew any doping methods: doping is of course forbidden, and the risks are enormous for those who get caught. Nevertheless, despite the Elimination of Doping in Sport established under Article 17 of the Convention of the Council of Europe in 1989, the Tour de France is a show that requires more and more superhuman efforts for the cyclists to draw the attention of the target audience, and that asks them to

8 Jean-François Caron, *Théorie du super soldat: La moralité des technologies d'augmentation dans l'armée* (Presses de l'Université Laval 2018) 102.

9 Caron, *Théorie du super soldat* (n 8) 76, 85.

cross several mountain passes classified out of category in the same day. There is a hypocrisy that pushes cyclists to surpass themselves by all means if they want to stay in the race.

The study done by Christine Thoër and Michèle Robitaille[10] indicates that for young students and workers, psycho-stimulant drugs are seen as effective products and their use to improve performance is considered legitimate as it is aimed at academic or professional success.

But the soldier influenced by his education, his environment, or his studies and who puts himself at the service of his country is above all a citizen, and is part of this community of individuals which constitutes the civil world.

Therefore, it appears that ethical principles should be applied differently in the army and in civil society. We already have examples of these. In civil society, differentiating diverse kinds of enhancement depending on gender will prevail, even if pregnancy must be preserved and protected. A growing and lucrative market for the compulsory treatment of potential pathological risks (within the framework of predictive medicine) is about to come, and so-called comfort enhancement techniques will invade our common life. To illustrate this last point, the use of anabolic steroids to acquire muscular mass is now a frequent practice within the civilian world. Albeit available only with a medical prescription, they can be easily obtained.

How will the Armies have to position themselves? Many questions can be raised on the matter:

- The tolerance of certain practices in the civilian sector (and not their acceptance) is contrary to military practice. For example, many students today take drugs before exams to boost their cognitive and physical performance. Those same students who then become soldiers will not understand why doping will be prohibited when facing danger and where their life is at a risk, while in the past they could take drugs to improve their performance on simple exams.
- NBICs and the transhumanist movement will encourage the Armed Forces to work towards the superhuman soldier, by finding the highest potential to transcend his current natural state and surpass his innate limits. It follows that, shaped by individual interests, a substantial pressure from civil society will arise.

10 Christine Thoër et Michèle Robitaille, 'Utiliser des médicaments stimulants pour améliorer sa performance: usages et discours de jeunes adultes québécois' 10 (2) *Drogues, santé et société* 143 <https://doi.org/10.7202/1013481ar> accessed 22 March 2020.

It should be ensured for the Armies to be prescribers of exemplary behaviours, by defining their enhancement policy in a clear way and on simple bases comprehensible to all.

For this purpose, it is illusory to believe that armies will be able to ignore such behaviours in the military units. The answer goes through a reinforced education on this subject, with the help of the military medical world, specific training of the officers, and a constant monitoring of the soldier on the field.

6 Section 3: Factors to Consider

Recognising the temptation for enhancement in the minds of the population due to its current use in society, the question arises how it will then fit into the social environment, subject however to easily accessible enhancement techniques.

6.1 *Social Environment*

- There could be a trend for enhancing the highest potentials (an Anglo-Saxon vision that favours elitism or an Asian vision that encourages the individual to stand out from the others) or for evening out differences by enhancing average performers (a more egalitarian Western view, such as in France). In the military world where an *esprit de corps* is prevalent, each army and even each corps will have to define what is to be favoured.
- A soldier might start to believe that: "if I'm not enhanced, I'll be excluded from the group. I must therefore be enhanced to become part of it." This will be even more apparent as collective practices will grow under the pressure of members of the group, who will no doubt exercise an influence on their comrades. Such a case has already happened, when an American soldier, whose body was intolerant of Red Bull and therefore rejected it, went to see his platoon leader, indicating that he could not go on a mission because he was not enhanced by Red Bull as his comrades were. Of course, there is an educational role that the commander must here ensure: to reassure.
- Military units have a natural tendency for some form of elitism in their military training. Will an enhanced or non-enhanced soldier be discriminated against during his life of service? This will be the case in units requiring utmost combatant efficiency where soldiers' capacities may falter, notably with age.

6.2 *Military Environment*

The enhancement of a soldier's performance is the result of operational interests. The degrees of danger in a military framework mean that enhancements must be made in accordance with (i) operational efficiency criteria and (ii) security norms. The enhancement activation procedure will then depend on a full range of contextual factors. Let us cite three examples:

- Enhancement through the absorption of doping substances to face long-lasting, serious threats (a pill for alleviating thirst, avoiding the need to sleep) – and thus fulfil a given military mission – even though the risks of absorbing such substances are far from neutral.
- A prerequisite for enhancement applied to the entire group (non-discriminatory) in that it's a last resort for protection against imminent enemy threats (e.g. chemical threats).
- The principle of the soldier in all-out war: "In any case, with little hope of survival, I may well get some enhancement and thus increase my chances for survival in the heat of battle; never mind the mid or long-term medical consequences".

An overall conceptual approach is illustrated in Figure 11.2 below. It intends to describe the decision-making process of taking a pharmacological substance in order to enhance the performance of a soldier in operation.

Globally, the decision-making process takes into account several levels of decision-making which must all be validated, each one participating in the global decision through a certain percentage symbolically called here Δ:

1. At the very beginning of this process, political authorities should have validated research on enhancement techniques and agreed whether potential uses comply with national and international regulations. They are the initiators of potential research on performance enhancements of the fighter.
2. Then the military command intervenes, which has to consider upstream the opportunities of enhancement according to the overall operational situation. For example, a proven chemical risk may imply the agreement by the Army Staff of a potential substance intake that protects the soldier against such attacks. And if the mission must be accomplished by any means (such as the battle of Verdun in WW1), the soldiers must be sustained by all possible means. But this same Army Staff must have previously agreed in principle to the use of pharmacological substances, in conjunction with the Army Health Service and the legal authorities. This, in order to assess all risks to the soldier, such as addiction, side effects, potential long-term risks, and compliance with legislation.

These two previous steps of the decision-making process are unavoidable as they are the official agreements of the higher authorities. They are basically taken upstream, and cannot be taken in the course of the military action. Nevertheless, two steps remain.

In the diagram described below, the decision "au contact/at the front line" is taken by the tactical leader, at the level of the section or the company.

3. Then comes the decision-making part of the military tactical leader, the penultimate part of the decision-making process.

First of all, his role is to take into account all the contextual elements of the situation, in particular the level of danger to which the military unit is exposed, the intensity of the combat in progress, the environment and the associated risks (open field position, temperature etc.), as well as the rules of engagement to respect. This perception of the environment must be completed by some indicators that the tactical leader will consider, such as the level of fatigue of his unit, its level of stress, external factors such as chemical aggression, etc. Once these contextual elements are known, he will make a risk estimate by considering two aspects: a) the need to accomplish the military mission he has been entrusted with and its level of criticality; then b) the impacts that the benefit of the enhancement can bring to the soldier, to the group, or even to the civilians potentially present on the scene of the action. He can then make his decision, considering that it is possible to proceed to a pharmacological enhancement. Nevertheless, he also has to consider the necessity of the increase through a wider prism, because he has to anticipate and predict the effects of this enhancement over a long time, as well as the sociological impact that it can have on the whole group. For example, if a substance prevents a soldier from sleeping for 72 hours, but makes him completely exhausted after this period of time so that he is no longer able to carry on the mission, can he take such a risk for the whole unit?

4. In the final step of the decision-making process, the individual himself must give his consent to this enhancement. This is the Δ corresponding to his own area of responsibility.

6.3 *Perception of the Combatant Himself*

We also here have to mention various reactions a combatant may have in confronting extreme situations:

- The potential addiction of a combatant's enhancement could be portrayed as follows: "If I'm not enhanced, I refuse to be deployed, as I am liable to be the cause for weakening the group".
- "Facing a determined foe, unconcerned by any value held by our Armies, it would certainly be quite frustrating if I'm not allowed to enhance myself whilst our enemies can" (e.g. CAPTAGON amphetamines used by ISIS terrorists).

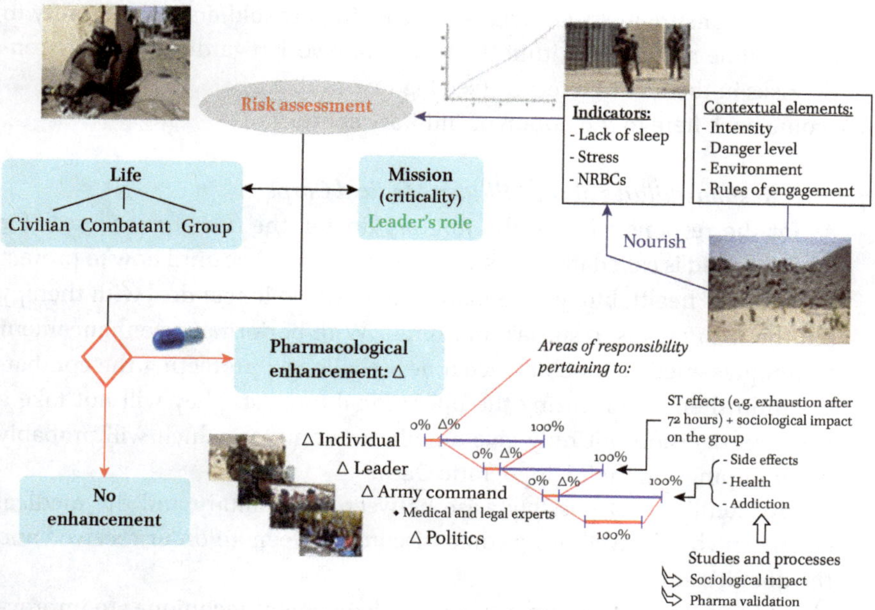

FIGURE 11.2 Decision-making process in military operations

The three factors mentioned above are in fact sub-parts of a broader question that I would describe here as the "military context". Any enhancement depends on the military context and must therefore be part of an ethical framework, with reference values centered on respect for the soldier.

7 Section 4: Responsibilities and Challenges Ahead

7.1 *Responsibilities of the Military*

Considering cost constraints and enhancement availabilities, choices will have to be made at the organisational level:

- In terms of military effectiveness, selected units are deployed on missions of vital importance and must be successful. Assuming that enhancement can avert setbacks, which units should thus be enhanced? Only commando units or the special forces?
- The difficulty for a leader to take an appropriate decision will possibly increase with this new parameter; i.e. enhancement. For a mission to succeed, a soldier may well be sent to his death. "Am I therefore in a position to prohibit the use of substances hazardous to health? Shouldn't I do the

utmost to ensure mission success by reducing my soldiers' vulnerability in battle while remaining within the legal framework regardless of the potential risks in the medium term?" (see Figure 11.2 above).

We come back here to the notion of "military context".

7.2 *Responsibilities of the Military Medical Corps*

– As for the responsibility of the military doctor, the use of substances for medical need is called into question: a doctor's role was until now to protect his patients' health but, with enhancement, we no longer deal with therapy but the with means to surpass our limits. With performance enhancement techniques, medical doctors face a new challenge: protecting the combatant from them or favouring the operational interest. They will not take a clear-cut decision but only give an advisory opinion which will probably never impinge on their Hippocratic Oath.
– A new conflict may possibly arise between the military and the medical corps, which may well bring some discord between an order received and the doctor's advice.
– Should the army adopt some specific enhancement techniques to improve operations and implement them once the young recruit has joined the forces?
– And, if harsh restrictions were to be applied for enhancement opportunities (i.e. lines not to be crossed mentioned above), what controls and screening mechanisms should be established within units to prevent individuals from breaking the rules and/or examine wrongdoings?

And what is more, establishing on-the-spot procedures during the critical phase of a mission, in the case of an emergency and/or in the pitch of battle (who should be enhanced?, in which combat phase?, for which type of position?, etc.).

7.3 *The Medical Prescription Law*

Considering that soldier performance enhancement is necessary, the military medical corps is changing in nature. We can then imagine that we must abandon the existing law of medical prescription and create a special legal framework for soldier enhancement, with its own particularities and based on the specificity of military status – especially in case of emergency where the risks for the soldier are very high, or for a specific military objective.

8 Section 5: The Enhanced Soldier as a Part of a Broader System

The question of the augmented soldier should not be seen in isolation, but in the context of other military developments[11] with which he is interconnected.

At what point or degree of enhancement do we consider that a soldier is no longer a simple human, but becomes integrated into a weapons system, or even becomes a "weapon" himself? Indeed, Article 36 of the Geneva Convention specifically states that any new weapon must be lawful. Therefore, on the legal side, would it be necessary to pass the soldier's enhancement through the prism of this Article?

An enhanced soldier could for example wear invasive implants, having autonomous intelligence, and be connected to a weapons system. This may exponentially increase the military effectiveness of both. Yet again, the questions of moral and legal responsibility here, as well as those of command responsibility, are issues to tackle. But they seem too distant in time for an immediate response to be required. The author of this paper proposes to debate them when the technology of these implants has become more advanced.

9 Conclusions

If military training has as its main objective to ensure an optimal skill level for the soldiers going into a tactical operation, new technologies allow us to envision an enhanced soldier whose performance will go beyond his own physical, physiological, or psychological limits.

However, if the definition of enhancement that we used in this article intentionally covers a very broad spectrum, the ethical questions arising from it are crucial and of great importance. It seems to us imperative that the answers we provide should not go against what is fundamental to our armies: that is to say, respect for human dignity. It seems then imperative to write a Code of Soldier Enhancement, based on a common European approach and respectful of the codes of ethics existing within each army of these countries.

This Code of Soldier Enhancement would help in establishing a relationship of trust between the soldier and the military hierarchy, based on a clearly defined military research framework, including precise assessment and certification processes, and transparency on potential side effects.

---

11 Ted Van Baarda, discussion, June 2018.

Finally, to conclude, in our society where everything is measured by the yardstick of performance, there is in my opinion a point of great importance: the training of a soldier and his operational condition must be seen as a global project, involving all the dimensions of being.[12] But if all that is visible is measurable, there remains a human part that is not measured, or very difficult to measure. It is the soldier's psychic component that feeds on his own inner strength, his psychological form, his metaphysical strength, and his relationships to others and the military community, for the benefit of the basic operational entity: the combat unit.

References

Boisboissel, Gérard de, 'Le soldat augmenté: regards croisés sur l'augmentation des performances du soldat' (2019) *Le soldat augmenté: regards croisés sur l'augmentation des performances du soldat. Fondation pour l'innovation politique* (18 décembre 2019) <http://www.fondapol.org/etude/le-soldat-augmente-regards-croises-sur-laugmentation-des-performances-du-soldat/> accessed 09 April 2020.

Caron, Jean-François, Théorie du super soldat: La moralité des technologies d'augmentation dans l'armée (Presses de l'Université Laval 2018).

Cusset, Pierre-Yves, 'Améliorer les capacités humaines: actualité d'un vieux rêve' (2015) 45 DSI Hors-série Le soldat augmenté, repousser les limites pour s'adapter, Décembre 2015, 8.

Hude, Henri, 'Quelle éthique du recrutement?' (2015) 45 DSI Hors-série Le soldat augmenté, repousser les limites pour s'adapter, Décembre 2015, 84.

'Le soldat augmenté – Les besoins et les perspectives de l'augmentation des capacités du combattant' (2017) Les cahiers de la Revue de la Défense Nationale (Décembre 2017) <https://iatranshumanisme.com/2018/02/28/le-soldat-augmente-cahier-de-la-rdn/> accessed 22 March 2020.

Maynié, Louis-Joseph, 'De pugnatoris trinitate. L'augmentation du combattant, d'une trinité à l'autre' (2019) *Le soldat augmenté: regards croisés sur l'augmentation des performances du soldat. Fondation pour l'innovation politique* (18 décembre) 72 <http://www.fondapol.org/etude/le-soldat-augmente-regards-croises-sur-laugmentation-des-performances-du-soldat/> accessed 14 April 2020.

12 Chef de bataillon Louis-Joseph Maynié, 'De pugnatoris trinitate. L'augmentation du combattant, d'une trinité à l'autre' (2019) *Le soldat augmenté: regards croisés sur l'augmentation des performances du soldat. Fondation pour l'innovation politique* (18 décembre) 72 <http://www.fondapol.org/etude/le-soldat-augmente-regards-croises-sur-laugmentation-des-performances-du-soldat/> accessed 14 April 2020.

Sandrine Turgis, 'L'augmentation du soldat à la croisée des droits de l'homme et du droit des conflits armés' (2017) Les cahiers de la Revue de la Défense Nationale (Décembre 2017) 171 <https://iatranshumanisme.com/2018/02/28/le-soldat-augmente-cahier-de-la-rdn/> accessed 22 March 2020.

Thoër, Christine et Michèle Robitaille, 'Utiliser des médicaments stimulants pour améliorer sa performance: usages et discours de jeunes adultes québécois' 10 (2) Drogues, santé et société 143 <https://doi.org/10.7202/1013481ar> accessed 22 March 2020.

Tonkens, Ryan, 'Morally Enhanced soldiers: Beyond Military Necessity', in Jai Galliott and Mianna Lotz (eds), Super Soldiers: The Ethical, Legal and Social Implications (Emerging Technologies, Ethics and International Affairs) (Ashgate, Farnham, United Kingdom 2015).

PART 5

Leadership

CHAPTER 12

Special Units and Emerging Technologies

Environmental and Organizational Features and Their Influence on Ethical Considerations

Tzippi Gushpantz

1 Introduction

In the year 2000, it became known that over one hundred naval special force troops who underwent regular diving training activities in the Kishon River, just south of the port city of Haifa, Israel, had become ill with cancer, and at least 27 of them had died as a result. A special independent commission was set up to investigate the matter, headed by the highly respected Meir Shamgar, former Chief Justice of Israel's Supreme Court.[1]

Since the 1960s, the Kishon had been used as a disposal site for the industrial waste of dozens of heavy industries in the Haifa Bay area, as well as sewage treatment runoff of the various municipalities and local authorities in proximity to the river.[2] Yet the stench of the place, the profoundly turbid water reported by the divers, the layers of oil covering the surface, the nature of the sludge present when diving – all failed to trigger any alarms among the commanding officers responsible for the training. Shockingly, this situation had already been reported in the 1950s by governmental and scientific authorities.[3] From the beginning of the 1970s it had already been proven that heavy industrial pollution prevented any life from existing in the Kishon waters.[4] At the same time, evidence was accumulating at the chemical laboratory of the Navy to indicate that poisonous materials were causing damage to the ships

1 Kishon Commision Report, Part I, p. 13. Quote taken from the protocol of the Inquiry Commission on the consequences of military activity in the Kishon River and the surrounding waters on the health of IDF soldiers who were active there. The Commission was headed by Judge Meir Shamgar. Any statement or reference originating in the Commission's protocols (all dating from the year 2000) is followed in brackets by the letter **P**, the date and month they were spoken in the Commission, and the page of the Hebrew transcript. The Commission' report was published in 2001. Statement or reference to the report itself are denoted **R**, followed by the page number.

2 R, 87.

3 R, 39.

4 R, 39, 48.

 | DOI:10.1163/9789004507951_014

anchored in the Kishon.[5] Yet not one single commanding or medical officer managed to put two and two together and consider the harm that might be caused to the soldiers who were training in a place so severely polluted as to be apparent for all to see.

Navy medical officers who accompanied these training exercises over the years began dealing with the possible dangers of this situation only towards the end of the 1980s.[6] Until then, the quality of the water was not a subject that anyone felt compelled to deal with, and the head of the Medical Corps considered the sludge to be 'an integral part of the medium in which the divers would have to carry out their duties'.[7] It was found that even after medical authorities began warning about the possible health dangers of contact with the Kishon water, no one in the senior command took decisive action to cease the training exercises there. In fact, training exercises and routine operations in the Kishon area continued until the end of the 1990s.

The Commission laid the blame on generations of Navy and Medical Corps officers who either knew, or should have known, better. It concluded that these bodies had functioned for decades without any systematic planning, checking of data, or effort to learn the reality of the situation.[8]

2 The Research Method: A Prism of 'real life'

The investigation of the affair by an external commission that functioned similarly to other governmental investigative bodies, created a unique opportunity: to use the extensive and intensive descriptions in the protocols as raw material for a qualitative case study research. The Commission summoned anyone and everyone connected in some manner to the training setup in the Kishon, not only at the time of the inquiry, but also for the three previous decades: commanders, medical officers, doctors, public and governmental offices, and entities involved in health who worked alongside them over the years. For example, naval medical officers who had served since the 1970s were called to testify.

Bearing the above in mind, and based on the ensemble of the commission protocols, I examined how this phenomenon could occur in an organization that has a well-publicized code of ethics which *specifically emphasizes the*

5 P. (21.8.), 45.
6 P. (13.9.), 37.
7 P. (6.9.), 10.
8 R, 224.

preservation of human life in training, as the former driving instructor wondered in retrospect: 'How could it happen, that normal people, (and I consider myself to be one), who saw this filthy water, and as a commander, it never occurred to me that it might also be dangerous'.[9]

By mapping and analysing the evidence according to the role context and over time, I was able to create a prism through which I could examine first-hand an organizational phenomenon as part of the fabric of real life.[10] My findings revealed and described in great detail the web of relationships by way of the conduct and perception of responsibility of the various commanding entities, as well as the functioning of the governing authorities around them. This wealth of data provides a very complete picture of the events in question and makes it possible to understand them within their social and historical contexts.[11] This is on quite a different scale to other studies in organizational behaviour and managerial ethics which attempt to explain ethical or unethical patterns of decision-making by examining attitudes and intentions towards hypothetical scenarios.[12] The fact that the same mode of action was adopted by generations of commanding officers made it possible not to focus on the characteristics and motivations of any particular officer, but rather to focus the analysis on the organizational-systemic context, and on the functional group – commanders in elite units – identify social and environmental connections, and analyse their impact on decisions and on the implementation (or lack thereof) of the ethical norms.

Identifying and mapping the many varied factors and processes that influenced the organizational culture of the Navy required 'shifting', from a research standpoint, between the formal level of the organization – the structural characteristics and the managerial frameworks, and the informal level – values, norms and mind-sets that moulded the organizational climate and culture.

---

9 P. (9.11.), 28.

10 Robert K. Yin, *Case Study Research: Design and Methods* (SAGE Publication 1984).

11 Jennifer Platt, 'Case Study in American Methodological Thought' (1992) 40 (1) *Current Sociology*, 17–48.

12 Michael E. Brown, Linda K. Treviño and David A. Harrison, 'Ethical Leadership: A Social Learning Perspective for Construct Development and Testing (2005) *Organizational Behavior and Human Decision Processes* 97 (2), 117–134; Logan M. Steele, Tyler J. Mulhearn, Kelsey E. Medeiros, Logan L. Watts, Shane Connelly and Michael D. Mumford 'How Do We Know What Works? A Review and Critique of Current Practices in Ethics Training Evaluation' (2016) *Accountability in Research. Journal Policies and Quality Assurance*, 23 (6) 319–350.

This was done in the full research.[13] In this article I will relate that part of my findings that focuses on environmental and organizational features.

How does this connect to the issue of advanced technologies, special units, and ethical considerations? My rationale is that mechanisms and processes that gave special unit commanders the legitimacy to take actions designed to fulfil the combat ethos while ignoring ethical norms, are relevant to a discussion on thinking and ethical decision-making in special units using advanced technologies.

The research findings reveal various features that help to explain the phenomenon: (a) environmental and institutional features; (b) structural features; (c) the situational context; (d) the organizational culture and climate. I will first present the theoretical aspects and then the key data for each of these, the conclusions to be drawn from them, and how these might pertain to the use of advanced technologies by special units and ethical considerations.

3 Environmental and Institutional Features

Systemic and sociological theories attribute decisive importance to the influence of the environment when analysing the features of an organizational phenomenon. They explain the organizational activity in contextual variables of structures and the adoption of social norms and values by the organizations, so that over time, one can find a match between the norms of the environment and those of the organizations acting within it. According to Edgar Carr[14] one cannot understand and analyse the behaviour of individuals without relating it to their interpersonal contexts, which include social, cultural, and political forces.

Sociological theories focus on identifying the influences of the institutional environments on the organizations, and especially when examining the question of how the institutions – the beliefs, rules, and norms around them – affect the organizational structure and their activity patterns.[15] The explanation for an organizational behaviour is mainly based on unwritten conventions and the

13 Tzippi Gushpantz, 'Kishon Divers Affair – Factors and Processes Shaping the Navy's Organizational Culture and Influencing the Ethical Norms and Their Implementation' (2013) PhD dissertation, Tel Aviv University.

14 Edgar H. Carr. *What is history?* (Penguin, London 1961).

15 Richard W. Scott, 'The Adolescence of Institutional Theory' (1987a) *Administrative Science Quarterly* 32 (4) 493–511.

organization's dependence on environmental factors and its values.[16] It was found that organizations display conformity with their environment and tend to establish various conventions that are prevalent in their social environment and in the organizational field they belong to.[17] The normative institutionalism approach claims that institutions affect the behaviour of the players by shaping their values, norms, interests, identities and beliefs.[18]

Were the passive approach of the senior commanding and medical officers to the growing accumulating pollution at the training site, and the lack of initiative in questioning whether diving in chemical substances might be dangerous, also the direct outcome of the social, institutional, and cultural contexts around them? Did the lack of control and orientation towards ecological issues within the military reflect the influence of norms at the systemic level?

The first part will present a sample of the findings of the monitoring of the Kishon waters over time. A look at the information gathered enables us to examine whether the mental block in understanding the scope of the pollution and the risks it posed was the result of a lack of clarity and availability of the data. In the second part I will present patterns of conduct of governing bodies regarding the emerging risk in the Kishon waters. This will reveal the norms and conventions pertinent to the environmental risks.

4 Monitoring of the Kishon and the Growing Risk

From the 1950s on, the Kishon was monitored by both state and scientific entities. The table below shows how the unauthorized, uncontrolled flow of industrial waste and sewage that continued into the late 1990s turned the Kishon into a reservoir of organic and inorganic chemical and biological substances.

16 Jeffrey Pfeffer and Gerald R Salancik, *The Eternal Control of Organizations: A Resource Dependence Perspective.* (Harper & Row, New York 1978).

17 Walter Powell and Paul. J. DiMaggio (eds), *The New Institutionalism in Organizational Analysis* (UCP, Chicago 1991); Lynne G Zucker, 'The Role of Institutionalism in Cultural Persistence' in Walter W Powell and Paul J DiMaggio (eds), *The New Institutionalism in Organizational Analysis* (UCP, Chicago 1991) 103–106.

18 Gerald F. Davis and Walter W. Powell, 'Organization Environment Relations' in M. D. Dunnette and L. M. Hough (eds), *Handbook of Industrial and Organizational Psychology* (Consulting Psychologists Press; Palo Alto, CA 1992) 315–375; John W. Meyer and Brian Rowan, 'Institutionalized Organizations: Formal Structure as Myth and Ceremony' in Walter W. Powell and Paul J. DiMaggio (eds), *The New Institutionalism in Organizational Analysis* (UCP, Chicago 1991) 41–62; Richard W Scott, *Organizations: Rational, Natural, and Open Systems* (2nd ed. Prentice-Hall, 1987b).

TABLE 12.1 Findings of the Kishon water monitoring and treatment of pollution risks

1957	The Kishon Monitoring Committee informs the Naval Commander of the discovery of severe pollution in the river. The Committee points out the damage to the fish: 'partial or complete annihilation of the fish [...] and the corrosion of vessels anchored in its waters, as a result of the influx of waste from industries in the area'.(R,39).
1970	The Ministry of Health conducts a comprehensive health survey of the Kishon, concluding it is heavily polluted by industrial waste that is destroying every living thing.(R,46,48).
1975	A comprehensive survey by the Ministry of Health determines that even if efforts are made to improve the state of the water, bathing or any kind of direct human contact with the water will not be possible. (R,61).
1978	The Water Commissioner issues 15 warrants against polluting factories demanding correction of the situation within five years.(R,65).
1989	Monitoring by the Seas and Lakes Authority indicates a high concentration of heavy metals in the river bed. This concentration rises significantly and equals that found in the most highly polluted rivers in the world.(R,69,73).
1993	Fourteen years after the issuing of warrants, not one factory has met the demands.(R,80).
1997	In 1997, after 4 people who fell in the polluted Yarkon River lost their lives, a warning went to the directors of the Ministries of Education, Defence and Health to cease any activity in the Kishon.(P.27.8,119)
2000-2001	First biological monitoring of the Kishon. Findings show very high toxicity and deterioration, an absolute lack of living organisms in the water.(R,88).

SOURCES: SHAMGAR COMMISION REPORT(2001), SHAMGAR COMMISION PROTOCOLS (2000).

Was the lack of alertness on the part of the commanding and medical officers regarding the above findings the result of environmental norms and conventions about the environmental risks and their health implications?

In order to answer this question, I will briefly present testimonies given by institutional and governmental figures, through which one can decipher the mind-sets and norms regarding this issue. I will later examine whether and how these were reflected in the testimonies of the commanding officers.

5 "A mirror of the era": Mind-Sets in the Institutional Environment Regarding the Risks of the Pollution

Director, Ministry for Ecological Preservation (1973–1989):

> The former director testified that it was only in 1982 that they began to enforce the law against deviant air pollution in the Haifa Bay area: 'This issue – quality of the environment – was shunned by most of the political establishment. We worked in a hostile setting with no authority. Anybody who could disrupt us did so. From the 1970s we published articles […]'[19]

Ministry of Heath Regional Physician (1988):

> Already in 1972 it was reported that the water was hazardous to humans […] The army never consulted us about diving 8[…].[20]

Director, Ministry for Quality of the Environment (1996–1999):

> … all the coastal streams are polluted by sewage or industrial waste.[21]

In 1997 heavy metals were found in the Kishon waters. The Managing Director personally called the Haifa Municipality in whose jurisdiction there were sailing training and fishing activities, and at the same time she publicized in all the media a notice to parents warning of risk to life. However, the Haifa Municipality informed her that 'water sports are important and vital, and one should not spread panic and stop the welcome activities taking place in the Kishon […].'
Director, Kishon River Authority since 1995:

> Our working assumption was that this was a flow consisting entirely of industrial and sanitary waste […] military activity. We approached anyone sailing in the river [i.e. marine sports] and warned them against sailing in the Kishon. This report also reached the Navy and we took the initiative to send it to the Chief Physician of the Navy. Nothing.[22]

19 P. (1.8.), 63–64.
20 P. (28.8.), 4–14.
21 P. (27.8.), 102 and the subsequent quotes are from pages 109, 101, 119–120, 121, 8.
22 P. (27.8.), 42–45.

The Director of the Ministry for Quality of the Environment in 2000–2002 noted that despite the letters of warning from the Ministry:

> We still see [in 2000] that kind of sailing in the Kishon, [...] and if we warn the Haifa Municipality about it, the answer we get – the Ministry of Health, which is legally responsible, is if children fall into the water they should rinse themselves off.[23]

It appears that the many years during which the polluting entities ignored court orders taken out against them and the feebleness exhibited by the authorities in handling the pollutants and in enforcing the prohibitions on those acting in the Kishon, reflect the low priority that ecological issues and their risks held on the public agenda of government decision-makers. Might this ensemble explain, even partially, the lack of alertness of the commanders to the connection between the risk being created in the river and the health of their subordinates?

Indeed, some quotes from senior officers' testimonies clarify the norms and attitudes on this issue within the military. For example, the Commander of the Navy (1985–1989):

> All this awareness and consciousness they are talking about didn't exist. And as far as I know, there was never any testing of the water. Quality of the environment began in the later eighties. All over the world it is known that port waters are polluted ... does that mean that this water is polluted and shouldn't be swum in? We didn't make this connection because it wasn't in anyone's consciousness.[24]

And the Commander of the Navy for 1989–1992 claimed:

> I suppose that if someone had come up to us and said, 'there's a danger there are toxic substances' ... nobody would have ignored it, not that we knew there were substances endangering the health of our soldiers; 'nobody came and said there was a health risk here.[25]

The medical bodies were an integral part of the exercises and operations of the Navy. A former Commander of the Navy said: 'They knew about every training

23 P. (24.8.), 7–8.
24 P. (9.11.), 25.
25 P. (9.11.), 25, 34.

exercise.'[26] Nevertheless, it was only in 1989 that the medical system began to express an opinion about aspects of the risk. The chief medical officers had no acceptable explanation as to why they had not done this any earlier.

> 'As someone coming from an elite unit, I trained there on several occasions; it was filthy, it was disgusting'; 'It never came up, because there was no awareness of the incidence of illness we are talking about now', 'today there is greater awareness of ecology.'
>
> CMO 1979–1983[27]

The head of the Institute for Marine Medicine from 1975 to 1994 mentioned that he had dived several times in the most polluted part of the Kishon. And yet, he stated: 'it was very dirty, a terrible smell. But it never occurred to me and there was no awareness that there were carcinogenic substances or anything like that.'[28]

In 1989, the Corps doctor (1988–1991), who was horrified to discover that soldiers were diving into a bath of chemicals, prohibited the continued activity but the commanding officers simply did not accept what he wrote. They did not comprehend the scope of the risk.[29]

Hence, the norms and mind-sets of the surrounding system might seem to legitimize not asking questions about the look and smell of the water and might explain the difficulty that anyone not connected to the medical profession – i.e. the combat commanders – might have in linking the signs of pollution to the long-term health implications for those training in the Kishon.

Regarding technologies, in an era of technological revolution characterized by rapid and significant changes, scholars and experts have to confront ethical issues and questions which are currently not covered by the existing laws and policies.[30] This lack of clarity and lack of certainty require us to formulate and justify new policies (laws, rules and customs) for acting in these new kinds of situations.[31]

26 P. (9.11.), 22.

27 P. (31.10.), 3.

28 P. (6.9.), 7.

29 P. (13.9.), 64.

30 James H. Moor, 'Why We Need Better Ethics for Emerging Technologies' (2005) *Ethics and Information Technology* 7(3), 111–119.

31 Paul W. Singer, 'The Ethics of Killer Applications: Why is it so Hard to Talk about Morality when it Comes to New Military Technology' (2010) *Journal of Military Ethics* 9(4), 299–312; Philip A. E. Brey, 'Anticipatory Ethics for Emerging Technology' (2012) *Nanoethic* 6, 1–13.

However, formulating and justifying new policies is made more complex by the fact that the concepts that we bring to a situation involving policy vacuums may not provide a unique understanding of the situation. The situation may have analogies with different and competing traditional situations. 'We find ourselves in a conceptual muddle about which way to understand the matter in order to formulate and justify a policy'.[32]

Scholars are trying to propose ways to cope with the unknown, even when applications or uses are not yet known. For example, Brey claims that it might be possible to identify and discuss 'generic ethical issues that are likely to manifest themselves as technology develops. Alternatively, we might "speculate on future devices, uses and social consequences"'.[33]

He further suggests that 'a systematic futures study would consider how the technology may be combined with various new and emerging technologies to yield possible new capabilities and functionalities not found in current artefacts'.[34]

This societal and governmental uncertainty, confusion, and lack of ethical knowledge may influence the perceptions and understandings of decision-makers within a military system who are dealing with emerging technologies.

Proposals such as the above require extensive interdisciplinary collaboration and might take a long time. The current ethical vacuum obliges commanding officers dealing with cutting-edge technology to determine what is to be considered right and proper in any given situation. The confusion and lack of policy, and the pressure to create *ex nihilo* mechanisms and processes that will enable rapid formulation of policies and procedures, might lead to a situation in which they might 'steer away from such dissections and stay within our old world and not foresee the new coming problem'.[35] Alternatively, it might reinforce the phenomenon of "a life of their own"[36] which is typical of elite

32 Moor (n 30) 115.
33 Brey, (n 31) 2.
34 Brey, (n 31) 2.
35 Singer (n 31) 301.
36 Paul DiMaggio, 'Constructing an Organizational Field as a Professional Project: U.S Art Museums,1920–1940' in Walter W. Powell and Paul J. DiMaggio (eds), *The New Institutionalism in Organizational Analysis* (UCP, Chicago 1991) 267–292; Joseph Galaskiewicz, 'Making Corporate Actors Accountable: Institution Buildings in Minneapolis, St. Paul' in Walter W. Powell and Paul J. DiMaggio (eds), *The New Institutionalism in Organizational Analysis* (UCP, Chicago 1991) 293–310.

units, and legitimize the establishment of unique ethical standards[37] in order to reduce ethical uncertainty.

This issue is addressed in the following section, which examines the influence of the structural and situational features on commanders of elite units and their impact on ethical considerations.

6 Structural Features

Large, complex organizations, such as military systems, run on well-established structures and arrangements of a ranking of authority and specialization in order to attain their goals.[38] On the assumption that specialization and a set of rules, procedures and control mechanisms are effective means of transferring information and coordinating activities among its different parts,[39] the organization establishes tight bonds between its constituent components – patterns and mechanisms that are typically highly structured and based on training and expertise.[40] At the same time, the organization must have more fluid and flexible informal patterns within its specialized sub-systems, such as elite units, to allow their decision-makers to respond to surrounding constraints in timely fashion.[41] However, the structural-functional differentiation of such sub-systems also leads to splitting and fragmentation of the responsibility between different factors within the organization.[42] Since different units fulfil different tasks, their compartmentalization and hierarchy may mean that each one only feels responsible for its specific area.[43] Where decision-makers are expected

37 Roger Friedland and Robert R. Alford, 'Bringing Society Back. In: Symbols, Practices, and Institutional Contradictions' in Walter W. Powell and Paul J. DiMaggio (eds), *The New Institutionalism in Organizational Analysis* (UCP, Chicago 1991) 232–263.

38 Frederick W. Taylor, *Scientific Management* (Routledge London 2004); James D. Thompson, *Organizations in Action: Social Science Bases of Administrative Theory* (Routledge, New York 2017).

39 Henry Mintzberg, *The Nature of Managerial Work* (Harper and Row 1973); Henry Mintzberg, *The Structure of Organizations* (Prentice-Hall 1979).

40 Paul R. Lawrence and Jay W. Lorsch, *Organization and Environment* (Irwin 1967); Max Weber, The Theory of Social and Economic Organization (Parsons and A.H. Anderson, trs and eds, Free Press 1947).

41 Mintzberg 1979 (n 46); Charles Perrow, *Complex Organizations: A Critical Essay* (Random House, New York 1986).

42 Richard M. Cyert and James M. March, *A Behavioral Theory of the Firm* (Prentice-Hall, Englewood Cliffs, New Jersey 1963).

43 Christopher D. Stone, Where the Law Ends: The Social Control of Corporate Behavior (Harper & Row Inc. 1975).

to have a broad, systemic perspective in order to make optimal choices for the organization, we might, instead, find a greatly narrowed view. The structural differentiation might lead them to rely on a set of solutions with which they are already familiar in order to facilitate the execution of their tasks.[44] But over time, this can lead to a lack of mental flexibility and initiative when it comes to resolving problems. The structural differentiation may reinforce loyalty to the goals of a specific unit and legitimize ignoring other broader goals of the organization. Thus, the flexibility afforded to special units to enable rapid responses may also lead to 'decoupling',[45] that state of reduced oversight and evaluation, that can widen the mismatch between the organization's ethical code, orders, and procedures and the means chosen to execute a particular task or mission. Scholars have noted that decoupling may also occur because it serves the interests of powerful organizational leaders, or because it allows organizational decision-makers to avoid implementing policies that conflict with their own ideological beliefs.[46]

Gary Weaver offered an additional aspect of structural influences on the behaviour of individuals and the formation of their moral-organizational identity. He claimed that the more members are able to create their own private space of identity – "a life of their own" – within the organization, the more they can preserve their own identity and cultivate it separately from the distinct identity of the workplace.[47]

Do the structural features of a military system influence the formation of patterns of activity that can be defined as deviating from the formal mechanism – the established orders, procedures and ethical norms? Does this, in turn, narrow the perspectives of elite unit commanders who might, even unwittingly, focus on their own particular tasks, rather than on the bigger picture?

In the case of the Kishon affair, the Institute of Marine Medicine was the main body in charge of testing the ongoing health of the elite units diving in the Kishon River, and it used to conduct tests every two years.[48] The tests examined specific diving skills, without it ever occurring to any of the doctors

44 Robert K. Merton, *Social Theory and Social Structure* (Free Press 1957).

45 Ludwig von Bertalanffy, *Organismic Psychology and Systems Theory* (Clark University Press 1968).

46 András, Tilcsik, 'From Ritual to Reality: Demography, Ideology, and Decoupling in A Post-Communist Government Agency' (2010) *Academy of Management Journal*, 53(6), 1474–1498. James D. Westphal and Edward J. Zajac, 'Decoupling Policy from Practice: The Case of Stock Repurchase Programs' (2001) *Administrative Science Quarterly* 46, 202–228.

47 Gary R. Weaver, 'Virtue in Organizations: Moral Identity as a Foundation for Moral Agency' (2006) *Organization Studies* 27(3), 341–368.

48 P. (6.9.), 7.

to also test the quality of the water for any long-term side-effects in might have on the divers' health. Indeed, the testimony of a former head of the institute revealed how many years of role differentiation can create an inability to think "outside the box": 'Our entire research attention for 20 years has been on physiological pathological aspects. [...] The problem of this polluted environment never came up as an issue the institute should be looking at.'[49] The institute's medical staff focused only on the tasks that had been defined for them: 'We worked only on physiological issues [...] that was our mandate'.[50]

Another example of mental inflexibility can be seen among the staff of the Navy's chemical laboratory, who were in charge of the condition of the boats and ships. While the diving training was going on, they focused only on the technical and chemical aspects of the shipyard, seeking solutions to the damage caused to the vessels. As early as 1953, the lab director published scientific articles about the corrosion caused by the pollution in the Kishon, a clear indication of toxic substances in the water.[51] This raises the question: given the effect of the pollution on metal, how come they did not see fit to pass on their findings to the medical institute staff who were responsible for the health of the divers?

The explanation of the Commander of the Navy to the Commission illustrates the effect of the deep role differentiation on the patterns of command thinking: 'The Marine Medical Institute deals with the physiology of the divers [...] the chemical lab of the Navy is definitely not an institution that is capable of doing anything with the water pollution [...] it is not its job to bring attention to the data'.[52] In other words, does this mean that everyone should stay "in their own sector" and not look, at the big picture?

Advanced technologies in the military are handled by experts who have the specific knowledge and skills to develop the next generation of sophisticated systems. Members of such a unit are carefully handpicked after several rounds of screening, and have to undergo intensive, in-depth training in a wide range of intelligence and technological fields.[53] The diverse purposes towards which the special technological units work and the need to make effective use of resources in order to attain and retain superiority in a dynamic environment[54]

49 P. (6.9.), 9, 13, 2.
50 P. (6.9.), 13.
51 P. (21.8.), 77.
52 P. (21.8.), 45.
53 From: the IDF website, Intelligence Corps and Unit 8200 <https://www.idf.il/en/minisites/military-intelligence-directorate/> accessed 15 November 2020.
54 From: the IDF website, Intelligence Corps and Unit 8200 <https://www.idf.il/en/minisites/military-intelligence-directorate/> accessed 15 November 2020.

makes it necessary to work according to patterns of specialization, with profound role differentiation. However, the risk of working in deep deracination patterns obliges the technological elite unit leaders to take steps to ensure that technology professionals do not choose to act only according to what has been defined as their mandate rather than thinking ethics. I will elaborate this notion later on.

The format of the activities of special units in the military system is typically dynamic and subject to change. Might the need to confront the various challenges cause a deviation from ethical considerations? We shall now discuss this question.

7 Contextual Features

Research studies confirm that the unique characteristics of a situation may affect the considerations and the decisions of decision-makers.[55] It has been found that in situations of overload or conflict, the norms that the individual adheres to and his or her actual orientation may prevent the consideration of other options or finding relevant information regarding the ethics of a situation.[56]

The difficulty of taking action in the face of diverse tasks and time constraints might be conflictual and lead to over-identification with one aspect of the job and the neglect or ignoring of others.[57] Janis and Mann confirm that strong commitment to an existing path of action influences the decision-maker to continue along the same path and refrain from considering alternatives.[58] The complexity of organizational goals influences the commitment to act according to declared organizational values.[59] Military personnel often

---

55 Linda K. Treviño, 'Ethical Decision Making in Organizations: A Person-Situation Interactionist Model' (1986) *Academy of Management Review* 11(3), 601–617.

56 Donald P. Robin, Eric Reidenbach and Paul J. Forrest, 'The Perceived Importance of an Ethical Issue as an Influence on the Ethical Decision-Making of Ad Managers' (1996) *Journal of Business Research* 35 (1), 17.

57 Steven L. Grover, 'Lying in Organizations: Theory, Research and Future Directions' Robert A Giacalone and Jerald Greenberg (eds) *Anti-Social Behavior in Organizations* (Sage, Thousand Oaks, CA 1997) 68–84.

58 Irving L. Janis and Leon Mann, Decision-making: A Psychological Analysis of Conflict, Choice, and Commitment (Free Press, New York 1977).

59 Nili Sukennik, *Organizational Mechanisms through which the Organization Copes with the Contradiction between its Goals, and Welfare and Safety* (Mangenonim irguni'im bemtza'utam mitmoded ha'irgun 'im hastira bein matarotav larevah vebetihut), PhD Dissertation, Tel Aviv University 2002.

have to carry out tasks in a dynamically complex environment[60] in which is necessary to act and respond quickly. This involves situations in which the rules and instructions are insufficiently clear, silent, or even contradictory.[61] Dealing with this complexity requires deep understanding and consideration of ethical aspects that are in play.[62]

In the case of the Kishon Divers Affair, the testimonies of the various commanders revealed how the uniqueness of the context influenced their perception of their role and their attitude regarding the pollution:

> The quality of the water never occurred to me. The concern was always about the tools.
>
> Flotilla commander, 1981–1983[63]

There was a clear tendency to identify with one aspect of the role – focusing solely on the operational ethos while ignoring all other aspects:

> 'Everything is examined in the operational context'; 'We never paid attention to whether it was healthy or unhealthy. The goal was to carry out the task.'
>
> UMI commander[64]

When the senior ranks of commanders are required to act quickly and effectively vis-à-vis various missions and in harsh field conditions, there can be a serious misreading of the situation. This might be expressed as a difficulty in focusing and recognizing the signs, as the navy commander described:

> The process by which we gather everything for the purpose of this matter [referring to the signs of pollution] were always right before our eyes, like everything else [other missions] that were right before our eyes, but we

---

60 Eric H. Kramer: Organizing Doubt: Grounded Theory, Army Units and Dealing With Dynamic Complexity (Copenhagen Business School Press 2007).

61 Ted van Baarda and Desirée E. M. Verweij, *Military Ethics: The Dutch Approach – A Practical Guide* (Martinus Nijhoff Publishers 2006); Moshe Ya'alon 'Leadership' [Manhigut] in Idan Asher (ed) *On Leadership* [Al manhigut] (IDF HQ/Education Officer and Galei Zahal [army radio station] 2007) 7–17.

62 Paul Robinson, Nigel de Lee and Don Carrick (eds), *Ethics Education in Military* (Ashgate, Aldershot 2008).

63 P. (22.11.), 4.

64 P. (22.11.), 60.

> didn't see them; it was either too close or too far, or we were focusing on something else, as often happens.[65]

We may conclude from this that special unit commanders have to act in a complex reality of overload and rapid responses and this can lead to short-sightedness, such as identifying with only one aspect of their role, for example, the operational ethos, while ignoring other aspects such as the ethical consideration, and even the specific ethical demand for safety in training.

Here too, commanders operating on the cutting-edge of technology must cope with time-sensitive issues to ensure the success of their missions, and this may come at the expense of ethical considerations. In other words, commanders operating in the forefront of technology deal with a variety of tasks as well as rapid changes in a competitive environment.[66] The desire to achieve technological superiority and to remain on the cutting-edge of technology might create similar pressures.

Does the conduct at the formal level actually reflect the basic assumptions of the commanders regarding their role and their missions? Is it the conventions that developed as a result of the interaction within the functional peer group that drive the patterns of actions? These questions are addressed below.

8 Organizational Culture and Climate: Shared Values and Perceptions

Researchers relate to organizational culture as a set of "fundamental assumptions": mind-sets and beliefs a group develops while dealing with problems of external adaptation and internal cohesion.[67] The more effective the mind-sets and beliefs in solving problems and carrying out tasks, the more they become accepted views that define the nature of the organizational "reality" and "truth".[68] Over time, these basic assumptions become fixed as objective, and members adhere to the values, symbols, and practices deriving from them.[69]

Studies confirm that the work peer group is the strongest influencing factor on an individual in an organizational context, since individuals adopt the beliefs and mind-sets of the people with whom they work and interact

65 P. (21.8.), 52.

66 Moor (n 30).

67 Gareth Morgan, *Images of Organization* (Sage 1986).

68 Mary E. Boyce, 'Collective Centering and Collective Sense-making in the Stories and Storytelling of One Organization' (1995) *Organization Studies* 16(1), 107–137.

69 Edgar H. Schein, *Organizational Culture and Leadership* (4th Jossey-Bass 2010).

closely.[70] Organizational units with high interaction and cohesion were found to formulate their own values and consensus[71] about "how we do things here".[72] Individuals and groups tend to be creative in rationalizing their actions whereby rules, procedures, and symbols are interpreted to suit the immediate preferred context.[73]

Leadership is the key factor that decisively impacts the patterns of action and the organizational behaviour.[74] In a strong organizational culture[75] such as the military system, with charismatic leadership,[76] the influence of the values and mind-sets of the leaders on the organizational culture is augmented. In the military system this may mean total identification between the values of the commander and the unit spirit. Shamir *et al* note that charismatic leader behaviours are not directed 'at individual subordinates or followers. Rather, they are ambient behaviours that are either directed at the unit as a whole (for instance, emphasizing the collective identity) or at no one in particular (for instance, leaders self-sacrifice).'[77] The critical point is that many leaders' behaviours go beyond face-to-face interactions,[78] yet the behaviours have a

---

70 Albert Bandura, Social Foundations of Thought and Action: A Social Cognitive Theory (Prentice-Hall 1986); Thomas M. Jones, 'Ethical Decision Making by Individuals in Organizations: An Issue-Contingent Model' (1991) *The Academy of Management Review* 16 (2), 366–395; Gary R. Weaver, Linda K. Treviño and Bradley Agle, 'Somebody I Look up to: Ethical Role Models in Organizations' (2005) *Organizational Dynamics* 34(4), 313–330.

71 Gil Luria, 'Climate Strength – How Leaders Form Consensus' (2008) *The Leadership Quarterly* 19(1), 42–53; Dov Zohar and Orly Tenne-Gazit, 'Transformational Leadership and Group Interaction as Climate Antecedents: A Social Network Analysis' (2008) *Journal of Applied Psychology* 93(4), 744–757.

72 Linda K. Treviño, Niki A Den Nieuwenboer and Jennifer J. Kish-Gephart '(Un)ethical Behavior in Organizations' (2014) *Annual Review of Psychology* 65(1), 635–660.

73 Friedland and Alford (n 44); Sukennik (n 66).

74 Micha Popper, *On Managers as Leaders* (Al menahelim kemanhigim) (Ramot – Tel Aviv University 1994); Bernard M Bass and Ruth Bass, *The Bass Handbook of Leadership: Theory, Research, and Managerial Applications* (4th ed, Free Press 2008); Schein (n 76).

75 Anat Rafaeli, 'What Is an Organization? Who Are the Members?' in Cary L. Cooper and Susan E. Jackson (eds) *Creating Tomorrow's Organizations* (John & Wiley, 1997) 122–138.

76 Jay A. Conger, *The Charismatic Leader: Behind the Mystique of Exceptional Leadership* (Jossey-Bass 1998); Jay A. Conger, Rabindra N. Kanungo, and Sanjay T. Menon, 'Charismatic Leadership and Follower Effects' (2000) *Journal of Organizational Behavior* 21 (7) 747–767.

77 Boas Shamir, Eliav Zakay, Esther Breinin and Micha Popper, 'Correlates of Charismatic Leader Behavior in Military Units: Subordinates' Attitudes, Unit Characteristics, and Superior Appraisals of Leader Performance' (1998) *The Academy of Management Journal*, 41 (4) 387–409, 392.

78 Ann E Tenbrunsel, Kristin Smith-Crowe and Elizabeth E Umphress, 'Building Houses on Rocks: The Role of the Ethical Infrastructure in Organizations' (2003) *Social Justice Research*, 16(3) 285–307.

large impact on the units the leader commands in terms of defining a leadership climate.[79]

The practical way to identify the values and basic assumptions of leaders is to examine how they are expressed within the organizational climate[80] through accepted practices, mind-sets, and consensus.[81] Studies on organizational ethics confirm the influence of these "significant others" – leaders and peer groups – on choices and decisions.[82] Regarding the military system, it is the high-ranking commanders who model and create the ethical climate.[83]

In my research, I found deep similarities among the functional peer group – high-ranking commanders – regarding their missions and task, and likewise between the commanders' mind-sets, opinions and attitudes and those of their soldiers. They all treated the pollution as "a given reality" of a special unit: 'Like a storm in the sea.'[84] The testimonies revealed deep loyalty to the notion of being able to realize the combat ethos: 'The mind-set was always to push to the edge of physical and mental ability' (Combat Diving Instructor 1981–1984).[85] They all rationalized the training in the well-known and visible pollution of the Kishon water as the appropriate way to prepare their soldier for a crucial day. The commanders explained the importance of maintaining combat readiness: 'If the soldier trained in difficult conditions he would be properly prepared' (UMI Commander 1980–1983); 'We thought that the murkier the water, the more real the simulation' (Naval Commander 1992–1996).[86]

The Kishon River was perceived as a professional and technical challenge for training the elite units: 'The Kishon is a successful operational simulation' (Naval Commander 1992–1995).[87] Diving in the Kishon became a built-in feature in the special unit's socialization process. The commanders explained: 'My

79 Leonard Wong, Paul Bliese and Dennis McGurk, 'Military Leadership: A Context Specific Review' (2003) *The Leadership Quarterly* (14) 657–692; Gushpantz (n 13); Tzippi Gushpantz, 'Senior Officers in the Kishon Diving Affair: Between Ethics and Acts' (2017) *Journal of Military Ethics* 16 (1–2), 38–55.

80 Schein (n 76).

81 Benjamin Schneider, Mark G. Ehrhart, and William H. Macey, 'Organization Climate and Culture' (2013) *Annual Review of Psychology* 64, 361–388.

82 Treviño (n 79).

83 Brett D Weigle and Charles D Allen, 'Keeping David from Bathsheba: The Four-Star General's Staff as Nathan' (2017) *Journal of Military Ethics*, 16 (1–2) 94–113.

84 P. (12.12.), 55.

85 P. (27.12.), 21.

86 P. (22.11.), 60; P. (26.11.), 15.

87 P. (26.11.), 2.

commanding officer dived with me, and now it is my turn to dive with my soldiers' (Flotilla Commander 1981–1984).[88]

We see the cohesion within the functional peer group: commanders, who had all undergone the same path of training in the Kishon, moulded a consensus about their tasks and missions – pushing physical boundaries as part of the preparation for combat readiness. Such consensus has tremendous influence on those who belong to the group. Testimonies show how, over time, the interpretation and opinions of the senior command slowly turned into professional opinions that defined truth and reality in the organization. In this way the Kishon with its "special" features was gradually attributed a special value for operational simulation: a technical challenge and a successful model. The reliance on their own experience and not on objective data enabled the emergence of a complete mental block regarding any ethical issues such as the long-term health of the divers, or even upholding the stated demand in the IDF code of ethics to maintain safety in training and not put soldier's lives at risk.

The conclusions we can draw from this are that a high level of cohesion among the commanders of special units might easily create an organizational blindness. Leaders can, even unwittingly, use creative bias to rationalize their values and propositions. They can mould an organizational culture which suits their mind-set and use the 'unit spirit' as a managerial tool to instil their own values and goals. In this case, by diving with their soldiers, the officers strengthened the norms and the identification with that 'unit spirit'. Allowing leaders' personal beliefs to mould an organizational culture can significantly reduce awareness of values and ethical consideration, if left unchecked.

The relevance to the technological sphere should be obvious. The cyber units dealing with the development of sophisticated technologies are perceived as elite teams to which only the brightest and the best are recruited.[89] The grand aura of secrecy surrounding these units because of the tremendous importance of their contribution to military superiority on the one hand, and the pressure to meet expectations and compete successfully against other military systems on the other, might well create among cyber unit commanders, the same kind of total loyalty to the technological ethos as well as the difficulty in recognizing ethical issues or the desire to confront such issues.

Such deep loyalty to the unit spirit and the ethos of technological superiority might reduce sensitivity to and awareness of ethical considerations in the use of emerging advanced technologies. The advantages of any new technology

88 P. (22.11.), 1.

89 From: the IDF website, Intelligence Corps and Unit 8200 <https://www.idf.il/en/minisites/military-intelligence-directorate/> accessed 15 November 2020.

are usually obvious, because they have often been created precisely in order to solve a certain problem, whereas it is all too easy to avoid asking the awkward questions about what the disadvantages might be, or what limitations should be imposed on their use.

9 Practical Question and Implications

The ethical behaviours and attitudes of peers are role models for ethical decision-making in significant ethical situations.[90] Units that interact intensively develop their own ethical-normative standard with decisive influence on the mind-sets and attitudes of their members and often impose conformity to group norms and values.[91] This ethical microcosm[92] might constrain organizational ethics and policies.

The above review points to the influence of structural and situational factors on the sensitivity, discretion and awareness of decision-makers, but mainly it points to the influence of the values and mind-sets of the cultural reference group (role peers) and of leaders.

So how should we proceed from here? My findings led me to ask the following questions, which, I believe, are just as relevant to the context of the use of emerging technologies: How can we make ethics the commanders' primary 'guiding spirit' despite uncertainty, the vacuum of rules, and lack of ethical instructions? How can we deepen the understanding that a particular issue, which may seem routine, actually requires careful reasoning and proper ethical choices?

Based on the experience of the IDF in the Kishon Affair, it seems that even having a clearly written code of ethics and conducting training sessions to upgrade the professionalism of commanding officers has insufficient impact on decision makers, especially in special units characterized by a high level of cohesion.

---

90 Thomas M. Jones and Lori V. Ryan, 'The Effect of Organizational Forces on Individual Morality: Judgment, Moral Approbation, and Behavior' (1998) *Business Ethics Quarterly* 8(3), 431–445.

91 Anke Arnaud and Marshall Schminke, 'The Ethical Climate and Context of Organizations: A Comprehensive Model' (2012) *Organizational Science* 23(6), 1767–1780; Celia Moore and Francesca Gino, 'Ethically Adrift: How Others Pull our Moral Compass from True North, and How We Can Fix It' (2013) *Research in Organizational Behavior* 33, 53–77.

92 Arthur P. Brief, Robert T. Buttram, and Janet M. Dukerich, 'Collective Corruption in the Corporate World: Toward a Process Model' in Marlene E. Turner (ed), *Groups at Work: Theory and Research* (Erlbaum 2001) 471–499.

Organizational culture and unit norms are apparently more powerful than values and ethics guidelines.[93] This means that ethics implementation processes must be structured and continually managed.[94] Mechanisms should be put in place to constantly reteach the notion of not discarding the 'bigger picture' of the overall goals and ethical norms of the organization they serve.[95] Ethical discourse in the organizational culture must be encouraged. How?

10 Implementing Ethics in the Praxis of Command

The leadership must be in charge of implementing ethics in the praxis of command, making it part of an officer's professionalism. They must be trained to apply the 'looking in the mirror' approach, constantly asking themselves the following questions:

- Do my decisions and conduct reflect the ethics of the organization?
- What messages do I convey to my peers and subordinates in my day-to-day dealings with them?

This concept can encourage a change in the organizational learning and implementation that favours ethics. The assessment processes of implementing ethics and learning about how the mind-sets, values, and beliefs of commanding officers are formed might help in the early detection of situations and preliminary signals of any interpretations – or rather, misinterpretations – by either individuals or groups that are not aligned with the values or fundamental guidelines of the organizations.

The clarification and moulding of attitudes and beliefs through a learning process requires delving into the roots of the matter.[96] Hence, organizational resources must be allocated to eliciting the consensus and the understandings created with the groups (units) and in the mechanisms that are developing at the informal level. There is no doubt that training courses alone cannot change

93 Gushpantz (n 13).

94 Eva van Baarle, Laura Hartman, Desirée Verweij, Bert Molewijk and Guy Widdershoven, 'What Sticks? The Evaluation of a Train-the-Trainer Course in Military Ethics and its Perceived Outcomes' (2017) *Journal of Military Ethics* 16 (1–2), 56–77; Asa Kasher, 'Teaching and Training Military Ethics: An Israeli Experience' in Paul Robinson, Nigel de Lee and Don Carrick (eds), *Ethics education in military* (Ashgate 2008) 133–146.

95 Ya'alon (n 68).

96 Peter M. Senge, The Fifth Discipline: The Art and Practice of the Learning Organization (Doubleday 1990).

or shape the organizational culture.[97] It is essential to work on an ongoing basis within the settings in which senior commanding officers are being trained on the issue of their interpretations of the mind-set regarding the role and the scope of responsibility involved, as part of their professional advancement.[98] I believe that it is only in such a manner that it will be possible to deal with informal learning patterns that are moulded through the interactions within a given unit that might end up in deviations from the fundamental rules of the organization.

Hence, what is required is a plan of action that will make it possible to work at the group level[99] whether it is within the formal or informal structure, in order to bring to the surface any hidden assumptions, as well as the mind-sets and expectations of the commanding officers. There are a number of methods to achieve this: a double learning circle focusing on diagnosing the reasons underlying the deviation in thinking and on ways to remedy and improve that thinking, and a three-way learning circle that closely examines the comprehension of the basic assumptions of the organization and the reasons why the deviations occurred.[100] The feedback process is essential to change existing paradigms and to prevent the formation of any new undesirable paradigms. Analysis of the values and mind-sets of the senior commanding officers – what there is – towards how they should be performing their duties – the values and norms established by the organization – and mapping these out might reflect, for example, the gap between mission orientation and purely operational risks[101] and the duty to accede to the fundamental rules and values and act accordingly, 'and this work never finishes'.[102]

Since we are in the midst of a 'conceptual muddle'[103] about how to understand the effects and implications of technological advances, and since the possibility of formulating and justifying new policies will take time and require the collaboration of multidisciplinary experts – ethicists, scientists and technology-oriented social scientists,[104] – this is precisely where we see the

97 Michael Kalichman, 'Rescuing RCR Education' (2014) *Accountability in Research* 21, 68–83; Steele (n 12).

98 Timna Shamali, 'Developing Leadership from Theory to Practice' (Pituach manhigut halacha lema'aseh) in Arieh Idan (ed) *Military Leadership* (Manhigut tzva'it) (2007) Broadcast University IDF Radio, as part of the College for National Security; Van Baarle (n 101).

99 Chris Argyris and Donald Schön, *Organizational Learning, Theory, Method and Practice* (Addison-Wesley 1996).

100 Argyris and Schön (n 106).

101 See Kasher before the Vinograd commission, 15.11.2006, p.17.

102 Van Baarle (n 101) 69.

103 Moor (n 30).

104 Singer (n 31).

importance of training officers in special units dealing with advanced technologies to "think ethically" and examine their unconscious paradigms.

Moor suggests developing more sophisticated ethical analyses to give guidance to a particular situation; to be more proactive in doing ethics, 'otherwise we leave ourselves vulnerable to a tsunami of the technological change'.[105]

The suggestion to have commanders "look at themselves in the mirror" as a norm, requires constant alertness, and hence its importance. Constant examination of decisions and choices minimizes the opportunity for the entrenchment of norms and mind-sets that deviate from the values of the organization.

Examination of commanding/managerial paradigms and mind-sets for their compatibility with the code of ethics enables identifying the gaps and leading changes at the formal level – role definitions, management patterns, work and control processes – and at the informal level: the message conveyed through personal example.

Defining ethical practices in general, and in the context of emerging technologies in particular, must be seen as an "ongoing and dynamic enterprise".[106] Some would prefer to 'work out' all the ethical issues ahead of time; others may suggest delaying the use of technological developments until ethics can "catch up".[107]

Such attitudes seem to be better than ignoring ethics until after damage has been inflicted. However, in reality, both attitudes have limitations, because it is impossible to anticipate every ethical issue that might arise from technologies we cannot yet even envision.[108]

To quote Moor:

> We have to do as much as we can while realizing applied ethics is a dynamic enterprise that continually requires reassessment of the situation. Like advice given to a driver in a foreign land, constant vigilance is the only sensible approach.[109]

Although looking into the "ethical future" in the context of emerging technologies will be no simple task, it does have one advantage – the fact that, as yet, there is no "baggage" of "well, we have always done it like this". In other words,

105 Moor (n 30) 119.
106 Moor (n 30) 118.
107 Bill Joy, 'Why the Future Doesn't Need Us' (2000) *Wired* 8(4).
108 Brey (n 31); Singer (n 31).
109 Moor (n 30) 17.

there are no ingrained mind-sets to be reversed. Senior commanding ranks will only have to make sure that such mind-sets are never allowed to develop.

References

Argyris, Chris and Donald Schön, *Organizational Learning, Theory, Method and Practice* (Addison-Wesley 1996).

Arnaud, Anke and Marshall Schminke, 'The Ethical Climate and Context of Organizations: A Comprehensive Model' (2012) *Organizational Science* 23(6), 1767–1780.

Baarda, Ted van and Desirée E. M. Verweij, *Military Ethics: The Dutch Approach – A Practical Guide* (Martinus Nijhoff Publishers 2006).

Baarle, Eva van, Laura Hartman, Desirée Verweij, Bert Molewijk and Guy Widdershoven, *'What Sticks? The Evaluation of a Train-the-Trainer Course in Military Ethics and its Perceived Outcomes'* (2017) Journal of Military Ethics 16 (1–2), 56–77.

Bandura, Albert, Social Foundations of Thought and Action: A Social Cognitive Theory (Prentice-Hall 1986).

Bertalanffy, Ludwig von, *Organismic Psychology and Systems Theory* (Clark University Press 1968).

Boyce, Mary E., 'Collective Centering and Collective Sense-making in the Stories and Storytelling of One Organization' (1995) *Organization Studies* 16(1), 107–137.

Brey, Philip A. E., 'Anticipatory Ethics for Emerging Technology' (2012) *Nanoethic* 6, 1–13.

Brief, Arthur P., Robert T. Buttram, and Janet M. Dukerich, 'Collective Corruption in the Corporate World: Toward a Process Model' in Marlene E. Turner (ed), *Groups at Work: Theory and Research* (Erlbaum 2001) 471–499.

Brown, Michael E., Linda K. Treviño and David A. Harrison, 'Ethical Leadership: A Social Learning Perspective for Construct Development and Testing' (2005) *Organizational Behavior and Human Decision Processes* 97 (2), 117–134.

Carr, Edgar H., *What is history?* (Penguin, London 1961).

Conger, Jay A., Rabindra N. Kanungo, and Sanjay T. Menon, 'Charismatic Leadership and Follower Effects' (2000) *Journal of Organizational Behavior* 21 (7) 747–767.

Conger, Jay A., The Charismatic Leader: Behind the Mystique of Exceptional Leadership (Jossey-Bass 1998).

Cyert, Richard M. and James M. March, *A Behavioral Theory of the Firm* (Prentice-Hall, Englewood Cliffs, New Jersey 1963).

Davis, Gerald F. and Walter W. Powell, 'Organization Environment Relations' in M. D. Dunnette and L. M. Hough (eds), *Handbook of Industrial and Organizational Psychology* (Consulting Psychologists Press; Palo Alto, CA 1992) 315–375.

DiMaggio, Paul, 'Constructing an Organizational Field as a Professional Project: U.S Art Museums, 1920–1940' in Walter W. Powell and Paul J. DiMaggio (eds), *The New Institutionalism in Organizational Analysis* (UCP, Chicago 1991) 267–292.

Eric H. Kramer: *Organizing Doubt: Grounded Theory, Army Units and Dealing With Dynamic Complexity* (Copenhagen Business School Press 2007).

Friedland, Roger and Robert R. Alford, 'Bringing Society Back In: Symbols, Practices, and Institutional Contradictions' in Walter W. Powell and Paul J. DiMaggio (eds), *The New Institutionalism in Organizational Analysis* (UCP, Chicago 1991) 232–263.

Galaskiewicz, Joseph, 'Making Corporate Actors Accountable: Institution Buildings in Minneapolis, St. Paul' in Walter W. Powell and Paul J. DiMaggio (eds), *The New Institutionalism in Organizational Analysis* (UCP, Chicago 1991) 293–310.

Grover, Steven L., 'Lying in Organizations: Theory, Research and Future Directions' Robert A Giacalone and Jerald Greenberg (eds) *Anti-Social Behavior in Organizations* (Sage, Thousand Oaks, CA 1997) 68–84.

Gushpantz, Tzippi, 'Senior Officers in the Kishon Diving Affair: Between Ethics and Acts' (2017) *Journal of Military Ethics* 16 (1–2), 38–55.

Gushpantz, Tzippi, *Kishon Divers Affair – Factors and Processes Shaping the Navy's Organizational Culture and Influencing the Ethical Norms and Their Implementation* (2013) PhD dissertation, Tel Aviv University.

IDF (Israel Defense Force). n.d. *IDF Code of Ethics* <https://www.idfblog.com/about-the-idf/idf-code-of-ethics/> accessed 02. November 2020 <http://www.jewishvirtuallibrary.org/ruach-tzahal-idf-code-of-ethics> accessed 02 November 2020.

Janis, Irving L. and Leon Mann, *Decision-making: A Psychological Analysis of Conflict, Choice, and Commitment* (Free Press, New York 1977).

Jones, Thomas M. and Lori V. Ryan, 'The Effect of Organizational Forces on Individual Morality: Judgment, Moral Approbation, and Behavior' (1998) *Business Ethics Quarterly* 8 (3), 431–445.

Jones, Thomas M., 'Ethical Decision Making by Individuals in Organizations: An Issue-Contingent Model' (1991) *The Academy of Management Review* 16 (2), 366–395.

Joy, Bill, 'Why the Future Doesn't Need Us' (2000) *Wired* 8(4).

Kalichman, Michael, 'Rescuing RCR Education' (2014) *Accountability in Research* 21, 68–83.

Kasher, Asa, 'Teaching and Training Military Ethics: An Israeli Experience' in Paul Robinson, Nigel de Lee and Don Carrick (eds), *Ethics education in military* (Ashgate 2008) 133–146.

Kishon Commision Report, Part I.

Lawrence, Paul R. and Jay W. Lorsch, *Organization and Environment* (Irwin 1967).

Luria, Gil, 'Climate Strength – How Leaders Form Consensus' (2008) *The Leadership Quarterly* 19(1), 42–53.

Merton, Robert K., *Social Theory and Social Structure* (Free Press 1957).

Meyer, John W. and Brian Rowan, 'Institutionalized Organizations: Formal Structure as Myth and Ceremony' in Walter W. Powell and Paul J. DiMaggio (eds), *The New Institutionalism in Organizational Analysis* (UCP, Chicago 1991) 41–62.

Mintzberg, Henry, *The Nature of Managerial Work* (Harper and Row 1973).

Mintzberg, Henry, *The Structure of Organizations* (Prentice-Hall 1979).

Moor, James H., 'Why We Need Better Ethics for Emerging Technologies' (2005) *Ethics and Information Technology* 7(3), 111–119.

Moore, Celia and Francesca Gino, 'Ethically Adrift: How Others Pull our Moral Compass from True North, and How We Can Fix It' (2013) *Research in Organizational Behavior* 33, 53–77.

Morgan, Gareth, *Images of Organization* (Sage 1986).

Perrow, Charles, *Complex Organizations: A Critical Essay* (Random House, New York 1986).

Pfeffer, Jeffrey and Gerald R Salancik, *The Eternal Control of Organizations: A Resource Dependence Perspective* (Harper & Row, New York 1978).

Platt, Jennifer, 'Case Study in American Methodological Thought' (1992) 40 (1) *Current Sociology*, 17–48.

Popper, Micha, *On Managers as Leaders* (Al menahelim kemanhigim) (Ramot – Tel Aviv University 1994); Bernard M Bass and Ruth Bass, *The Bass Handbook of Leadership: Theory, Research, and Managerial Applications* (4th ed, Free Press 2008).

Powell, Walter and Paul. J. DiMaggio (eds), *The New Institutionalism in Organizational Analysis* (UCP, Chicago 1991).

Rafaeli, Anat, 'What Is an Organization? Who Are the Mem Exact bibliographical references are missingbers?' in Cary L. Cooper and Susan E. Jackson (eds), *Creating Tomorrow's Organizations* (John & Wiley, 1997) 122–138.

Robin, Donald P., Eric Reidenbach and Paul J. Forrest, 'The Perceived Importance of an Ethical Issue as an Influence on the Ethical Decision-Making of Ad Managers' (1996) *Journal of Business Research* 35 (1), 17.

Robinson, Paul, Nigel de Lee and Don Carrick (eds), *Ethics Education in Military* (Ashgate, Aldershot 2008).

Schein, Edgar H., *Organizational Culture and Leadership* (4th Jossey-Bass 2010).

Schneider, Benjamin, Mark G. Ehrhart, and William H. Macey, 'Organization Climate and Culture' (2013) *Annual Review of Psychology* 64, 361–388.

Scott, Richard W., 'The Adolescence of Institutional Theory' (1987a) *Administrative Science Quarterly* 32 (4) 493–511.

Scott, Richard W., *Organizations: Rational, Natural, and Open Systems* (2nd ed. Prentice-Hall, 1987b).

Senge, Peter M., *The Fifth Discipline: The Art and Practice of the Learning Organization* (Doubleday 1990).

Shamali, Timna, 'Developing Leadership from Theory to Practice' (Pituach manhigut halacha lema'aseh) in Arieh Idan (ed) *Military Leadership* (Manhigut tzva'it) (2007) Broadcast University IDF Radio, as part of the College for National Security.

Shamgar [Judge Meir] Report 2001. Report of the Inquiry Commission on the Consequences of the Military Activity in the Kishon River and Surrounding Waters for the Health of IDF Soldiers Trained There (Doch va'adat hahakira be'inyan hahashlahot shel pe'ilut tzva'it benachal hakishon umeimei hasviva al bri'utam shel hayalei tzahal shehuf'alu bamakom), Part 1. Tel Aviv: Misrad Habitachon (Ministry of Defense).

Shamgar Commission. 2000–2001. *The Shamgar [Judge Meir] Commission Report.* The protocols of the Shamgar Commission were published in full on the Commission website via the Tel Aviv University website: tau.ac.ilq~bhkishon. This URL is no longer active. (Protokolim shel va'adat Shamgar pursemi bemlo'am be'atar hava'ada betoch atar haibternet shel Universitat Tel Aviv, http://www.tau.ac.ilq~bhkishon . Kayom haktovet eina pe'ila.)

Shamir, Boas, Eliav Zakay, Esther Breinin and Micha Popper, 'Correlates of Charismatic Leader Behavior in Military Units: Subordinates' Attitudes, Unit Characteristics, and Superior Appraisals of Leader Performance' (1998) *The Academy of Management Journal*, 41 (4) 387–409.

Singer, Paul W., 'The Ethics of Killer Applications: Why is it so Hard to Talk about Morality when it Comes to New Military Technology' (2010) *Journal of Military Ethics* 9(4), 299–312.

Steele, Logan M., Tyler J. Mulhearn, Kelsey E. Medeiros, Logan L. Watts, Shane Connelly & Michael D. Mumford 'How Do We Know What Works? A Review and Critique of Current Practices in Ethics Training Evaluation' (2016) *Accountability in Research. Journal Policies and Quality Assurance*, 23(6) 319–350.

Stone, Christopher D., *Where the Law Ends: The Social Control of Corporate Behavior* (Harper & Row Inc. 1975).

Sukennik, Nili, *Organizational Mechanisms through which the Organization Copes with the Contradiction between its Goals, and Welfare and Safety* (Mangenonim irguni'im bemtza'utam mitmoded ha'irgun 'im hastira bein matarotav larevah vebetihut), PhD Dissertation, Tel Aviv University 2002.

Taylor, Frederick W., *Scientific Management* (Routledge London 2004).

Tenbrunsel, Ann E, Kristin Smith-Crowe and Elizabeth E Umphress, 'Building Houses on Rocks: The Role of the Ethical Infrastructure in Organizations' (2003) *Social Justice Research*, 16 (3) 285–307.

Thompson, James D., *Organizations in Action: Social Science Bases of Administrative Theory* (Routledge, New York 2017).

Tilcsik, András, 'From Ritual to Reality: Demography, Ideology, and Decoupling in A Post-Communist Government Agency' (2010) *Academy of Management Journal*, 53(6), 1474–1498.

Treviño, Linda K., 'Ethical Decision Making in Organizations: A Person-Situation Interactionist Model' (1986) *Academy of Management Review* 11(3), 601–617.

Treviño, Linda K., Niki A Den Nieuwenboer and Jennifer J. Kish-Gephart '(Un)ethical Behavior in Organizations' (2014) *Annual Review of Psychology* 65(1), 635–660.

Weaver, Gary R., 'Virtue in Organizations: Moral Identity as a Foundation for Moral Agency' (2006) *Organization Studies* 27(3), 341–368.

Weaver, Gary R., Linda K. Treviño and Bradley Agle, 'Somebody I Look up to: Ethical Role Models in Organizations' (2005) *Organizational Dynamics* 34(4), 313–330.

Weber, Max, *The Theory of Social and Economic Organization* (Parsons and A.H. Anderson, trs and eds, Free Press 1947).

Weigle, Brett D. and Charles D. Allen, 'Keeping David from Bathsheba: The Four-Star General's Staff as Nathan' (2017) *Journal of Military Ethics* 16 (1–2) 94–113.

Westphal, James D. and Edward J Zajac, 'Decoupling Policy from Practice: The Case of Stock Repurchase Programs' (2001) *Administrative Science Quarterly* 46, 202–28.

Wong, Leonard, Paul Bliese and Dennis McGurk, 'Military Leadership: A Context Specific Review' (2003) *The Leadership Quarterly* (14) 657–692.

Ya'alon, Moshe, 'Leadership' [Manhigut] in Idan Asher (ed) *On Leadership* [Al manhigut] (IDF HQ/Education Officer and Galei Zahal [army radio station] 2007) 7–17.

Yin, Robert K., *Case Study Research: Design and Methods* (SAGE Publication 1984).

Zohar, Dov and Orly Tenne-Gazit, 'Transformational Leadership and Group Interaction as Climate Antecedents: A Social Network Analysis' (2008) *Journal of Applied Psychology* 93 (4), 744–757.

Zucker, Lynne G., 'The Role of Institutionalism in Cultural Persistence' in Walter W Powell and Paul J DiMaggio (eds), *The New Institutionalism in Organizational Analysis* (UCP, Chicago 1991) 103–106.

CHAPTER 13

Preparing Leaders of Character for Complex Conflict

Christopher Luedtke and Christopher Miller

1 Introduction

This chapter explores perspectives on the evolving nature of conflict and consequent challenges facing military professionals in democratic nations. To succeed in proactively defending the societies they serve, modern militaries must deliver both traditional principled service and adapt to achieve reliable excellence in complex, rapidly evolving military tasks where even the boundaries of their responsibilities, vis-à-vis other national security entities, are increasingly ambiguous. The preparation of military leaders is therefore of the utmost importance. The United States Air Force Academy's approach to developing 'leaders of character' is a useful frame to illuminate foundational aspects of commissioned officer development, amid such rapid technological and social change, that are relevant to interested scholars and practitioners beyond the US Department of the Air Force.

It is our fundamental contention in this essay that while evolving technologies present extraordinary challenges for societies in general, and militaries in particular, the development of leaders of character remains the *sine qua non* of military success. In the context of the future profession of arms, we define a leader of character as one who lives honorably, lifts others to their best possible selves, and who elevates the performance of their organisation to excellence in common and noble endeavors. Individual leaders and organisations which exhibit these attributes are likely to best manage the human and technical challenges of the complex and rapidly changing conflict environment we all face. As a means of exploring the link between character-based leadership and military success in complex conflict, we will examine key values, goals, outcomes, and frameworks that guide Air Force Academy cadet development throughout the four-year program and contribute to the overarching objective of 'developing leaders of character'. These elements are part of an academic, military, and athletic experience that culminates for each cadet in an undergraduate Bachelor of Science degree and a commission in either the US Air Force or US Space Force. Even as the Academy builds on decades of success

 | DOI:10.1163/9789004507951_015

in blending traditional educational paths and leadership experiences, it – and similar institutions within and beyond the United States – face imperatives to redouble their emphasis on understanding new conflict-affecting technologies and warfare concepts, how they interact with the human aspects of the military profession, and then adjust traditional pedagogy and paradigms to make leader development continue to deliver the results democratic militaries need.

The need for a forward-looking preparation of officer-leaders is a recurring assertion throughout much of recent human history, but today's pace of technological change is inarguably driving more rapid, less predictable evolution in nearly every aspect of human interaction than at any previous time. The character of war is equally subject to rapid evolution and the consequences of change are significant. Even a superficial survey of the conflict environment that Academy graduates may have to deal with – in social, geopolitical, technological, ethical, and organisational terms – suggests that preparing graduates for careers that measure in tens of 'Moore's Law' cycles requires a blended approach that recognises both continuity and adaptability.

To arrive at that blended approach, it is critical to first look forward at what future leaders must understand and master. We will touch on some key technological trends bearing on the future of war, such as cyber conflict, information and disinformation, remotely piloted vehicles, space, and artificial intelligence. There are significant knowledge and consensus gaps regarding their application and acceleration in warfare, and a host of difficult practical and ethical decisions lie ahead in each of these areas – all issues which clearly bear on preparation of future leaders for the moral/ethical and leadership challenges associated with employment of these technologies.

With this backdrop, the task at hand is to shape the contemporary priorities most likely to lead to the sound foundation and adaptable mental constructs needed to enable effective service. A valuable approach to thinking about how to achieve that goal has been advocated as part of the Air Force Academy character and leadership program by a distinguished member of the Academy's third graduating class, Lieutenant General Ervin Rokke. He maintains that effective education of a military force requires a continuous, relentless reconciliation of three essential factors: *Immutable values*, the *changing character of successive generations* entering military service, and the *changing character of conflict*.[1] As a means of facilitating that reconciliation, we will first discuss the

1 Ervin J. Rokke, unpublished essay, 'Time to Revisit the Profession of Arms: A Perfect Storm' (2017).

changing character of conflict – perhaps the most conceptually cloudy of the three factors.

2 Future Conflict Is a Moving Target

It is beyond the scope of this paper to dwell on the details of technological change, but it is useful to survey some of the most salient technological trends facing militaries and the ways in which they challenge traditional paradigms for thinking about military conflict.

By far the most omnipresent trend is the explosion in the quantity, velocity, and importance of reliable information to militaries and especially to the societies they serve. It is nearly impossible to overstate the relevance of the cyber domain and potential impact of 'information warfare' for modern societies. From financial transactions to control and function of electrical and other key industrial infrastructures, the more developed and modern nations have become increasingly reliant on cyber-enabled systems that are universally operated but inconsistently protected.[2] In the United States, the military is responsible for defending its own information systems (both administrative and those integral to weapon systems); it plays a supporting role in other Federal cyber efforts, but has almost no responsibility to protect key electronic infrastructure in the same way it would traditionally be expected to protect older systems accomplishing the same function. The potential impact of this trend is perhaps most clearly illustrated if we consider a thought experiment contrasting the military missiles and guns that defended against bombers prosecuting high-explosive attacks on transportation infrastructure in WWII, with a cyberattack on aspects of electrically powered autonomous transportation a few decades from today. The potential effect is the same yesterday and tomorrow, i.e. denial of transportation with the economic and military impact that such paralysis can cause. The means of attack and defense, and the identity and responsibilities of those attacking and defending, are far less clear in the future case.[3] Innumerable other examples of the impact of information operations on nations' security exist in recent history, including exploitation of information to mask, enhance, and conduct military operations; election interference in, and conducted by, multiple entities; cyber-enabled intellectual property theft affecting military systems; and the list goes on. The key

2 Cyberspace Solarium Commission Report (March 2020) 8–19.

3 Christopher D. Miller, 'Yesterday at War with Tomorrow: Rebooting the Profession of Arms' (2020) 7 *Journal of Character and Leadership Development* 108.

characteristic that militaries must consider is the information environment's interpenetration of previously definable and defendable physical borders, and its implications for the role and capabilities of military professionals.

The December 2019 creation of the United States Space Force is one of several markers of the relevance of space-based systems for terrestrial life, and a recognition of the fact that conflict affecting space – whether or not actually conducted in orbit – is a matter of national security concern. Space-faring nations have clear interests and make the greatest direct use of all kinds of space systems, but all nations have a stake in the space environment and benefit indirectly from viable space systems that enhance weather prediction, precision agriculture, navigation, communication and many other services that are increasingly taken for granted and essential to development and economic progress. Both military and civilian entities are increasingly engaged in space activities and interact in ways that affect national security and prosperity. Personal risk and proximate killing are nearly absent as considerations for military space professionals; the demands of stewardship of a unique global commons, and moral aspects of indirect effects of space-related warfare, are omnipresent. A key characteristic of the growth of importance of space for the military profession is that 'warfare' in space demands ethical decision-making different in its complexity and personal impact when compared to the calculus of millennia-old violent combat. In shorthand, valor's connection to value is less clear.

Remotely operated weapons pose yet another new and evolving challenge. Similar to cyber- and space-domain warfare, military professionals who operate remote weapon systems of current and future types are far less exposed to personal, reciprocated physical risk than their counterparts in more traditional kinetic warfare systems. Yet the technologies of human-directed remote weapons allow them to be closely engaged with the targets they attack even more acutely than any combatant using more traditional long-range weapons like manned aircraft-delivered bombs or bullets or long-range missiles or artillery. For those who use violence remotely, then, a key characteristic is a different experience of conflict that is not without risk of moral injury.

Artificial intelligence (AI) – a term that has multiple technical meanings and instantiations and which is certainly not universally understood, especially when applied to the military context – poses yet another set of ethical and practical challenges to future military leaders. From those who design, program, or make decisions to use a weapon that uses artificial intelligence to identify or destroy a target, to those who design or use AI-enabled systems to analyze intelligence and inform military and civilian decision-makers making life-or-death decisions, those involved with AI have potentially immense systemic impact on the way militaries operate and their success or failure. AI has the potential to either radically enable, practically overrule, or simply confuse human ethical and practical decision-making. The key characteristic of AI's impact on the military profession will be the necessity of many in the military to understand its strengths and limitations at tactical, operational, and strategic levels, to communicate these factors clearly to national decision-makers, and to build inclusive and interactive teams across the civil-military boundary as AI systems are developed and deployed.

Finally, the logical extension of capability in 'traditional' weapon systems is itself an important shaping factor for the future military profession, and one that accentuates the impact of many of the technologies mentioned above. Hypersonic attack weapons are just one salient example of a technology that may only achieve a traditional effect more rapidly (i.e. kinetic strike on a preselected target) – yet the impact on leaders in tactical decision-making or strategic deterrence and escalation planning and execution is substantial. Just as importantly, the cost and development timelines of highly sophisticated space, air, maritime and land weapon systems make their numbers inevitably smaller than previous generations of weapons. This in turn affects the way leaders must think about training, retention, attrition, resilience, basing, deployment, risk-taking, and many other considerations. And while military leaders throughout time have had to account for similar factors, the sum of technological change in weapons systems arguably poses a far more complex and therefore difficult problem than in years past.

Thus, we suggest that it is in the *character of conflict* that the velocity of change is greatest and the language we use to describe it least helpful. Developing the cognitive skills that will enable future leaders to understand and navigate complexity is imperative, and an essential part of that development is in fostering a willingness to examine and where necessary modify deeply held and unspoken assumptions about the nature of conflict and the military profession.

Millenia of history have shaped a pervasive, often unspoken Western assumption that the activity known as war, when it involves military force, is about lines on a map. Human experience of war has shaped our language and public discourse around sacrifice, physical action, proximate conflict, comradeship strengthened by shared risk and privation, and stakes that clearly and compellingly involve life and death. Such powerful shared assumptions, particularly in the US, are both compelling and confining when it comes to comprehending evolving conflict modalities. On a practical level, that same experience has been systematically codified in various 'principles of war' which proceed directly from the demands of waging physical combat, such as mass, maneuver, simplicity, surprise and others. The nominal course of an armed conflict is codified in US Joint doctrine, in which each phase is a 'definitive stage or period during a joint operation in which a large portion of the forces and capabilities are involved in similar or mutually supporting activities for a common purpose …'[4]

Current US joint combat operations notional phases include shaping, deterring, seizing initiative, dominating, stabilising, and enabling civil authority.[5] While not necessarily omnipresent or sequential in any given conflict, they are rooted in assumptions that military action will largely focus on physical control of territory and lines of communication, because these things have historically been prerequisites for maintaining the security of people and nations, or the objectives for acquisitive powers desiring to accumulate greater resources. Military action and military virtues are also intimately associated – as elaborated in literature from Homer's *Odyssey* to Hackett's *Third World War*, and in history from Thucydides to Toynbee – with physical risk, physical force, and explicit coercion or threat of coercion. This dominant historical experience led political scientist Samuel Huntington, writing in 1957, to define the core competence of the American profession of arms as the 'management of violence'.[6]

Immediately following the Second World War and in the opening decades of the Cold War, it was logical for Huntington to closely associate the profession of arms with management of violence, and his elaborations of that core military skill adequately described the societal responsibility then assigned to the American military. In the early 1970s, Morris Janowitz advanced an alternative view, still firmly anchored in the Cold War's underlying tension between fear of nuclear Armageddon and the reality of continued use of conventional arms, that the

> use of force in international relations has been so altered that it seems appropriate to speak of constabulary forces, rather than of military forces … continuously prepared to act, committed to the minimum use of force, [seeking] viable international relations, rather than victory, because [they have] incorporated a protective military posture.[7]

4 US Department of Defense, 'Joint Publication 3-0, "Joint Operations"' (US Department of Defense 2017) xvii.

5 US Department of Defense, 'Joint Publication 3-0' (n 4) v-8.

6 Samuel P. Huntington, *The Soldier & the State: The Theory and Politics of Civil-Military Relations* (Belknap Press 1957) 11.

7 Morris Janowitz, *The Professional Soldier: A Social and Political Portrait* (rev edn, The Free Press 1971) 418.

Janowitz posited that military and civilian technologies and functions would become increasingly intermingled, with consequences for the nature of that force, noting that 'the effectiveness of the military establishment depends on maintaining a proper balance between military technologists, heroic leaders, and military managers.'[8]

Much more recently, Paula Thornhill articulated this contrast, in concepts of military organisation and identity, when she noted that the American military faces a dichotomy between a historically-validated, force-employment-focused 'overseas' paradigm and an emerging 'guardian' paradigm, echoing in some respects Huntington and Janowitz' models, with their differing emphases on where, how, and under what circumstances force is an appropriate tool for militaries, and the composition of the force wielding it.[9]

Regardless of the causes of armed conflicts – whether religious, ethnic, ideological, resource, or miscalculation, the idea that peace and war are two somewhat mutually exclusive sides of a single coin has been a consistent thread throughout the history of warfare, shaping the way states have organised, trained, equipped and conceived of using their military forces. Yet this dichotomous world is increasingly less representative of the environment for which service academies must prepare their graduates. Nor is it sufficient to use the metaphor of the multi-level chessboard that some have used to depict conflict and competition in diplomatic, informational, military and economic strata; this metaphor still implies a single, physical game and finite numbers of players.

Instead, modern conflict can be conceived as an indefinite space where threads of interests – possessed by states, organisations, alliances, and even individuals – fill an ever-evolving space, like beams of light. Where those interests intersect and reinforce each other, there is coexistence and cooperation; but where they collide there is conflict in one or more domains for some period of time. The interests are continuously variable, changing the position and size of the nodes of intersection where they collide or cohere. Major war can flare at any of these nodes when conflicting interests are vital or perceived to be; and depending on the domain, geography, and other factors, the conflict may be more or less visible to the people and nations involved.

Sharply contrasting with World War I a century ago, where logistical preparations and operations plans were concrete, pervasive and time-consuming,

---

8 Janowitz (n 7) 424.

9 Paula G. Thornhill, *The Crisis Within: America's Military and the Struggle Between the Overseas and Guardian Paradigms* (RAND Corporation 2016) <https://www.rand.org/pubs/research_reports/RR1420.html> accessed 22 November 2020.

and battle was joined with great violence on now-hallowed physical battlefields, modern conflict is capable of forming in the silicon of sensors and artificial intelligence that shape human perception, and can develop in microseconds to minutes, not months. Stanley Hoffmann, writing in 1965, addressed the stability of systems in an international conflict by asserting that 'when one major actor's decision to discard [moderation] coincides with or brings about a revolution in the technology of conflict or a change in the basic structure of the world (or both), the system is particularly unstable.'[10]

Young officers commissioning into any service today simply must be educated to perceive and comprehend that kind of instability. Air Force Academy graduates face intangible threats, unlike tanks massed on a border or bombers overhead, which are far outside common experience. For example, few people across the globe know which spacefaring nations provide their personal phones with satellite navigation and timing signals, which organisations launch and maintain them, or how interwoven with society they've become – yet some of these systems have military origin, all have military application, and in all cases, have tremendous impact on modern daily life. Other technologically sophisticated systems, from power distribution to on-demand logistics to daily news and information, are similarly taken for granted but increasingly vital in a global and networked economic environment.

In short, these young officers will depend upon, operate, or oversee technically sophisticated systems that function in, or are dependent upon, multiple domains – from the terrestrial and physical to the orbital and virtual. Given that each domain is a channel for competition among potentially hostile actors, the military operational environment is very different from even thirty years ago, and it is this environment that our graduates must be prepared to master – requiring far more sophisticated cognitive skills than what was demanded of the soldiers, sailors, airmen and marines of old.

3 The Changing Character of American Society

From the World War II 'Greatest Generation,' to the 'baby boomers,' to millennials and beyond, demographers and sociologists have produced many sophisticated analyses of generational characteristics; and popular stereotypes exist in abundance. Military leaders frequently address and continuously manage

10 Stanley Hoffmann, *The State of War: Essays on the Theory and Practice of International Politics* (Praeger 1965) 92–93.

the challenges and opportunities they observe in younger service members. Beyond stereotypical characterisations of and conventional wisdom, generational characteristics are important: they affect interactions between and among cohorts of serving military members, the organisational cultures they create, and their ability to understand and master the strategic, operational, and tactical considerations necessary for success in discharging their professional responsibilities.

Not only are the characteristics of successive generations important, but evolving policy and societal imperatives shape which members of any given generation enter the Academy, consequently affecting the Academy's organisational culture and cadet experience. Lieutenant General Jay Silveria, the Air Force Academy's twentieth Superintendent, addressed this evolving dynamic:

> We come to the Air Force from across the country and around the globe, each of us with varied backgrounds and experiences, which are vital to how we exchange ideas, challenge assumptions and broaden our horizons. Diversity is one of the truest reflections of our nation's ideals, and part of the fabric of our military. It is crucial, not because it is in vogue, but because it makes us better, stronger and more effective as a fighting force. As Airmen we have a single mission: Fight and win the nation's wars, be it in the sky or in space and even cyberspace.[11]

The combination of generational characteristics and increasing demographic diversity implies the cohorts of young men and women entering the Academy are less formal, less instinctively comfortable with hierarchical organisations, and far more omnivorous in their information consumption habits; they are more 'connected' than previous generations and less inclined to seek information coming solely through a hierarchical chain of command as their only or most important source of guidance. Unlike generations of predecessors, where direct supervisors, peers and subordinates formed perceptions of each other in a largely first-person sense, entering generations of cadets often encounter each other in third-person virtual arenas that change with the speed of Twitter, Facebook, YouTube, Snapchat, Jodel and countless other social media platforms.

As Remi Hajjar observed in 2014, these kinds of postmodern dynamics

11 Jay Silveria, 'Air Force Academy Leader: Why Diversity?' *CNN Opinion* (2018) <https://www.cnn.com/2018/02/14/opinions/air-force-academy-superintendent-why-diversity-opinion-silveria/index.html> accessed 22 November 2020.

> influence the culture of the US military, including the world-wide growth of ambiguity, multiculturalism, the information age, increased civilians in military positions, greater questioning of traditions, authority, ideas, and plans, and the rise of a multi-mission postmodern military that bears prominent and influential warrior and peacekeeper–diplomat cultural orientations and tools, as well as other cultural spheres.[12]

In other words, both cadets and the military profession they are joining are changing. The character of the generation entering the US Air Force Academy today is very different than in 1955, when the first class entered. Those differences encompass new strengths and new weaknesses, so the Academy experience must evolve to reinforce the strengths and mitigate the weaknesses – while recognising that the evolution will be as much discovered as designed in the interactions between the teachers and the taught.

4 The Air Force Academy's Character & Leadership Development Construct

We consider it useful to share the approach that the United States Air Force Academy has taken, and is taking, toward developing leaders of character. In early 2019, Air Force leadership reiterated the Academy's mission: 'to educate, train, and inspire men and women to become officers of character, motivated to lead the United States Air Force in service to the nation.'[13] Since graduating its first class of cadets in 1959, the institution has remained focused on the development of the qualities of character and leadership necessary in the profession of arms and functionally required of officers in the Air Force and since December 2019, in the Space Force.

The Academy's course of instruction combines study and experiences through academic, military and athletic pillars to prepare cadets for the physical, moral and intellectual challenges they will face as officers. The program emphasises a broad liberal education to deal with technological, ethical, cultural and human issues they will likely face in the future. Coupled with the scholarly journey are ethical, leadership, military training and athletic experiences providing developmental opportunities for cadets. It is through this

12 Remi M. Hajjar, 'Emergent Postmodern US Military Culture' (2014) 40 (1) *Armed Forces & Society* 122.

13 United States Air Force, 'Air Force Mission Directive 12' (5 March 2019) 1.

experiential learning that cadets practice, falter, learn and develop the qualities and skills expected from them in the profession of arms.

The US Air Force Academy values a culture of assessment and feedback and recognizes a potential paradigm shift defining the Profession of Arms has the potential to outpace the development program we offer cadets. As such, the Academy seeks to ensure the four-year development program reinforces the professional values and innovative leadership necessary for graduates to grasp, comprehend and lead through the difficult challenges they will face in a non-linear and unpredictable future.

5 Character Development in Higher Education and the Profession of Arms

From its colonial beginning, higher education in the United States has had a role in the character and moral development of its students. The early American educational system combined intellectual development and moral development as inseparable requirements for an enlightened graduate.[14] According to Rudolph, the early American college had developed an 'impressive arsenal' for developing students.[15] One of these influences was a senior level core course that was commonly taught by the college president. This final capstone course focused on moral and intellectual philosophy. Rudolph described how the college president's powerful stature and the moral philosophy course was considered 'essential to the formation of true character' in the students.[16] Even today, the mission statements of many US colleges and universities acknowledge their roles in promoting character in their students.[17]

Moral and character research has roots in developmental theory in which an individual progresses in moral and character development as he/she proceeds through various age/education stages in his/her life.[18] In their summary

14 Frederick Rudolph, *The American College and University* (2nd edn, University of Georgia Press 1990).

15 Rudolph (n 14) 140.

16 Rudolph (n 14) 140.

17 Anne Colby and William M. Sullivan, 'Formation of Professionalism and Purpose: Perspective From the Preparation for the Professions Program' (2008) 5 (2) *University of St. Thomas Law Journal* 404–427.

18 Lawrence Kohlberg, 'Moral Stages and Moralization: The Cognitive-Developmental Approach' in Thomas Lickona (ed), *Moral Development and Behavior: Theory, Research, and Social Issues* (Rinehart & Winston 1976) 31–53; Jean Piaget, The Moral Judgment of the Child (first published 1932, The Free Press 1965).

of research studies concerning change in moral development by year in college, Pascarella and Terenzini (1991) concluded that students typically make dramatic gains in moral and character development during college.[19] Based on the consistent empirical evidence available, Rest concluded that 'cognitive restructuring of one's moral thinking seems to be more related to formal education than to passage of years.'[20] In 1985, Rest and Thoma came out even stronger asserting that formal education was the most consistent and powerful correlate with moral judgment.[21]

Researchers continue to publish on the impact of college on the development of the 18–25 year old cohort and that the college experience involves growth in student understanding of the nature of truth and beliefs, values and their relation to the self, professional responsibilities and commitments, political identity, and other critical aspects of adult life.[22] The college experience with this age cohort is vital to personal and moral growth.[23]

Identifying and committing to values and beliefs is an important component within a character development program. The higher education and military profession environment provide a unique context to frame character development. In her research, Shannon French provided insights into the important influence of military values as they shaped warrior cultures.[24] Stated values frame the culture and artifacts that reinforce an individual's development within an organisation. Edgar Schein indicated that cultural norms, values, beliefs about what is important and virtuous, and how the group reinforces the commitment to these organisational values is important to the development

19 Ernest T. Pascarella and Patrick T. Terenzini, *How College Affects Students* (Jossey-Bass 1991).

20 James R. Rest, *Development in Judging Moral Issues* (rev edn, University of Minnesota Press 1979) 112.

21 James R. Rest and Steven J. Thoma, 'Relation of Moral Judgement Development to Formal Education' (1985), 21 *Developmental Psychology* 709–714.

22 Patricia M. King & Karen Strohm Kitchener, 'Reflective Judgement: Theory and Research on the Development of Epistemic Assumptions Through Adulthood' (2004) 39 (1) *Educational Psychologist* 5–18.

23 Christopher J. Luedtke 'A Longitudinal and Qualitative Descriptive Study of Cadet Moral Judgment' (PhD Dissertation, The Florida State University College of Education 1999); Anne Colby, 'Fostering the Moral and Civic Development of College Students' in Larry P. Nucci and Darcia Narvaez (eds), *Handbook of Moral and Character Education* (1st edn, Routledge 2008) 391–413; Ronald L. Dufresne and Evan H. Offstein, 'Holistic and Intentional Student Character Development Process: Learning from West Point' (2012) 11 (4) *Academy of Management Learning & Education* 570–590; James R. Rest and Darcia Narvaez (eds), *Moral Development in the Professions* (Lawrence Erlbaum Associates, Inc. 1994).

24 Shannon E. French, *The Code of the Warrior: Exploring Warrior Values Past and Present* (first published 2003, Rowman and Littlefield Publishers 2005).

of individuals within the group.[25] More recently, researchers have identified the importance that environmental context has on an individual's character development.[26]

Character development in higher education must be fully integrated to be effective. According to Berkowitz and Bier, an integrated character development program has applicability to student motivation, achievement, positive social behaviour, promoting moral reasoning, shaping identity, and building mutual trust. Essential to the character development program integration is the requirement for professional development of the college faculty, coaches, staff, and leadership in order for them to understand, implement, and reinforce character development as role models.[27] Huitt and Vessels contend that effective character development is complex combining formal instruction, exemplary leadership and reinforcing activities that allow students to increase their understanding through practice.[28]

Beyond higher education's role in character and moral development, it offers leadership development opportunities. Combining both character and leadership development has captured the interest of additional academics, such as Sendjaya (2005) who argues that 'morality is a necessary component of leadership' ...'its absence could turn an otherwise powerful leadership model (i.e. transformational leadership) into a disastrous outcome.'[29] Ciulla (1995) maintains that for leadership to be superior, it has to include both technical competencies and moral capacities.[30] It is insufficient for leaders to be effective but unethical. Sendjaya further asserts 'the ultimate goal of leadership education is to create good leaders who are both effective and ethical, strategically equipped with technical and moral proficiencies.'[31] Kraack (1985) argued that leadership experiences had an important impact on character development as

---

25 Edgar H. Schein, *Organizational Culture and Leadership* (2nd edn Jossey-Bass 1992).

26 Richard M. Lerner and Kristina Schmid Callina, 'The Study of Character Development: Towards Tests of a Relational Developmental Systems Model' (2015) 57 (6) *Human Development* 322–346.

27 Marvin W. Berkowitz & Melinda C. Bier, 'Research-Based Character Education' (2004) 591 (1) *The Annals of the American Academy of Political and Social Science* 72.

28 William G. Huitt and Gordon G. Vessels, *Character Development: Looking Back, the Eclectic Ideal* (Early Twenty-First Century 2015).

29 Sen Sendjaya 'Morality and Leadership: Examining the Ethics of Transformational Leadership' (2005) 3 (1) *Journal of Academic Ethics* 75.

30 Joanne B. Ciulla, 'Leadership Ethics: Mapping the Territory' (1995) 5 (1) *Business Ethics Quarterly* 5–25.

31 Sendjaya (n 29) 84.

leaders had to reason through ethical and moral dilemmas that they faced in their decision-making.[32]

For American military service academies, the intersection of character/moral development research and leadership development research has been a consistent focus. In a recent journal article, Developing Leaders of Character at the United States Military Academy, the authors concluded,

> when higher education gives explicit attention to these outcomes, as West Point and other military academies do, we argue that the undergraduate experience is a particularly effective setting for promoting advances in character development.[33]

Lisa Kuhmerker, founder of the Moral Education Forum, has recognised the military's initiative and leadership in the area of character education programs and called for inquiry into moral education in the military training environment with specific interest in the values the military is trying to inculcate in recruits and how recruits interpret the values training they receive. She stated,

> In a democracy where the military is under the direction of a civilian government structure, civilians have an obligation to inform themselves about the values taught in their military institutions.[34]

Building on the experience of other service academies since graduating its first class of cadets in 1959, the Air Force Academy has maintained a primary mission focus on the character development of its students, holding that given the right environment, cadets will develop an understanding of the moral values expected in the military profession. The institution believes,

> Cadets arrive at the institution at a time of their lives when they are naturally interested in questions and values … although they may not possess

32 T. Kraack, 'The relation of moral development to involvement and leadership experiences' (Unpublished Doctoral Dissertation, University of Minnesota 1985).

33 Kristina Schmid Callina, Diane Ryan, Elise D. Murray, Anne Colby, William Damon, Michael Matthews and Richard M. Lerner, 'Developing Leaders of Character at the United States Military Academy: A Relational Developmental Systems Analysis' (2017) 18 (1) *Journal of College and Character* 9–27.

34 Lisa Kuhmerker, "Moral development research designed to make a difference: Some gaps waiting to be filled," (1995) 20 (4) *The Moral Education Forum* 2–10, 6.

> professional military character when they arrive here, the right institutional environment will help them develop it.[35]

Utilising the work of Thomas Lickona, the Academy has historically defined good character as having three interrelated parts: moral knowing, moral feeling, and moral behaviour.[36] The Academy wanted to graduate officers who could judge what is right, care deeply about what is right, and then do what they believe to be right. The philosophy called for the interrelationship of the cognitive component of moral knowing, the affective component of moral feeling, and the behavioural component of moral action. Good character is thought to be present when these three components work together to do the right thing for the right reason.[37]

6 The Mandate for Developing Leaders of Character

Certainly, developmental and academic research suggests the value of developing leadership and character in future military officers, but the federal military academies in the United States draw guidance, resources and direction on their purpose and mission from higher level government authorities, just as other nations' military education institutions are similarly guided by their governments. For United States military academies (Military Academy, Naval Academy and Air Force Academy) Department of Defense Instruction 1322.22 directs that they:

> Provide, each year, newly commissioned officers to each Service that have been immersed in the history, traditions, and professional values of the Military Services and developed to be leaders of character, dedicated to a career of professional excellence in service to the Nation. The accession of those officers generates a core group of innovative leaders capable of thinking critically who will exert positive peer influence to convey and sustain these traditions attitudes, values, and beliefs essential to the long-term readiness and success of the Military Services.[38]

35 United States Air Force Academy Center for Character Development, 'Character Development Manual' (Unpublished Manuscript, 1994) 2.

36 US Air Force Academy 'Character' (n 35) 17.

37 US Air Force Academy 'Character' (n 35) 21.

38 United States Department of Defense, 'Department of Defense Instruction 1322.22' (United States Department of Defense 2015) 1.

In 2017, the US Secretary of Defense James Mattis authored an expectation memorandum to all Department of Defense service members and employees. The memorandum entitled 'Ethical Standards for All Hands' served as the Defense Secretary's personal effort to express his ethical expectations for personnel to be an honorable example, stressing that ethics were vital in the profession of arms. The memorandum embraces innovation, but not at the expense of ethical standards. The Secretary states,

> To ensure each of us are ready to do what is right, without hesitation, when ethical dilemmas arise, we must train and prepare ourselves and our subordinates … I want our focus to be on the essence of ethical conduct: doing what is right at all times, regardless of the circumstances or whether anyone is watching.[39]

US Air Force Mission Directive 12 further clarifies mission focus for the US Air Force Academy, mandating the Academy:

- Instill in cadets commitment to the Air Force core values.
- Be a leadership laboratory that provides cadets opportunities to learn and develop values-driven leadership through practice.
- Deliver an accredited Bachelor of Science degree program based on a core curriculum that includes a strong foundation in science, technology, mathematics, and engineering, complemented by a foundation in the social sciences and humanities [and] instill in cadets the intellectual curiosity, innovative spirit, and desire for self-improvement that will follow them throughout their Air Force careers.
- Develop an appreciation and understanding of the spectrum of Air Force operations in the context of the joint force.
- Challenge cadets with a wide range of competitive opportunities to develop habits of excellence, both as individuals and as teammates.[40]

Air Force Instruction 36–2014 defines a leader of character as one who has internalised the Air Force's core values, lives by a high moral code, treats others with mutual respect and demonstrates a strong sense of ethics. The warrior ethos is the embodiment of the warrior spirit: tough mindedness, tireless

39 James Mattis, 'Secretary of Defense Memorandum: Ethical Standards for All Hands' (United States Department of Defense 2017).

40 United States Air Force, 'Mission Directive' (n 13) 2–3.

motivation, an unceasing vigilance, a willingness to sacrifice one's life for the country, if necessary, and a commitment to be the world's premier air, space and cyberspace force.[41]

Consistent with this higher-level guidance, the Air Force Academy has further defined its roles, responsibilities and intentions in a number of institutional documents. The most recent revision of the Academy's strategic plan defines its vision, mission, and goals to unify the academic, athletic and military mission elements toward a common set of objectives. The plan emphasizes:

> The lieutenants we commission must be innovative Airmen of character, steeped in the warrior ethos. Innovation, warrior ethos, and character are embedded in the Academy's institutional outcomes and guide how we develop and deliver our programs and experiences to produce 21st century leaders. It is paramount that our graduates lead with impeccable character, guided by the core values of our Air Force and Academy. The fundamental notion of treating others with respect and dignity underpins our graduates' ability to lead their fellow Airmen and shape an appropriate culture and climate in the Air and Space Forces they will guide into a historic new era.[42]

Further, the strategic plan conveys a vision that makes clear the Academy's intent to graduate principled leaders capable to grappling with complex future military challenges, as it seeks to be 'the Air and Space Forces' premier institution for developing innovative leaders of character ready to lead in future conflict.'[43]

With that mission and vision in mind, the Air Force Core Values serve as the essential foundation for cadet leadership and character development.

Core values are qualities that outline an organisation's highest priorities and deeply held beliefs. Core values define what an organisation believes and how the organisation is reflected amongst personnel internal to the organisation and interactions external to the organisation. Core values are deeply integrated amongst personnel within the organisation clearly linking the professional belief systems and organisational actions.[44]

---

41 US Air Force, 'Air Force Mission Directive' (n 40) 6.

42 United States Air Force Academy, 'US Air Force Academy Strategic Plan' (United States Air Force Academy 2020) 5.

43 US Air Force Academy, 'Strategic Plan' (n 42) 6.

44 Susan M. Heathfield, 'Core Values Are What You Believe' (2019) <www.thebalancecareers.com/core-values-are-what-you-believe-1918079> accessed 25 November 2020.

The Air Force core values, *Integrity First*, *Service before Self*, and *Excellence in All We Do*, are a statement of those timeless institutional values and principles of conduct that provide the moral framework for military activities. They 'provide a foundation for leadership, decision-making, and success, no matter the level of an Airman's assignment, the difficulty of the task at hand, or the dangers presented by the mission.'[45]

The Air Force core values are a commitment each cadet makes when they enter the Academy; they are central to each day as cadets attend academic classes, pursue scientific research, conduct military training, hone their leadership through experience, compete in athletic events and pursue aviation activities. By internalizing the core values and practicing their application across the range of Academy experiences, cadets gain the skills and confidence to operate in a fast-moving, dynamic, and complex environment. Cadets must gain confidence that their commitment to, and experience with, the core values will guide their leadership when time and information limitations are against them. Education, training, experience and practice, and reflection helps these values become second nature and contribute to the officer being better prepared in all situations. These values provide a foundation for leadership, decision-making, and success that will guide the Air Force officer in their leadership role.

Nested under the Academy mission statement are institutional goals and objectives to refine focus on cadet development activities, ensuring an integrated course of instruction using academic, military and athletic pillars to develop character and leadership in cadets. The goals and objectives foster a balance between classroom, role modelling, athletic competition, military development and experiential/participatory opportunities supporting character and leadership development. The leader of character development effort is further designed to link in-depth intellectual, technical, physical and military skills and competencies for leadership and innovation in air, space and cyberspace for Air Force and Joint operations.[46]

The collective higher expectations levied upon the profession of arms, and specifically the US military, serve as the mandate for character and leadership development efforts at the US Air Force Academy. Both Department of Defense and Air Force Instructions provide mission expectations and direction for the Academy to develop leaders of character. With a firm understanding of the

45 United States Air Force, 'Air Force Doctrine Volume II: Leadership' (Curtis E. Lemay Center 2015) 13.

46 US Air Force, 'Doctrine Volume II' (n 45).

impetus for developing leaders of character at the Academy, we turn to how the Academy pursues this mission.

7 How the US Air Force Academy Develops Leaders of Character

The Academy is organised around three primary organisations which make unique contributions to developing leaders of character through academics and research, military training and experiences, and athletic pursuits. The Dean of Faculty leads the rigorous Bachelor of Science undergraduate degree program. The cadets pursue a broad liberal education with strong emphasis in Science, Technology, Engineering, and Math (STEM), as well as deep pursuit of the Social Sciences and Humanities. The Commandant of Cadets leads the cadet military training and leadership development experience through a 47-month curriculum. This experience continues beyond the formal training venues to the cadet dormitories where students live and work together organised as a military squadron with associated leadership and follower roles distributed to facilitate experiential development. Lower ranking cadets fulfill follower roles focused on personal responsibility and accountability, while more senior cadets serve as leaders with responsibility and accountability for the others. The Athletic Director leads athletic programs designed to foster initiative, teamwork, confidence and competition as contributions to the development of cadets into leaders of character, including 25% of cadets who participate in intercollegiate competition sanctioned by the National Collegiate Athletic Association (NCAA). Cadets also complete physical education courses and compete in intramural athletic competitions.

These three mission elements – academic, military, and athletic – are designed to work together in a concerted effort to reinforce development of leaders of character. In order to facilitate the pursuit and assessment of necessary officer competencies, the Air Force Academy identified nine outcomes for the mission elements to align their programs, curriculum, and assessment. While their precise formulation is specific to the Air Force Academy, these Institutional Outcomes are likely to be applicable in some degree to any modern military education and training program. They are:

> *Critical Thinking*
> Upon graduation, graduates will be required to identify and solve complex problems and effectively respond to situations they have not previously confronted. Acting responsibly in an ever-changing world of ill-defined problems requires critical thinking. Academy graduates will

be able to think through complex problems with self-aware, informed, and reflective reasoning for problem-solving and decision-making in the absence of ideal information.

Application of Engineering Methods
Graduates will recognise the engineering and technical challenges of the Air Force mission and the physical capabilities and limits within their assigned career fields and weapon systems. Graduates will be problem solvers that use engineering principles to devise enhanced capabilities essential to achieving and maintaining Air Force dominance in air, space, and cyberspace.

Scientific Reasoning and the Principles of Science
Graduates will be science-proficient officers who can make decisions in a world increasingly influenced by scientific and quantitative data. Officers will be proficient in the Nature of Science, Scientific Reasoning, and the Principles of Science.

The Human Condition, Cultures, and Societies
Academy graduates will be required to interact with a wide range of individuals, to include those representing cultures and societies different from their own. To foster success in these interactions, the Academy focuses cadet understanding of the human condition, cultures, and societies in both domestic and international environments.

Leadership, Teamwork, and Organisational Management
The Academy develops leaders through implementation of the Officer Development System (ODS) which will be discussed further in this chapter. ODS utilises the PITO model, which organises leadership capabilities development into Personal Leadership, Interpersonal Leadership, Team Leadership, and Organisational Leadership.

Clear Communication
Clear communication is a complex, nuanced and teachable practice essential for successful officers and leaders of character. Effective use of oral, visual, written, and aural modes of communication signifies the professional competence and knowledge expected in a leader while engendering the trust of those being led. Officers must routinely assess context, understand purpose, develop processes, know audiences, and employ the materials necessary to plainly convey intentions.

Ethics and Respect for Human Dignity
When deciding how to act, a leader of character comprehends moral knowledge and ethical alternatives, respects the dignity of all affected persons, uses ethical judgment in moral decision-making to select the best alternative, and acts consistently with that judgment so as to develop habits of moral excellence.

National Security
National Security commonly refers to 'the ability of the state to protect the fundamental values and core interests of a society'. Within the broader objective that cadets be prepared to 'defend our nation in air, space, and cyberspace', this Outcome emphasises not only the operational, tactical, and technological capabilities necessary to do so but also the broader political context in which military force must be employed.

Warrior Ethos and Airmen as Citizens
Warrior ethos is the embodiment of the warrior spirit: tough mindedness, tireless motivation, an unceasing vigilance, a willingness to sacrifice one's life for the country, if necessary, and a commitment to be the world's premier air, space and cyberspace force. The warrior ethos proficiencies comprise a structure that is based on the intellectual development inherent to the Profession of Arms. The Warrior Ethos is described in Air Force Doctrine Document 1–1 as 'exhibiting a hardiness of spirit despite physical and mental hardships … It compels one to fight through all conditions to victory, no matter how long it takes and no matter how much effort is required. Warrior Ethos is grounded in the refusal to accept failure … it reminds us that the unlimited liability of the profession of arms may require one to sacrifice their life to save others and accomplish the mission.'[47]

To optimise the Outcomes' collective impact throughout the academic, military, and athletic programs, the Academy has identified cross-functional teams for each Outcome that include faculty and staff from all mission elements. They are responsible to the institutional leadership for integrating the Outcomes in curriculum and programs and assessing cadet and institutional effectiveness in these areas.

---

47 United States Air Force Academy, 'US Air Force Academy Outcomes' (2018) <www.usafa.edu/academics/outcomes/> accessed 25 November 2020.

As mentioned above, the Officer Development System (ODS) is a guiding doctrine to develop leaders of character over the four years they attend the Academy. In 2003, a multi-disciplinary team of military and civilian faculty and staff from across the Academy collaborated in the development of ODS, with publication and introduction to cadets through a series of lectures and workshops in 2004.[48] Importantly, this developmental framework allows cadets to direct their own intellectual, physical, social, and spiritual development and enables them to guide others' development, a critical leadership skill. Fourteen years later, ODS remains the leadership development framework guiding cadet development.

ODS is developmental in intent as cadets move through followership and leadership levels that become progressively broader and more complex as a cadet gains experience, becomes more responsible, and matures. The ODS process involves all the mission elements at the Academy and encompasses every dimension of a cadet's life – intellectual, professional, physical, ethical, spiritual, and social – while remaining focused on character development.

Contemporary theories describe leadership in terms of the interpersonal relationship between leaders and followers rather than defining leadership solely by the position power a leader holds. This shift from a focus on instrumental towards relational bases of power in leadership reflects increased inclusion of interpersonal style. For example, one such theory describes transformational leadership as a process in which leaders engage with others and create a connection that raises the level of motivation, performance, and morality of both the leader and followers. Transformational leaders are attentive to the needs of their followers and try to help followers achieve their fullest potential.[49]

The ODS encompasses these sorts of considerations, outlining a framework for the development and interactions that cadets will experience as they participate across the academic, military, and athletic activities at the Academy. ODS has two main components or models, the Personal, Interpersonal, Teamwork and Organisational Model (PITO) and the Leadership Growth Model (LGM).

The PITO model describes and defines the competencies for each level of the cadet developmental process. Cadets develop their follower-leader

48 Heidi L. Smith and Christopher Luedtke, 'Military Missions and Their Implications Reconsidered: The Aftermath of September 11th' in Giuseppe Caforio and Gerhard Kümmel (eds), *Contributions to Conflict Management, Peace Economics and Development* (Elsevier Ltd 2005) 377–398.

49 Bernard Bass, *Leadership and Performance Beyond Expectations* (Free Press 1985); Peter Guy Northouse, *Leadership: Theory and Practice* (Sage Publications 1997).

competencies through the four areas, mastering personal accountability, advancing to interpersonal skills, then to team leadership, and finally shifting to organisational leadership. Each aspect of the leadership development hierarchy includes, leverages and further develops previous skills. Figure 13.1 provides a depiction of the cadet's development through the PITO leadership model. A four-degree represents a cadet in their first year at the Academy while a first-degree represents a cadet in their final year at the Academy, serving in cadet leadership positions. Of note in the figure, a four-degree is focused on building their proficiency in personal responsibility and accountability represented by the colour purple. By the time a cadet is in their final year as a first-degree, their skills show competency across the PITO model represented pictorially with an organisational leader using personal skills, interpersonal skills, team leadership skills, and organisational leadership competency .

In mapping leadership objectives for each cadet at each phase, the ODS provides a progressive, deliberate process tailorable to meet individual needs. As a more junior cadet develops their personal responsibility and accountability

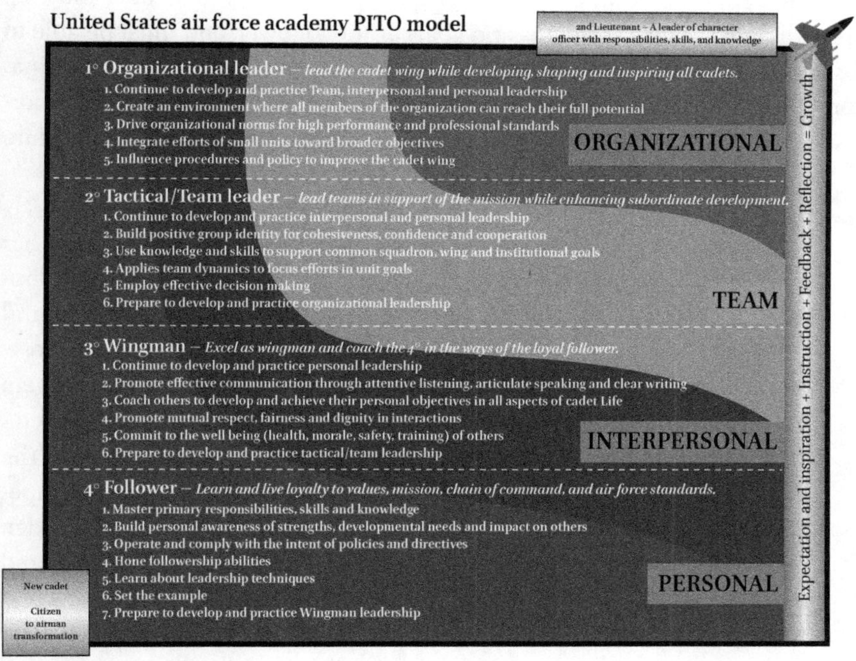

FIGURE 13.1 Air Force Academy Personal, Interpersonal, Teamwork and Organisational (PITO) Model[a]

a United States Air Force Academy, 'United States Air Force Academy Pamphlet 36-3527' (United States Air Force Academy 2013) 13.

under the supervision and mentoring of more senior cadets, the more senior cadets develop their interpersonal, team and organisational leadership skills through mentoring, coaching and responsibility for leading the organisation.

The ODS Leadership Growth Model (LGM) builds on the PITO framework, empowering and guiding interaction in the development process. It depicts how the leader and follower collaboratively approach the education, training, experiences and challenges that develop the leader competencies in the PITO model. Figure 13.2 depicts this interactive component between the leader and follower.

By providing a guide for leadership growth, the LGM captures the interpersonal, transformational process desired between cadets at the Academy. The core of the relationship between leader and follower is a mutual focus on follower development, where the leader coaches and mentors the follower and growth occurs as a result of an iterative process involving four steps: (1) establishing expectations and offering inspiration, (2) providing instruction, (3) feedback regarding performance, and (4) reflection on lessons learned. Leaders and followers must develop a number of interpersonal skills to successfully apply the LGM. In order to inspire the follower, the leader must be keenly attuned to the emotions and goals of the follower, and must be able to communicate in a way that is inspiring to the individual follower (a combination of Inspirational Motivation and Individualised Consideration in transformational leadership theory). Providing instruction and feedback will require leaders to nurture and counsel followers.[50] According to the LGM:

> In the first stage, the leader critically appraises the situation, his or her own skills, and the skills of the follower; the leader then sets developmental expectations with the follower. The leader also provides inspiration to the follower by developing a shared understanding of purpose. In the next stage, the leader provides the essential instruction to help the follower meet the leader's, follower's, and organisation's expectations and objectives. As the follower works toward these objectives, the leader coaches and mentors the follower, assesses the follower's competency and provides feedback throughout their engagement. The leader, during the instruction and feedback stages, must integrate coaching and mentoring techniques to help bridge the gap between expectations and results. Finally, the reflection stage (where the leader and follower review their expectations, instructions, and feedback) crystallises any lessons

50 Smith and Luedtke (n 40).

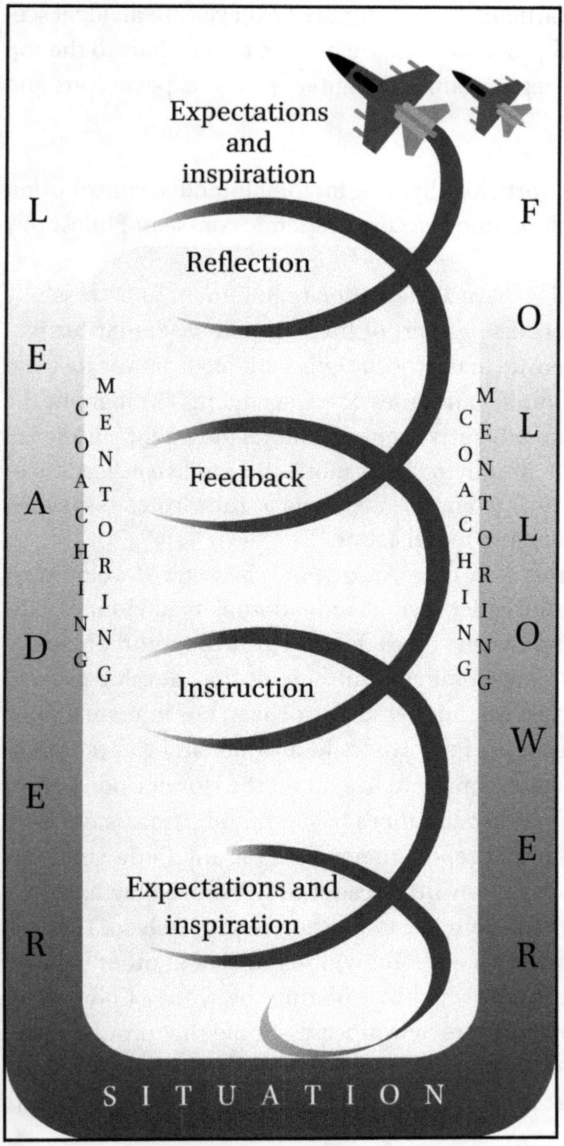

FIGURE 13.2 Air Force Academy Leadership Growth Model (LGM)[a]
a US Air Force Academy, 'Academy Pamphlet 36-3527' (n 50) 15.

> learned and prepares participants to enter the next cycle. In an ideal scenario, a participant will progress from the bottom of the chart to the top of the spiral and then begin again at a higher level of expectations and inspiration.[51]

Two additional activities are worth highlighting for their intended contribution toward cadet character development: the core academic course in Philosophy and the Cadet Honor Code.

All Air Force Academy cadets have a graduation requirement to successfully complete a core Philosophy course as part of the required academic curriculum. Cadets learn ethical theories and expectations with focus on the just war tradition, the law of armed conflict and rules of engagement. 'Throughout the course, cadets enhance their deliberative capacity, moral judgment, and sensitivity to ethical nuance while improving their motivation to live as leaders of character. Cadets also gain tools to analyse accounts of the virtues associated with excellent moral judgment and moral action.'[52]

An important pillar of the Air Force Academy's character development efforts has historically been the cadet-owned and -administered Honor Code. It represents an ethical commitment by each cadet to live honorably and a developmental opportunity to live that commitment as they develop as leaders. The Honor Oath states: 'We will not lie, steal, or cheat, nor tolerate among us anyone who does. Furthermore, I resolve to do my duty and to live honorably, (so help me God).'[53] Cadets commit to live under the Honor Code as they enter the Cadet Wing after the first summer's basic training. Consistent with the Code, 'Cadets are expected to report themselves for any Code violation. Furthermore, they must confront any other cadet they believe may have violated the code and report the incident if the situation is not resolved. This creates an atmosphere of trust and accountability unparalleled at other colleges or universities.'[54] If a cadet is suspected of violating the Honor Code, other cadets administer an administrative review process; should that process result in convening an Honor Board, a panel of cadets review the alleged violation of the Honor Code. If a cadet is determined to be in violation, the cadet could

---

51 US Air Force Academy, 'Academy Pamphlet 36-3527' (n 50) 15–16.

52 US Air Force Academy, 'Philosophy' (2018) <https://www.usafa.edu/academic/philosophy/> accessed 25 November 2020.

53 United States Air Force Academy Admissions, 'Honor Code' (2018) <https://www.academyadmissions.com/the-experience/character/honor-code/>.

54 US Air Force Academy Admissions, 'Honor Code' (n 55).

face accountability ranging from an honor probation designed to rehabilitate the cadet, to potential expulsion from the Academy.

In a comprehensive longitudinal study of the moral/character development of the US Air Force Academy Class of 1999, Luedtke found that the honor code, peer and faculty interaction, the core academic course in ethics, reflection, leadership responsibility, social interaction, discussion, and role-modelling all emerged as positive events/relationships in cadet moral judgment development.[55] The restrictive Academy environment, peer pressure, poor role modelling, and institutional dogma emerged as key events/relationships that had a negative impact on cadet moral judgment. Importantly, the longitudinal study also found linkages between advances in moral development and leaders experiences. Additionally, the Academy honor code emerged as a significant moral experience for cadets. No other researchers have previously identified an institutional honor code as a significant moral influence on developmental experience questionnaires. In the Air Force Academy context, living under the honor code appears to encourage cadets to reflect about moral issues as they assess ethical considerations regarding their own commitment not to violate the code or tolerate others that have violated the code.[56]

The long-standing Honor Code and the core Philosophy course at the Academy are important developmental experiences in each cadet's four years. In previous longitudinal research conducted at the Academy, cadets identified both the core Philosophy course and the cadet Honor Code as having a reflective and developmental impact on their commitment toward becoming Leaders of Character.[57]

As effective and powerful as each of these models, outcomes, and codes and educational experiences have been, the Academy has redoubled its efforts over the last decade to put in place a unifying construct to help prepare graduates to lead ethically and effectively in the challenging future conflict environment. The Leader of Character Framework, first published in 2011 and more recently articulated in 2020, is increasingly seen as an effective means to provide cadets and faculty with a means of connecting key character and leadership attributes with a practical framework for developing them. It is designed to facilitate development of a professional whose embodiment of the core values motivates others to do the right thing, for the right reasons, and who fosters the continuous development of their own and others' individual and collective capabilities. Leaders of character demonstrate moral excellence reflected

55 Luedtke 'Study of Cadet Moral Judgment' (n 23).
56 Luedtke (n 23).
57 Luedtke (n 23).

in their values and behaviour. They set a personal example for all, whether in their units, organisations or society.

As defined in this framework, a leader of character:

- *Lives honorably* by consistently practicing virtues embodied in the core values
- *Lifts others* to their best possible selves; and
- *Elevates performance* to a common and noble purpose.[58]

The framework also outlines a developmental process for achieving these aspirations. In it, individuals *own* pursuit of their identities as leaders of character; both individual and institution *engage* in purposeful experiences to foster identity development; and leaders *practice* habits of thought and actions. An important part of the 'practice' is inculcating the strength of character required to translate ethical decision into right action – what the framework calls crossing the 'decision-action' gap. Consistently achieving this result requires developing the *awareness* an ethical choice exists; *reasoning* about that choice; *deciding* consistent with the values of a leader of character; and importantly, *acting* in line with that decision.[59]

8 Immutable Values

With this background in Academy leadership and character development processes, we now return to complete our discussion of an overarching theme of effective military leadership development introduced early in this chapter: preparing for the future by continuously reconciling the *changing character of conflict*, the *changing character of successive generations* entering military service, and the *immutable values* of the military profession.[60]

We briefly surveyed the first two of these three ideas – change in conflict and in those entering the military profession – and detailed the mechanisms the Academy has employed to prepare its graduates to serve. In the remaining narrative, we will suggest how this idea of reconciliation, for the US Air Force

58 Center for Character and Leadership Development, 'Developing Leaders of Character at the United States Air Force Academy: A conceptual framework' (United States Air Force Academy 2011).

59 Douglas Lindsay, John Abbatiello, David Huston and Scott Heyler, 'Developing Leaders of Character', (2020) 7/2 *Journal of Character and Leadership Development* 25–28 <https://jcli.scholasticahq.com/article/13606-developing-leaders-of-character> accessed 25 November 2020.

60 Rokke (n 1).

Academy and any similar institution, may be even better achieved by focusing on development of the attributes we ascribe to a leader of character. The values which underpin the definition are invariant. In light of changes in the character of conflict and of society, however, the manifestation of each leader of character trait is likely to show up differently depending on the context in which they apply. The expression of these leadership and character attributes – living honorably, lifting others, and elevating performance – can and must evolve with the context in which they exist, and recognizing that reality gives educators and leaders the greatest chance of developing a future military force that remains both effective in complex, changing circumstances and firmly connected to the enduring military values that reinforce societal trust and confidence in the profession.

9 Living Honorably

In the Air Force's authoritative publication on Core Values, Integrity is said to be realised when thoughts and actions align with what one knows is right; 'doing the right thing, all the time, whether everyone is watching or no one is watching.'[61] The virtues which demonstrate one values integrity include honesty, courage, and accountability.

The Academy processes outlined above all operate to build the understanding and practice of integrity, beginning with lessons in the honor code and introduction to the Profession of Arms during Basic Training, through a multidisciplinary Officership curriculum in subsequent years, and through purposeful interactions in other academic, military and athletic settings. It does so with entering populations of cadets that come from a far wider cross-section of society than even ten or twenty years prior; as a former Air Force Chief of Staff and Academy graduate expressed it in a 2014 interview,

> On the character side, we draw people in from a huge funnel of character. A huge spectrum out here of how people behave, how they act, what their families think, what part of society they come from, all the things that drive people. So their character funnel's like this [gestures with arms outstretched] when they come in the door ... Our job is to compress that into a character funnel that's about that wide [gestures indicating a small

61 United States Air Force, 'America's Air Force: A Profession of Arms' (2015) 6.

> distance] – the way we expect them to behave, the way we expect them to treat each other, the way we expect them to perform.[62]

The virtues of honesty, courage, and accountability form a sound basis for such acculturation, but interpretation is essential.

As one example, the US ideal of an apolitical officer corps remains intact in law and policy, but the velocity of modern media, the blurring of physical and virtual arenas for political expression, and the intensity associated with contemporary political disagreements makes it more complex to educate incoming cadets on appropriate participation in politics. Research by Army colonel Heidi Urben found that mid-grade and younger officers in surveyed populations are active in social media and often post political and/or partisan expressions, such as 'friending' political figures, or posting critical comments on such figures.[63] This has the potential of posing long-term integrity challenges as political views, expressed in the moment, become a public record with which military officers must contend as their rank and responsibilities increase – and which may be used by others to form judgments, accurate or inaccurate, about their trustworthiness.

Similarly, conduct which historically has been known only to those directly involved, or ascribed to youth or temporary bad judgment, is today a potential matter of electronic record and the subject of potential immediate and delayed scrutiny.

On a strategic level, contemporary cadets face a far more complex ethical decision-making landscape than their counterparts in recent decades. Honorable service is profoundly defined by ethical decision making in conflict, and remotely-operated weapon systems and evolving legal constructs in space and cyberspace make the right decision far less obvious than compliance with the physical (and normally clear-cut) strictures of the Hague and Geneva conventions. George Lucas, in calling for a clearer definition of ethical behaviour in cyberspace, notes that '… the ideals of best practice and the limitations on acceptable practice arise from the deliberations and experience of members of the community of practice themselves, and reflect their shared values, to which they *voluntarily hold themselves accountable*.'[64]

---

62 William Burnette and Jay P. Fullam, 'Interview with Gen Mark A. Welsh III' (2015) 3 (1) *Journal of Character and Leadership Integration* 11.

63 Heidi A. Urben, *Like, Comment, Retweet: The State of the Military's Nonpartisan Ethic in the World of Social Media* (NDU Press 2017) 37.

64 George Lucas, *Ethics and Cyber Warfare: The Quest for Responsible Security in the Age of Digital Warfare* (Oxford University Press 2017) 163.

From an Air Force Academy perspective, we cannot write the prescriptions of legal and ethical frameworks still in flux: whether through philosophy courses, law courses, or practical experience with sub-scale remotely-piloted vehicles, we must lead our graduates to know ethical guidance when it is clear, consult others when it is not, and realise that seeking 'the good' and acting to achieve it is essential to their service and a critical component of their identities as honorable military professionals.

10 Lifting Others

The Leader of Character definition calls for *lifting others to be their best possible selves*. It builds on the integrity *of* the leader to serve those *around* the leader. At one level, this is simply a prioritisation of transformational, rather than transactional, leadership. It is focused on enhancing each member of the team in the expectation that their contribution to the team will be better and higher, and because it is the right thing to do in an organisation and society that value the individual. At a higher level, this aspect of the definition is also aligned with the core value of Service Before Self,[65] whose sub-components are duty, loyalty, and respect.

In educating an increasingly diverse student body, the Academy must consistently demand and facilitate interpersonal understanding – within the framework of the PITO model mentioned above – so that the perspectives of each team member are sufficiently understood, and the contributions of each team member valued. At each stage in the four-year curriculum, cadets must see and practice appropriate forms of challenging, supporting, developing, and inspiring others. In this way, graduates bring a mindset to subsequent decades of leadership, in which they have internalised a mindset that allows them to span cultural, generational, and experiential boundaries to take advantage of diverse character and cognitive strengths in every organisation.

At a strategic level, graduates who internalise the element of lifting others and the core value of service before self are also better prepared to embrace and master the challenges of an increasingly complex conflict operational and interpersonal environment. In developing an other-oriented leadership style, leaders will arguably be better able to understand the perspectives, priorities, capabilities and limitations of the individual and organisational partners that they will need in order to comprehend and master modern multi-domain warfare.

65 United States Air Force (n 63).

Indeed, the model of the heroic, solitary leader – while still fully applicable to some combat settings under some circumstances – is less likely to be needed or to succeed than those who can mobilise diverse resources to meet complex problem-sets. The leader who lifts others will be successful in motivating them to contribute more consistently and more effectively than one who does not.

Thus this element, too, serves a useful purpose in forming a constructive foundation to interpersonal relations for complex problem-solving, independent of the exact nature of the challenges that graduates will face.

11 Elevating Performance

The third element of the Academy's leader of character definition is that of elevating performance to a common and noble purpose. If the first element (living honorably) can be said to strengthen the core of the leader, and the second element (lifting others) can be said to enhance the leader's team, then this element completes the whole by giving purpose to leader and team development, enabling the building of diverse and inclusive teams to solve multi-faceted problems, and connecting to the societal responsibility entrusted to the Air Force, for which the Academy develops leaders of character in the first place.

As with the previous elements, there are both timeless and timely aspects to this integrative aspect of the definition. It is the most difficult to precisely determine, a measurement difficulty it shares with the Air Force core value of 'Excellence in All We Do' – which is explicitly not a demand for perfection in everything from everyone. Instead, it calls on service members to continuously advance their craft and increase their knowledge; to approach the mission 'with the mindset of stewardship, initiative, improvement, pride, and a continued commitment to anticipate and embrace change.'[66]

Preparing graduates to achieve excellence over time in a difficult-to-predict future is not a new challenge, but the means by which the Academy aims to achieve it are evolving. Decades of a broad core curriculum, with relatively deep exposure for each cadet to basic sciences, engineering, social sciences and humanities, is the baseline. This reflects both the technological nature of the Air Force's subject matter and the human dynamics that drive conflict, and it has been refined but not fundamentally changed over time. Relatively new, however, is an increased attention to boundary-spanning cognitive education, experience and development as an essential adjunct to the baseline liberal

66 United States Air Force (n 63).

education and discipline-based academic major. This takes the form of more intentional planning of the military curriculum in a coherent 47-month program; a greater number of inter- and multi-disciplinary courses; and a greater number of integrative experiences, such as cadet participation in remotely piloted aircraft training, a simulated Air Operations Centre, cadet satellite construction and launch, and a variety of cadet research opportunities both within the Department of Defense and with outside entities. In addition, the Academy recently took a decision to create an Institute for Future Conflict in order to enhance the focus and interconnection of academic disciplines and military training with regard to preparation for future conflict.

By providing such experience – oriented toward robustly achieving the Outcomes discussed above – the Academy reflects the likelihood that expertise in core academic discipline and military specialty training remain important but are not sufficient to prepare graduates for complex decision-making to come. The linear development of an officer or enlisted member in a single career field is a timeworn model whose value as 'the rule' is increasingly debatable. Take combat pilots, for example, where mission success has historically depended on personal situational awareness, skill in maneuver, and versatility in using relatively platform-focused weapon systems. Future generations of combat pilots will inevitably operate in much larger, more interconnected mental and electronic spaces. Cyber professionals already operate in an environment that changes literally daily and sometimes far faster. All competitive conceptual frameworks will change more rapidly than they have in the past, mandating a continual learning approach that accepts risk and change as a given, not phenomenon to be trained out.

As the Academy uses its institutional outcomes to drive interdisciplinary cognitive education, experience and development, it increases the probability that cadets will develop the instincts and foundation required to understand changing environments and to recognise and inspire the continued achievement of excellence.

12 An Evolving Profession

We conclude this discourse by returning to its purpose: providing some insights into the business of *preparing leaders of character for complex conflict*. Effective, modern military education requires us to acknowledge and account for increasing blurring of the traditional boundaries between war and peace; the expansion of domains in which competitors and combatants seek advantage; and the rising unreliability of traditional military ethos and assumptions to meet the full range of multi-domain, military and non-military, threats that exist today and into the foreseeable future. In the case at hand, that of the US Air Force Academy, it also requires acknowledging the authority and accumulated experience contained in senior Department of Defense and Department of the Air Force leadership direction, and the reality that violent military conflict on a large scale – fitting the classical definition of war – has not disappeared. These two threads of thought are compatible and mutually reinforcing as they come together in core elements present throughout the Air Force Academy's course of instruction:

- An officer development system that includes a structured approach to personal, interpersonal, team and organisational leadership and an interactive leadership growth model;
- A traditional honor code that provides a foundation for cadet assimilation and acceptance of Air Force Core Values;
- Institutional Outcomes which span disciplinary boundaries and promote holistic approaches to understanding rapidly evolving, non-traditional national security challenges and operational demands; and
- A leader of character definition that facilitates ongoing management of three threads essential to preparing leaders for the future: the nature of conflict, the nature of society, and unchanging values.

No educational institution or course of instruction graduates students perfectly prepared for life's challenges, and the Air Force Academy shares with every other university an added challenge: without hyperbole, it must prepare its graduates for the potentially lethal, highly adversarial environments of air and space, in which their readiness to compete and win affects themselves, the viability of their nation, and ultimately, world peace and stability. It is with this in mind that we acknowledge the difficulties, stress the importance, and share these perspectives on preparing leaders to serve their nations ethically and effectively in coming years.

The views expressed in this chapter are those of the authors and do not necessarily reflect the position of the United States Air Force Academy, the Department of the Air Force, the Department of Defense, or any other government office or agency. Clearance number "USAFA-DF-2020-410"

References

Bass, Bernard, Leadership and Performance Beyond Expectations (Free Press 1985).

Berkowitz, Marvin W. and Melinda C. Bier, 'Research-Based Character Education' (2004) 591 (1) *The Annals of the American Academy of Political and Social Science* 72–85.

Burnette, William and Jay P. Fullam, 'Interview with Gen Mark A. Welsh III' (2015) 3 (1) *Journal of Character and Leadership Integration* 6–25.

Center for Character and Leadership Development, 'Developing Leaders of Character at the United States Air Force Academy: A conceptual framework' (United States Air Force Academy 2011).

Colby, Anne and William M. Sullivan, 'Formation of Professionalism and Purpose: Perspective From the Preparation for the Professions Program' (2008) 5 (2) *University of St. Thomas Law Journal* 404–427.

Colby, Anne, 'Fostering the Moral and Civic Development of College Students' in Larry P. Nucci and Darcia Narvaez (eds), *Handbook of Moral and Character Education* (1st edn, Routledge 2008).

Cyberspace Solarium Commission Report (March 2020).

Dufresne, Ronald L. and Evan H. Offstein, 'Holistic and Intentional Student Character Development Process: Learning from West Point' (2012) 11 (4) *Academy of Management Learning & Education* 570–590.

French, Shannon E., *The Code of the Warrior: Exploring Warrior Values Past and Present* (first published 2003, Rowman and Littlefield Publishers 2005).

Hajjar, Remi M., 'Emergent Postmodern US Military Culture' (2014) 40 (1) *Armed Forces & Society* 118–145.

Heathfield, Susan M., 'Core Values Are What You Believe' (2019) <www.thebalancecareers.com/core-values-are-what-you-believe-1918079> accessed 25 November 2020.

Hoffmann, Stanley, *The State of War: Essays on the Theory and Practice of International Politics* (Praeger 1965).

Huitt, William G. and Gordon G. Vessels, *Character Development: Looking Back, the Eclectic Ideal* (Early Twenty-First Century 2015).

Janowitz, Morris, *The Professional Soldier: A Social and Political Portrait* (rev edn, The Free Press 1971).

Joanne B. Ciulla, 'Leadership Ethics: Mapping the Territory' (1995) 5 (1) *Business Ethics Quarterly* 5–28.

King, Patricia M. and Karen Strohm Kitchener, 'Reflective Judgement: Theory and Research on the Development of Epistemic Assumptions Through Adulthood' (2004) 39 (1) *Educational Psychologist* 5–18.

Kohlberg, Lawrence, 'Moral Stages and Moralization: The Cognitive-Developmental Approach' in Thomas Lickona (ed), *Moral Development and Behavior: Theory, Research, and Social Issues* (Rinehart & Winston 1976).

Kraack, T., 'The relation of moral development to involvement and leadership experiences' (Unpublished Doctoral Dissertation, University of Minnesota 1985).

Kuhmerker, Lisa, "Moral development research designed to make a difference: Some gaps waiting to be filled," (1995) 20 (4) *The Moral Education Forum* 2–10.

Lerner, Richard M. and Kristina Schmid Callina, 'The Study of Character Development: Towards Tests of a Relational Developmental Systems Model' (2015) 57 (6) *Human Development* 322–346.

Lindsay, Douglas, John Abbatiello, David Huston and Scott Heyler, 'Developing Leaders of Character', (2020) 7/2 *Journal of Character and Leadership Development* <https://jcli.scholasticahq.com/article/13606-developing-leaders-of-character> accessed 25 November 2020.

Lucas, George, *Ethics and Cyber Warfare: The Quest for Responsible Security in the Age of Digital Warfare* (Oxford University Press 2017).

Luedtke, Christopher J. 'A Longitudinal and Qualitative Descriptive Study of Cadet Moral Judgment' (PhD Dissertation, The Florida State University College of Education 1999).

Mattis, James, 'Secretary of Defense Memorandum: Ethical Standards for All Hands' (United States Department of Defense 2017).

Miller, Christopher D. 'Yesterday at War with Tomorrow: Rebooting the Profession of Arms' (2020) 7 *Journal of Character and Leadership Development*.

Northouse, Peter Guy, *Leadership: Theory and Practice* (Sage Publications 1997).

Pascarella, Ernest T. and Patrick T. Terenzini, *How College Affects Students* (Jossey-Bass 1991).

Piaget, Jean, *The Moral Judgment of the Child* (first published 1932, The Free Press 1965).

Rest, James R. and Darcia Narvaez (eds), *Moral Development in the Professions* (Lawrence Erlbaum Associates, Inc. 1994).

Rest, James R. and Steven J. Thoma, 'Relation of Moral Judgement Development to Formal Education' (1985), 21 *Developmental Psychology* 709–714.

Rest, James R., *Development in Judging Moral Issues* (rev edn, University of Minnesota Press 1979).

Rokke, Ervin J., unpublished essay, 'Time to Revisit the Profession of Arms: A Perfect Storm' (2017).

Rudolph, Frederick, *The American College and University* (2nd edn, University of Georgia Press 1990).

Samuel P. Huntington, *The Soldier & the State: The Theory and Politics of Civil-Military Relations* (Belknap Press 1957).

Schein, Edgar H., *Organizational Culture and Leadership* (2nd edn Jossey-Bass 1992).

Schmid Callina, Kristina, Diane Ryan, Elise D. Murray, Anne Colby, William Damon, Michael Matthews and Richard M. Lerner, 'Developing Leaders of Character at the United States Military Academy: A Relational Developmental Systems Analysis' (2017) 18 (1) *Journal of College and Character* 9–27.

Sendjaya, Sen, 'Morality and Leadership: Examining the Ethics of Transformational Leadership' (2005) 3 (1) *Journal of Academic Ethics* 75–86.

Silveria, Jay, 'Air Force Academy Leader: Why Diversity?' *CNN Opinion* (2018) <https://www.cnn.com/2018/02/14/opinions/air-force-academy-superintendent-why-diversity-opinion-silveria/index.html> accessed 22 November 2020.

Smith, Heidi L. and Christopher Luedtke, 'Military Missions and Their Implications Reconsidered: The Aftermath of September 11th' in Giuseppe Caforio and Gerhard Kümmel (eds), *Contributions to Conflict Management, Peace Economics and Development* (Elsevier Ltd 2005).

Thornhill, Paula G., *The Crisis Within: America's Military and the Struggle Between the Overseas and Guardian Paradigms* (RAND Corporation 2016) <https://www.rand.org/pubs/research_reports/RR1420.html> accessed 22 November 2020.

United States Air Force Academy Admissions, 'Honor Code' (2018) <https://www.academyadmissions.com/the-experience/character/honor-code/>.

United States Air Force Academy Center for Character Development, 'Character Development Manual' (Unpublished Manuscript, 1994).

United States Air Force Academy, 'United States Air Force Academy Pamphlet 36–3527' (United States Air Force Academy 2013).

United States Air Force Academy, 'US Air Force Academy Outcomes' (2018) <www.usafa.edu/academics/outcomes/> accessed 25 November 2020.

United States Air Force Academy, 'US Air Force Academy Strategic Plan' (United States Air Force Academy 2020).

United States Air Force, 'Air Force Doctrine Volume II: Leadership' (Curtis E. Lemay Center 2015).

United States Air Force, 'Air Force Mission Directive 12' (5 March 2019).

United States Air Force, 'America's Air Force: A Profession of Arms' (2015).

United States Department of Defense, 'Department of Defense Instruction 1322.22' (United States Department of Defense 2015).

Urben, Heidi A., *Like, Comment, Retweet: The State of the Military's Nonpartisan Ethic in the World of Social Media* (NDU Press 2017).

US Air Force Academy, 'Philosophy' (2018) <https://www.usafa.edu/academic/philosophy/> accessed 25 November 2020.

US Department of Defense, 'Joint Publication 3-0, "Joint Operations"' (US Department of Defense 2017).

Short Afterword from a German Perspective

Bernhard Koch

The increased use of armed drones in Afghanistan and Pakistan in the first years of President Barack Obama's administration has led to new attention being paid to emerging military technologies. In many Western societies, especially in Germany, the use of armed drones has been met partly with scepticism, but even more with indignant rejection. There were accusations that people were being illegally executed without trial, and the question of whether the collateral victims were justifiable was – rightly – hotly debated.[1] This public rejection of American drone use also overshadowed the efforts of the German armed forces to acquire armed drones for their own Afghanistan mission. The German military leadership, too, was always heard and read to say that they did not want to use drones in the same way as the United States. It remained unclear, however, which practice was referred to (negatively) in the demarcation, and what kind of deployment scenarios were envisaged. This blanket dismissal of the American use of drones was and is also inadequate in another respect: it overlooks how extensive the legal and ethical debate in the Anglo-American region and in Israel on the question of the use of armed drones already was. Much can be learned from these debates, and this book represents a further contribution to the ethical discussion of emerging military technologies that has been called for time and again. It is not the first in this field, nor will it be the last.[2] But it was important that Euro-ISME also took up the topic at one of its major annual conferences in Toledo in 2018, because especially in continental Europe the ethical discussion can still gain significantly by including arguments from other discourse contexts. It is no longer just about Unmanned Combat Aerial Vehicles (UCAVs), i.e. armed drones, but

1 On the problem of proportionality cf. (e. g.): Bernhard Koch, 'Is Proportionality a Matter of Attitude? A short Reflection about an Aspect of Virtue in Armed Conflict' in Bernhard Koch (ed.): *Chivalrous Combatants? The Meaning of Military Virtue Past and Present* (Nomos, Baden-Baden 2019), 139–160.

2 We can think of (e. g.): Bradley Jay Strawser (ed), Killing by Remote Control. The Ethics of an Unmanned Military (Oxford 2013); and: Ezio di Nucci and Filippo Santoni de Sio (eds), Drones and Responsibility. Legal, Philosophical and Socio-Technical Perspectives on Remotely Controlled Weapons (Routledge 2016); Michael J. Boyle (ed), Legal and ethical Implications of Drone Warfare (Routledge 2017); David Cortright, Rachel Fairhurst and Kristen Wall (eds), Drones and the Future of Armed Conflict. Ethical, Legal and Strategic Implications (The University of Chicago Press, 2014).

 | DOI:10.1163/9789004507951_016

about the use of "artificially intelligent" control technologies in all areas of the use of military technology, up to and including what are very sweepingly called "Lethal autonomous weapons systems" ("LAWS").

Ethics is a reflective discipline that first classifies moral judgements and then situates them in their context of justification, and thus questions them with regard to their normative prerequisites. Particularly in the case of ethics of technology, it is not so easy to say "yes" or "no" to a certain technology or a concrete technical device. The danger that (supposed) ethics is sometimes only used for one's own interests cannot be dismissed. I briefly illustrate this with the debate on armed drones. There we have to distinguish between three questions:

a. Are there situations in which this instrument can be legitimately used?
b. Should this instrument be (developed and) procured?
c. What rules should apply to the use of this instrument?

The first question has an ethical focus, but in the case of armed drones, hardly anyone (except very staunch pacifists) will argue that there are no situations at all in which they could legitimately be used. This information, however, does not predetermine the answer to question b): For even in the case of a possible legitimate use of a certain technical instrument, it still has to be weighed up (and in this case weighed up politically) whether there are not other and better ways to achieve the goals one has set out to achieve; questions of (even societal) costs and benefits are also at stake here.[3] In the German armed forces, the partial permission to use armed drones in certain situations was too quickly inferred to imply some kind of obligation on the part of the state to acquire such drones as well. The argumentative bridge was established by referring to the "protection" of soldiers: Those who withhold armed drones from soldiers in action are denying them necessary protection and would thus not be doing justice to their dignity. But the argument is problematic, because the "protection" provided by offensive weapon systems such as drones is not the same as the protection provided by purely defensive "systems" such as helmets or interceptor missiles. Such a broad notion of protection would ultimately justify the

---

3 Of course, other questions are important, e.g. the implications for the military profession, and – an ethical issue in the narrow sense – the implications for behavious of soliders and virtues. Cf: Bernhard Koch, 'Virtues for Peace. What Soldiers Can Do and Where Military Robotics Fails' in Florian Demont-Biaggi (ed), *The Nature of Peace and the Morality of Armed Conflict* (Palgrave Macmillan, Cham (CH) 2017), 223–242. – In this sense, Dobos [Ned Dobos, *Ethics, Security, and the War Machine* (Oxford University Press 2020)] also rightly asked this question the other day in relation to the institution of the armed forces as a whole: The fact that there are legitimate military missions is not itself a sufficient reason to maintain the institution of the military.

acquisition of any weapon system and thus become meaningless. Moreover, there is something totalizing about the protection argument. Demanding complete protection in the private sphere would mean, for example, no longer buying a small car or – in times of a pandemic – avoiding public life altogether. Protection must always be weighed up. That is why the political process is so important here.[4] – If the decision is made to acquire the instrument, then great importance must be attached to the principles of use (c), especially in the case of weapons that are designed to injure and kill people.[5] It is not unlikely that – according to the famous dictum of Abraham Maslow: To him who has a hammer, every problem looks like a nail – the availability of a technical instrument already makes us assess the problem-situation differently ("cognitive bias").

In the case of autonomous weapon systems[6] – even if we have to keep in mind that we are no longer simply dealing with "things" here, but with the relationship between man and machine (resp. "software") – comparable questions arise:

---

4 In Germany, in political discussions it is widespread to say, "Every dead person is one dead person too many." – A sentence that is correct in a banal way. But a state cannot guarantee liberty rights and be a "life protection machine" at the same time. This is true in the pandemic, and it is also true for the profession of soldiers: Because soldiers take on more risks than other occupational groups, they are owed more respect in this respect. For sure there are limits of the risks they have to accept, but there is no *a priori* deduction of these limits.

5 In Germany (July 2020) the Ministry of Defense sent a report to the German Parliament in favour of the aquistion of drones (https://www.bmvg.de/resource/blob/274160/f5d26b7af1a024551e4aafc7b587a01d/200703_BMVg_Bericht%20-Drohnendebatte-.pdf [06/01/2022]) but most relevant questions, e. g. who can become a target, whether drones are aimed at the destruction of enemy capacities and equipment or at killing enemy combatants remain unclear. The only constant argument is that drones are needed for the "protection" of Bundeswehr soldiers, but even here the concept of "protection" remains unclear. Government officials could have learned a lot from the ethical and legal discussions during the Obama administration in the U.S. – For German discussion cf: Bernhard Koch, 'Die ethische Debatte um den Einsatz von ferngesteuerten und autonomen Waffensystemen' in Ines-Jacqueline Werkner and Marco Hofheinz (Hrsg.), *Unbemannte Waffen und ihre ethische Legitimierung* (Springer VS, Wiesbaden 2019) 13–40; Bernhard Koch, 'Bewaffnete Drohnen und andere militärische Robotik. Ethische Betrachtungen' in Christof Gramm and Dieter Weingärtner (Hrsg.), *Moderne Waffentechnologie. Hält das Recht Schritt?* (Nomos, Baden-Baden 2015) 32–56.

6 The Institute for Theology and Peace in Hamburg (ITHF) was involved in the report of the Office of Technology Assessment at the German Bundestag on Automous Weapons Systems through an ethical expert opinion, the results of which are now also available: https://www.tab-beim-bundestag.de/de/untersuchungen/u30600.html [06/01/2022]. On the issue of LAWS cf. e. g. Alex Leveringhaus, *Ethics and Autonomous Weapons* (Palgrave 2015); Nehal Bhuta, Susanne Beck, Robin Geiß, Hin-Yan Liu and Claus Kreß (eds), *Autonomous Weapons Systems: Law, Ethics, Policy* (Cambridge University Press, Cambridge 2016).

a) Is there a conceivable situation in which an autonomous weapons system could be legitimately used? In the debate, it is argued that killings by autonomous weapon systems fundamentally violate human dignity. This argument needs to be explored in more depth; those who find it viable can probably conclude the discussion here. Questions b) and c) would thus be more or less settled, if a violation of human dignity can never be accepted. A second argument avers an unacceptable responsibility gap for autonomous systems; if it were valid, the use of autonomous weapon systems would also be excluded in principle. Sometimes this argument is conflated with the dignity argument. Personally, I think the dignity argument is fundamentally valid because a machine cannot provide the basic recognition that we should presuppose for any interpersonal interaction to be morally justifiable. Perhaps, however, the dignity argument is not convincing, and there are conceivable situations in which such an instrument could also be permitted. Then we are faced with question b).

b) Should it be possible to develop and procure an autonomous weapon system? As with drones, it is then a matter of weighing up. As an ethicist, one cannot simply deduce or prescribe a result here, but the weighing up is the subject of a political process in which many different points of view flow in. It is not only a question of "May we procure autonomous weapon systems?", but also a question of "Do we want to?" Does it fit with our image of ourselves and of human beings?

The ethicist must refer here to the enormously important arguments from the security policy discussion. (Applied ethics must of course look to empirical research, including sociology of technology and psychology of technology). So even if one can conceive of an artificial, isolated scenario in which it is conceivable that an autonomous weapons system might be legitimately deployed, a more expansive consideration may conclude that the disadvantages of having such systems in the world far outweigh the marginal advantages they might offer in certain situations. The risks of these systems are simply too high.

One could now say that this negative answer to b) settles question c). In principle, this is true, but due to the technical complexity of the systems, which are not simply a "thing", but often are software or include "hybrid" technologies or "dual use" technologies, there is probably also much to be done in the area of regulation, which, however, requires a careful knowledge of the technologies.

Some are convinced that ethics should definitely show that LAWS are always and under all circumstances prohibited. Others, on the other hand, want ethics to provide a kind of fundamental certificate of harmlessness, which is at most restricted by certain limits. For both of them, these considerations, which distinguish levels of competence, are unsatisfactory because the ball is at least partly played back into the field of politics and technology; but the risks posed by such systems alone give every reason to advocate for an enforceable ban on autonomous weapons systems and effective arms control in this area. Nevertheless, some uncertainties remain, because ethical argumentation is never completely free of assumptions about values, human images, social attitudes and more. Scientific ethics is something other than moralising. Often, it only establishes conditional relationships without being able to definitively decide the factual question. In this sense, the debate on emerging military technologies will of course continue.

References

Bhuta, Nehal, Susanne Beck, Robin Geiß, Hin-Yan Liu and Claus Kreß (eds), *Autonomous Weapons Systems: Law, Ethics, Policy* (Cambridge University Press, Cambridge 2016).

Boyle, Michael J. (ed), *Legal and ethical Implications of Drone Warfare* (Routledge 2017).

Cortright, David, Rachel Fairhurst and Kristen Wall (eds), *Drones and the Future of Armed Conflict. Ethical, Legal and Strategic Implications* (The University of Chicago Press, 2014).

Dobos, Ned, *Ethics, Security, and the War Machine* (Oxford University Press 2020).

German Federal Ministry of Defence, *Bericht des Bundesministeriums der Verteidigung an den Deutschen Bundestag zur Debatte über eine mögliche Beschaffung bewaffneter Drohnen für die Bundeswehr* (Report) (July 2020) <https://www.bmvg.de/resource/blob/274160/f5d26b7af1a024551e4aafc7b587a01d/200703_BMVg_Bericht%20-Drohnendebatte-.pdf> accessed 6 January 2022.

Koch, Bernhard 'Bewaffnete Drohnen und andere militärische Robotik. Ethische Betrachtungen' in Christof Gramm and Dieter Weingärtner (Hrsg.), *Moderne Waffentechnologie. Hält das Recht Schritt?* (Nomos, Baden-Baden 2015) 32–56.

Koch, Bernhard, 'Die ethische Debatte um den Einsatz von ferngesteuerten und autonomen Waffensystemen' in Ines-Jacqueline Werkner and Marco Hofheinz (Hrsg.), *Unbemannte Waffen und ihre ethische Legitimierung* (Springer VS, Wiesbaden 2019) 13–40.

Koch, Bernhard, 'Virtues for Peace. What Soldiers Can Do and Where Military Robotics Fails' in Florian Demont-Biaggi (ed), *The Nature of Peace and the Morality of Armed Conflict* (Palgrave Macmillan, Cham (CH) 2017), 223–242.

Koch, Bernhard, 'Is Proportionality a Matter of Attitude? A short Reflection about an Aspect of Virtue in Armed Conflict' in Bernhard Koch (ed.): *Chivalrous Combatants? The Meaning of Military Virtue Past and Present* (Nomos, Baden-Baden 2019), 139-160.

Leveringhaus, Alex, *Ethics and Autonomous Weapons* (Palgrave 2015).

Nucci, Ezio di and Filippo Santoni de Sio (eds), *Drones and Responsibility. Legal, Philosophical and Socio-Technical Perspectives on Remotely Controlled Weapons* (Routledge 2016).

Strawser, Bradley Jay (ed), *Killing by Remote Control. The Ethics of an Unmanned Military* (Oxford 2013).

TAB Büro für Technikfolgenabschätzung beim Deutschen Bundestag, *Autonome Waffensysteme. Endbericht zum TA-Projekt*, Reinhard Grünwald/Christoph Kehl, Arbeitsbericht Nr. 187, Berlin Oktober 2020 < https://publikationen.bibliothek.kit.edu/1000127160 > accessed 6 January 2022.

TAB Büro für Technikfolgenabschätzung beim Deutschen Bundestag, *Report of the Office of Technology Assessment at the German Bundestag on Automous Weapons Systems through an ethical expert opinion* <https://www.tab-beim-bundestag.de/de/untersuchungen/u30600.html> accessed 6 January 2022.

Index

www.ingramcontent.com/pod-product-compliance
Lightning Source LLC
Chambersburg PA
CBHW071227230926
51849CB00001B/49
9789004507944